Corporations, Classes and Capitalism

For Jill, Michael and Susan

Corporations, Classes and Capitalism

Second, completely revised, edition

John Scott

Lecturer in Sociology, University of Leicester

Hutchinson

London   Melbourne   Sydney   Auckland   Johannesburg

Hutchinson and Co. (Publishers) Ltd

An imprint of the Hutchinson Publishing Group

17–21 Conway Street, London W1P 6JD
and 51 Washington Street, Dover, New Hampshire 03820, USA

Hutchinson Publishing Group (Australia) Pty Ltd
16–22 Church Street, Hawthorn, Melbourne, Victoria 3122

Hutchinson Group (NZ) Ltd
32–34 View Road, PO Box 40–086, Glenfield, Auckland 10

Hutchinson Group (SA) (Pty) Ltd
PO Box 337, Bergvlei 2012, South Africa

First published 1979
Second, completely revised, edition 1985

© John Scott 1979, 1985

Set in 10 on 12 point Times by
J&L Composition Ltd, Filey,
North Yorkshire

Printed and bound in Great Britain by
Anchor Brendon Ltd,
Tiptree, Essex

British Library Cataloguing in Publication Data

Scott, John, *1949*–
    Corporations, classes and capitalism.—2nd ed.
    1. Capitalism
    I. Title
    330.12'2   HB501

Library of Congress Cataloging in Publication Data

Scott, John, *1949*–
    Corporations, classes and capitalism.

    Bibliography: p.
    Includes index.
    1. Capitalism. 2. Corporations. 3. International
business enterprises. 4. Industry and state. I. Title.
HB501.S47 1985   330.12'2   85–14314

ISBN 0 09 161381 7

Contents

Figures

Tables

Not all percentage figures add up to the totals stated. This is because of rounding-off in the original sources.

Preface and acknowledgements

This book differs markedly from its predecessor, both in coverage and in argument. I have added new sections on corporate structure and the labour process and have completely rewritten and re-arranged the remaining material. The updating of the empirical information from more recent studies has meant that most of the tables in Chapters 3 and 4 are new, and I have also altered and updated many other tables. Much of the tabular material in the first edition was based upon recalculations from secondary sources, but most of the British material in the present edition is now based on my own original research. This original data is mainly to be found in Tables 15, 18, 19, 22, 23, 29, and 44, and partly in Tables 17 and 54. In addition, original material from associated projects is contained in Tables 24 and 32. I have also considerably expanded the material on economies other than Britain and America, largely because of the growth of research since the completion of the first edition. This extended comparative focus has led me to clarify the central thrust of my argument concerning impersonal possession and control through a constellation of interests, and to recognize more clearly the differences between the Anglo-American and other patterns of development.

My colleagues in the Research Group on Intercorporate Structure continued to be a source of inspiration, especially Meindert Fennema, Beth Mintz, Frans Stokman, and Rolf Ziegler, who commented on many of the ideas developed in the first edition. Above all, however, I gratefully acknowledge the help of Catherine Griff in the production of much of the British data. Mike Schwartz suggested I contribute a chapter on Europe to a book which he is editing, and this became the nucleus of the ideas presented in Chapter 5. Any English-speaking researcher faces difficulties in handling Japanese data, and I have been lucky to have received considerable help and information from Hiroshi Okumura and Yoshiaki Ueda, who generously provided some of their own data and gave me detailed comments on my discussion of Japan in Chapter 5. Howard Newby carried out his editorial task above and beyond the call of duty, and correctly forced me to make those changes to which I had tried to turn a blind eye. The final manuscript was typed by Betty Jennings, who unfailingly produced accurate copy with a remarkably quick turn round.

John Scott
January 1985

1 The debate over big business

The business enterprise is a powerful and pervasive influence on our everyday life, though few people realize the extent of the connections between their own experiences and the world of 'big business' and 'high finance'. The products and services that are used in the course of routine daily activities – food, newspapers, cars, houses, credit cards, and so on – are produced by large business enterprises for the mass market and depend upon other products and services – such as machine tools, aircraft, printing presses, computers, and international finance – which businesses produce to sell to one another. The majority of those in paid employment are paid by these same businesses to work in factories, shops, and offices producing these goods and services. News reports on the movement of the *Financial Times* share index, the sterling balances, and the international currency markets in which these enterprises are involved are not peripheral to 'real' news events but are important determinants of the availability of goods, services, and jobs in everyday life. 'Consumers' and 'workers' are inextricably tied into a web of connections which stretch from the corner shop to the Tokyo money market.

The significance of this web of connections is masked from everyday experience by the disjunction between the homely and familiar products that we regularly use and the unreal corporate entities that appear only in the financial pages of the newspapers. The large enterprise is invariably an anonymous entity known by meaningless corporate initials or a meaningless corporate acronym: Exxon, TI, AE, GM, LWT, ITT. Even where a corporate name is widely known and recognized, the range and spread of its interests is generally unknown. Some examples will perhaps bring home the significance of what is being claimed.

Most people in Britain, and many in other parts of the world, will have heard of Unilever and will know that it has some connection with margarine and detergents, but few are aware of exactly how big and important it is in the world today. Unilever is a joint British and Dutch organization consisting of about 700 separate companies operating in all parts of the world. About a quarter of its world-wide sales total is in margarine, cooking oil, and dairy products, a quarter is in other foods, one-fifth is in detergents, and the rest is in paper, plastics, packagings, chemicals, animal foods, cosmetics, plantations, timber, office equipment, building materials, department stores, textiles, shipping, and numerous other activities. Unilever does not use its own name for the products it sells, but has a mass of well-known and competing brand names: in Britain alone it uses such names as White Cap, Spry, Krona, Stork, SB, Summer County, Echo, Outline, Crisp 'n' Dry, Blue Band, Flora, Cookeen, Batchelors, Unox, Walls, Eldorado, John West, Mattessons, MacFisheries, Snackpots, Cup-a-Soup, Vesta, Surprise, Birds Eye, Sure, Shield, Sunsilk, Impulse, Harmony, Twink, Surf, Omo, Drive, Radiant, Sunlight, Lemon Liquid, Vim, Domestos, Lifebuoy, Lux, Pears, Rexona, Breeze, Astral, Comfort, Persil, Handy Andy, Frish, Jif, Pepsodent, Gibbs, Signal, and Close-Up.

Unilever epitomizes the mixture of corporate anonymity and household familiarity, but it is by no means unusual. Imperial Group, for example, has interests in cigarettes, tobacco, snuff, brewing, wine, hotels, snack foods, frozen foods, and many other areas through such brands as Wills, Players, Ogdens, JPS, Embassy, Courage, Lea and Perrins, Golden Wonder, Ross, Young's, and Wotsits, and the spread of interests found in S. Pearson is even more diverse. Almost 300 subsidiaries extend S. Pearson's activities into newspapers, films, books, television, oil, china, banking, agriculture, funfairs, zoos, and waxworks. Its trade names run from Penguin and Ladybird books, through Madame Tussaud's and Warwick Castle, to Chateau Latour and Royal Doulton. The Prudential, widely known as an insurance company through 'the man from the Pru', shows clearly the links between our personal life insurance and the corporate world. It is Britain's largest insurance company, is involved in pensions and re-insurance, and is an investor in almost every major enterprise: it owns 6 per cent of Marks and Spencer, 7 per cent of General Electric, 3 per cent of Hawker Siddeley, 3 per cent of ICI, and so on.

The power and significance of big business has been recognized by many social scientists, but a variety of interpretations have been placed upon it (Holland 1975; Averitt 1968; Miller 1975).* Central to the contending interpretations has been the long-running debate over ownership and control. The classical entrepreneur of the nineteenth century both owned and controlled the business, but social changes have broken this immediate and direct link. The legal innovation of the 'company' or 'corporation', which spread rapidly at the end of the nineteenth century, introduced the possibility that the 'owners', those who subscribed to the shares which provided its capital, could become divorced from effective control over the operation of the business. The shareholders vote at an annual meeting on the appointment of a board of directors to manage the business, but their power of control over the business depends upon their ability to control this board.[1]† As the body of shareholders becomes larger and more diverse, such control becomes progressively more problematic. Not only do shareholders differ among themselves, they have also to contend with the entrenched interests of the directors and the conflicting interests of the managerial, technical, clerical, sales, and manual workers who are employed by the company. The 'enterprise' is a social organization based around a 'parent' corporation and its various 'subsidiary' companies,[2] and within the enterprise there is an inherent struggle for control between the various groups which have a stake in its future (Child 1969a, p. 14). The debate over the separation of ownership from control lies at the heart of the wider debate over big business, and the main lines of this debate must now be discussed.

The main interpretations which have been placed upon the enterprise and corporate power have their roots in two themes in social thought, each of which has provided the basis of a well-developed theory of the development of industrial capitalism. These are the themes of 'industrialism' and 'capitalism' (Giddens 1973, pp. 141–2; Turner 1975). The theme of industrialism refers to the transformation of human labour through the application of inanimate sources of energy to productive activity, and the associated physical proximity of workers and machines in a system of factory production. On the other hand, the theme of capitalism

---

* Full references quoted in the text are contained in the Bibliography beginning on p. 270.
† Superior figures refer to the Notes at the end of each chapter.

refers to the organization of production in terms of a search for the realization of profit for privately owned capital and the broader system of market exchange for which commodities are produced. While industrial capitalism can be seen as the conjunction of these two processes, the two most influential theories of industrial capitalism have each stressed one theme to the virtual exclusion of the other. These are the theories of industrial society and capitalist society.

Managerialism and the theory of industrial society

Much sociology since the work of Saint-Simon and Comte has centred around a concept of modern society as a specifically industrial society (Giddens 1976; 1971, p. 245ff.; 1973, ch. 8; Kumar 1978).[3] The clearest statements of this theory are to be found in a number of influential works produced in the 1950s and 1960s, in particular the works of Aron, Bell, Galbraith, and Kerr, and it has been a central component in the sociology of Parsons and the economics of Rostow. The theory holds that the basic features of culture and society are to be explained in terms of the unfolding of tendencies inherent in the determining industrial technology.[4] Technology is based upon the growth and application of scientific knowledge, and modern society expresses the rational, scientific organization of production:

Modern societies are defined first and foremost by their organisation of labour; that is, by their relationship to the external world, their use of machinery, the application of scientific methods, and the social and economic consequences of the rationalisation of production [Aron 1967, p. 15. See also Lenski 1966, pp. 298–9].

The industrial society follows from the development of technology; such is the 'logic' of industrialism (Kerr *et al.*1960, pp. 42–3; Aron 1968, p. 53).[5]

Galbraith is perhaps the most forceful advocate of the view that the central dynamic of industrial society – its rational technology – is to be found in the large business enterprise, arguing that the core of the economy consists of about 500 'technically dynamic, massively capitalized and highly organized corporations' (Galbraith 1967, p. 9; Pavitt and Worboys 1977, ch. 4). Within the large enterprise the increasing scale of production requires such great amounts of capital that the number of shareholders increases to the point where no individual or group of individuals is able to use their 'ownership' as a basis for 'control'. As Galbraith characteristically argues: 'Corporate size, the passage of time and the dispersion of stock ownership do not disenfranchise the stockholder. Rather, he can vote but his vote is valueless' (Galbraith 1967, p. 80). The resulting power vacuum creates the conditions under which professional, salaried managers are able to usurp effective control; they become a new social class capable of consolidating the development of industrialism. The capitalist propertied class is replaced by a managerial class, which is 'broad and diffuse . . . with several loosely integrated components', and which is based not on property ownership but on 'occupational status and occupational earnings' (Parsons 1954a, p. 431; Lenski 1966, p. 352).

The most sophisticated statement of this view is that of Bell, who argues that the rise of the managers is the end result of a long process. A series of economic crises at the beginning of the twentieth century led to the enhanced power of the investment bankers who took over and reconstructed the failing enterprises. This stage of 'finance capitalism' waned as the power of the bankers declined: the professional managers who had been recruited became the indispensable 'corporate organizers' (Bell 1957, pp. 40–1). As inheritance through the family became less important and technical skill became more important, there was a 'break-up' of the old ruling class; the mere possession of wealth was no longer a guarantee of access to economic power (Bell 1958, p. 50ff.; Lenski 1966, p. 343).[6] Parsons and Smelser (1957, p. 289) claim that 'the kinship-property combination typical of classical capitalism' has given way to 'bureaucratization', to a situation in which the theories of Weber are more relevant than those of Marx. The growth of a differentiated managerial hierarchy has been explained by Bendix as a consequence of the increased scale of corporate production: 'As the enterprise increases in size, it becomes necessary for the owner-manager to delegate to subordinates responsibility for many functions, which he has performed personally in the past. Subsequently, it becomes necessary to delegate further managerial functions' (Bendix 1956, p. 226). Dahrendorf has built such arguments into his own attempts to reconstruct Marx's sociology, arguing that class relations depend not on legal ownership but are 'relations of factual control and subordination in the enterprises of industrial production'. As such, classes are identified by their 'exercise of, or exclusion from, authority' (Dahrendorf 1959, pp. 21, 136; Bendix 1956, p. 13). He concludes that

Control over the means of production is but a special case of authority, and the connection of control with legal property an incidental phenomenon of the industrialising societies of Europe and the United States [Dahrendorf 1959, pp. 136–7].

The basis of managerial authority, however, is the knowledge and technical expertise which makes them indispensable to the large enterprise. Technically educated specialists are required in increasing numbers by the advance of technology, and so management becomes more 'professional':

As industrialisation reaches an advanced state, the enterprise emerges as an organisation of high-talent managerial resources, with product development specialists, production engineers, and planning departments, all co-ordinated and directed by divisional and top managers [Kerr *et al.* 1960, p. 146].

In the work of Aron and Kerr this is depicted as a necessary feature of any industrial society, capitalist or communist: 'There are certain leading roles to be performed in any industrial society, and consequently the same kinds of men appear to perform them' (Aron 1968, p. 59). All that differs is the route by which such societies travel to this destination; industrial societies are converging towards a common structural pattern. Galbraith has christened the technical bureaucracy the 'technostructure', arguing that its knowledge is the basis of its power within the enterprise and in the wider society. Power in the economy is an attribute of that factor which it is hardest to obtain or replace; and in the modern economy, where the large enterprise is able to finance its investments from its profits, capital is relatively abundant and specialist talent is in short supply. Power has passed from organized capital to the 'organized intelligence' represented by

the association of men of diverse technical knowledge, experience or other talent which modern industrial technology and planning require. It extends from the leadership of the modern industrial enterprise down to just short of the labour force and embraces a large number of people and a large variety of talent [Galbraith 1967, p. 56; 1952; Bell 1953].

The stress which the theory of industrial society places on the role and power of corporate management has led it to be identified with 'managerialism', but there are in fact two quite distinct variants of the managerial position. The predominant viewpoint among proponents of the theory of industrial society is what Nichols (1969) has termed 'non-sectional managerialism'. It has been argued that the separation of ownership and control produces important shifts in the motivation of business leaders. Managers are able to depart from the profit motivation of the old capitalist entrepreneurs because they are no longer constrained by the demands of the shareholders. Managerial motivation is, therefore, based upon a wider outlook which avoids purely sectional interests and embodies a sense of social 'responsibility'. The role of the manager comes to be seen as one of 'trust', a fiduciary role on behalf of the community as a whole, and corporate policy becomes 'benevolent' and even 'soulful' (Kaysen 1957; Mayo 1949; Drucker 1951). This heralds the age of 'People's Capitalism' (Berle 1960) in which the large enterprise is able to 'judge society's needs in a more conscious fashion and . . . to do so on the basis of some explicit conception of the "public interest"' (Bell 1974, p. 284).[7]

Others, however, have taken a more hard-headed approach to management and have formulated a variant of 'sectional managerialism', which has prevailed among economists. According to this version of managerialism, the separation of ownership and control allows management to give free reign to their own sectional self-interest and so corporate policy reflects a drive to maximize such things as growth, revenue, and managerial salaries (Galbraith 1967). The traditional theory of the firm, an integral part of the neo-classical theory of relative prices, assumed that market mechanisms guided the behaviour of profit-maximizing enterprises and ensured an appropriate level of output. Many writers have pointed out that this model made the unrealistic assumption that enterprises had accurate knowledge of their demand curve and their marginal revenues and costs, and the separation of ownership and control further undermined the theory by implying that the new managerial controllers were not even committed to the goal of profit maximization. Furthermore, the large enterprise has the power to increase its autonomy in the market and so its managers are able to co-ordinate the flow of resources in comparative freedom from market forces: 'the visible hand of management replaced what Adam Smith referred to as the invisible hand of market forces' (Chandler 1977, p. 1). Managerialists hold that this new view of enterprise has to be incorporated into alternative theories of pricing behaviour, though there is considerable disagreement about the nature of such an alternative. A common starting point has been Simon's analysis of rational choice. Simon claims that managerial administration involves the rational selection of a particular course of action from the range of possible actions, and rational choice depends not upon the market situation as it 'really' is but on the situation as it appears to the management. The 'logic of the situation' facing managers always involves incomplete knowledge, so any choice can only be 'satisfactory' and never 'optimal' (Simon 1945, ch. 4; March and Simon 1963, ch. 6). Enterprises do not 'maximize', they 'satisfice'. But what do they satisfice if their managers are not committed to profits? Williamson (1964) and Marris (1964) have argued that salaried managers are motivated by the rewards associated with their occupational position: they pursue salary, fringe benefits, work autonomy, and prestige, all of which are associated with the size of the enterprise. Thus, managers attempt to ensure the growth of their department and their enterprise, subject only to earning sufficient profits to keep the shareholders quiescent. Large and rapidly growing enterprises provide the rewards which managers pursue.[8]

The theory of industrial society embodies a coherent and, to many, convincing interpretation of the position of the business enterprise in modern industrial capitalism. The growth in the scale of production which is required by the development of technology results in a separation of ownership and control and, therefore, a 'managerial revolution', the rise to power of a new managerial class. Non-sectionalist managerialists claim that this class is the carrier of a new social ethic of responsibility, while sectionalist managerialists argue that, like any class, it pursues its own self-interest. The sectionalist argument has been widely used as the basis for attempts to construct a new perspective in microeconomics, but the non-sectionalist position has not proved attractive enough to be taken as the basis for an alternative economic theory. The sectionalist argument, therefore, has taken the lead in theoretical and empirical work. In the course of this book many criticisms of the theory of industrial society will be made, but it will be argued that any adequate understanding of big business must recognize the real, though limited, achievements of sectional managerialism.

Marxism and the theory of capitalist society

The theory of capitalist society is rooted in the work of Marx, though the form in which it has influenced research on the modern business enterprise owes more to the statement of the position in the work of Lenin. Although Marx's discussion of capital and his posthumously published remarks on the joint stock company have provided a source of material for later writers, it is the analysis in Lenin (1917a) which laid the foundations for the development of the orthodox Marxist theory which has acquired the status of textbook knowledge in Soviet Marxism. It is this orthodoxy which has supplied the concepts employed in many Marxist analyses of big business.

In *Imperialism*, Lenin traced the growth of industrial concentration and combination from the apex of competitive capitalism in the 1860s to the growth of monopoly capitalism in the 1890s. The introduction of the joint stock company in this period was seen as the harbinger of socialist production because it 'drags the capitalists, against their will and consciousness, into some sort of new social order, a transitional one from complete free competition to complete socialisation' (Lenin 1917a, p. 23). The society of the period from 1890 to 1917 represented the 'highest stage' of capitalism and its partial transcendence: 'Production becomes social, but appropriation remains private' (ibid., pp. 56, 119). This 'transitional' character of the joint stock company derives from its separation of the increasingly socialized productive assets from the still privatized appropriation of surplus value. The physical productive force, 'real capital' or 'functioning capital', is separated from the shares, bonds, and mortgages which comprise 'money capital'. Property owners withdraw from directly productive activities and concentrate upon their claims to money capital (Kuusinen *et al.* 1959, p. 252; Ryndina and Chernikov 1974, pp. 112ff., 186–9; Menshikov 1969, p. 11ff.).

The spread of the joint stock company encourages the monopolization of the economy through the growth of individual enterprises and through the cartels, trusts, shareholdings, and interlocking directorships which link enterprises together (Lenin 1917a, pp. 39, 45ff.). Both industry and banking become monopolized at the same time. Industrials monopolize productive capital and the banks 'grow from modest middlemen into powerful monopolies having at their command almost the whole of the money capital of all the capitalists and small businessmen' (Lenin 1917a, p. 28; Eaton 1963, p. 191). Monopolized capital in banking and manufacturing fuses into 'finance capital', capital which is not restricted to one particular sphere of activity.[9] The major banks own shares in industry, and industrial combines own shares in banks. The expansion of the credit system – manifested in the development of savings banks, insurance companies, investment trusts, pension funds, and so on – consolidates the dominance of finance capital over real capital (Rochester 1936, p. 13; Ryndina and Chernikov 1974, pp. 179–80). Finance capital is structured into 'financial groups' or 'empires of high finance', which are 'a method by which a handful of financial magnates can establish and extend their rule over a vast number of industrial, financial and other enterprises' (Ryndina and Chernikov 1974, p. 182). This is achieved through establishing centres of co-ordination and control over subordinate production units. The nucleus of the financial group is a closely linked group of monopolies which pursues a common policy and exerts control over a large number of operating companies in various branches of the economy. Interlocking directorships, cross-shareholdings, and other types of connection create 'associations of capital which at most have a common direction and at the least a common interest in avoiding conflicts of interest' (Aaronovitch 1961, p. 79, emphasis removed; 1955, pp. 12, 54ff.; Rochester 1936, p. 104). Perlo (1957, p. 15) claims that the 'ties which interlock the monopolies have become tighter and more complex. The control of corporations is more and more centralised in knots of financial power'. As capitalism develops, so these financial groupings are transformed 'from purely family groups into broad coalitions consisting of many families of financial magnates' (Ryndina and Chernikov 1974, p. 186; Rochester 1936, pp. 104–6; Menshikov 1969, p. 216).

Perlo has argued that the leaders of these financial groups are themselves connected into a nation-wide 'spider web':

Strong ties of ownership cemented with interlocking directorates link financial institutions of different kinds in an inner circle of coordinated power. Similar strands extend from the inner circle to the great corporations of industry, transport and utilities, through which billions of profits extracted from the population of this and other countries are funneled to the central oligarchy [Perlo 1957, pp. 61–2; Ryndina and Chernikov 1974, p. 182ff.; Bukharin 1915, p. 72].

This inner circle of finance capitalists, rentiers dependent on the income earned from money capital, are parasitic upon those who actually manage productive capital (Lenin 1917a, p. 56; Bukharin and Preobrazhensky 1920, pp. 141–8; Rochester 1936, p. 85). Recruited from the wealthy families and big banks they form a financial oligarchy, a clique of 'a few hundred or at most a few thousand men of wealth' who comprise the dominant social class (Perlo 1957, p. 13; Eaton 1963, p. 193; Aaronovitch 1961, p. 70). The members of the oligarchy determine the general policies which are implemented by their subordinate managers:

The financial oligarchy . . . does not, as a rule, itself take part in the direction of the hundreds and thousands of industrial companies, banks, railways and other enterprises which it controls. The 'activity' of the financial groups comes down more and more to expanding its domination by way of the acquiring of controlling blocks of shares in ever new companies and by various financial machinations. The immediate direction of the enterprises passes over gradually into the hands of hired directors [Kuusinen *et al.* 1959, p. 252].

While finance capitalists play an essential role in the reproduction of capitalist relations of production, they no longer play any significant role in the technical development of the forces of production. Actual control over production is in the hands of the managers, engineers, and clerks, though this is not to be seen as a managerial revolution. The finance capitalists retain the power to hire and fire, to decide policy, and to appropriate the proceeds of production (Kuusinen *et al.* 1959, p. 292; Menshikov 1969, pp. 80–1, 132–4, 318–20).

At the level of the economy as a whole, there is a tendency for an ever greater proportion of economic activity to fall into the hands of a small number of financial groups. Bukharin went so far as to claim that there was a tendency for the entire national economy to become 'a single combined enterprise with an organisation connection between all the branches of production' (Bukharin 1915, p. 70). Competition between groups is the driving force behind monopolization, and the formation of cartels, trusts, and other monopolistic forms is the means through which the capitalist class, against its will, brings about the incipient socialization of production. But it is also the means through which extra profit can be earned. Capital flows freely from the less to the more profitable sectors under conditions of atomistic competition, and so there is a tendency for the rate of profit earned by each unit of capital to be equalized. Competitive conditions generate a rising 'organic composition of capital', a continual displacement of labour by machinery,[10] and hence generate a tendency for the rate of profit to fall (Kozlov 1977, pp. 447ff., 214ff.). This does not necessarily occur under monopoly conditions because market barriers inhibit the free movement of capital and so there is no equalization of profits. Higher profits can be earned in the monopoly sectors dominated by the financial groups, but unprofitable sectors stagnate and require state support if they are to survive. Monopolization is associated with an interlocking between finance capital and the state, this partnership guaranteeing the conditions for domestic profitability and ensuring the international expansion of the national monopolies:

State power has become the domain of a financial oligarchy; the latter manages production which is tied up by the banks into one knot. This process of the organisation of production has proceeded from below; it has fortified itself within the framework of modern states, which have become an exact expression of the interests of finance capital [Bukharin 1915, p. 108].

'State monopoly capitalism' is the form of state–economy relationship appropriate to the stage of 'general crisis' initiated by the First World War and the Russian revolution. This general crisis is an all-pervasive disintegration of the system which requires an increasingly interventionist state (Kuusinen *et al.* 1959, p. 258; Rochester 1936, p. 287ff.; Aaronovitch 1955, pp. 66, 73ff.). The state takes on more and more economic functions such as the maintenance of profitability, creating demand, reallocation of national income, direct state enterprise, international military and political involvement, etc., but there are important changes in its internal structure (Kuusinen *et al.* 1959, pp. 267–9; Varga 1928, p. 66). Orthodox Marxist writers of the 1920s saw the fascist states of Italy and Germany as indicative of the form of state which would emerge in the other capitalist societies (Varga 1928, p. 12), but the more general claim is simply that dictatorship is more appropriate than democracy for monopoly capitalism. State monopoly capitalism continually evolves in this direction, with the state machine acting in the interests of the most powerful capitalist groups and serving the interests of the financial oligarchy (Aaronovitch 1955, p. 75):

Finance capital is not one interest among many which may lobby an impartial government and whose legitimate rights such a government should seek to satisfy. It is built into and controls the entire government and administration of this country for its own profit and against the wider interests of the nation [Aaronovitch 1961, p. 162].[11]

Internationally, state monopoly capitalism is expressed in imperialism and militarism. Owing to declining opportunities for profitable investment in their national economies, the monopolistic groups export capital throughout the world. The competitive struggle for colonies in which to invest brings about the increased chances of military conflict between rival national monopolies. An international division of labour develops, in which the industrial development of the colonies is subordinated to the needs of the imperialist powers (Lenin 1917a, p. 77). Colonial development is aimed at the production of the minerals, raw materials, and agricultural products which are required by capitalists in the imperial centres. The conflict of national capitalist groups produces a world economy in which the 'anarchy' of capitalist production is reproduced at the international level.

The idea that contemporary capitalism is in a 'transitional' phase, a stage which contains certain important features of the socialist future, has been more difficult to sustain as time has elapsed since Lenin's restatement of Marx's views on this matter. It may still seem possible to describe contemporary industrial capitalism as the 'highest stage' of capitalism, but to regard it as 'transitional' seems to deny the apparent stability of this stage of capitalist development. The orthodoxy has continued to pay lip service to the idea, but other Marxist writers have tried to arrive at alternative interpretations of the consolidation of 'late capitalism'.[12]

Althusserian writers such as Bettelheim (1970) and Poulantzas (1968; 1974) have responded to this by arguing that the *legal* changes involved in the joint stock company have not had the assumed *economic* consequences. It is argued that law is a condition of existence of social relations of production, but is determined, in the last instance, by those relations. The labour contract is a reflection of the wage labour relation, and property titles are reflections of the relation of 'economic ownership' over the means of production. Thus, a distinction is made between the ideological form of legal property, which survives as a purely nominal right to income from corporate capital, and the economic ownership relation which structures the appropriation and distribution of economic value through control over investments and capital accumulation (Bettelheim 1970, pp. 69, 134–5; Poulantzas 1974, p. 18). The implication of this is that there is no necessary connection between being a shareholder and having effective control over the means of production. Those shareholders with a large percentage holding may, depending on the overall distribution of shares, be able to participate in economic ownership, but it is also possible for those without shares to participate in the same way. The functions attached to economic ownership become embodied in a managerial hierarchy, all of whose members perform the 'global function of capital'. Those executives at the top of the hierarchy and their subordinate managers are 'supports' of capitalist relations of production, but only the former, together with the big shareholders and financiers, occupy the 'place' of capital. Abstract classes are defined as structural places in the relations of production, but the particular agents who occupy these places constitute the concrete social classes which can be identified in particular societies (Poulantzas 1974; Carchedi 1975).

From a different perspective, and on the basis of radically different assumptions, Baran and Sweezy (1966) also have concluded that the basic relations of capitalist production continue to exist in a modernized form (see also Braverman 1974). These writers take over much of the sectionalist managerialist position, but place this in the context of Marxist theory. To distance themselves from any implication that industrial enterprises are exclusively dependent on banks for investment funding they write not of 'finance capital' but of 'monopoly capital' – capital in its monopoly form regardless of sector. The orientation of the large enterprise towards the rational pursuit of growth or revenue involves no fundamental departure from the conditions of capitalist production – and if profits are pursued there is no departure from the goal of capitalist production. The managerial enterprise expresses these conditions in a particularly clear and systematic way, devoid of any of the irrational characteristics of the family enterprise. The continuing constraint of market profitability ensures the continuity of capitalist relations. This form of 'Marxist managerialism', therefore, sees the rational action of the large enterprise as the visible hand of monopoly capital.

A more radical position has been taken by Marcuse, Habermas, and the Frankfurt School of critical theory. Drawing on similar arguments to those of the theory of industrial society, they trace out some of the implications of the development of industrial technology (Marcuse 1964). Habermas (1973) argues that the expansion of technology requires a number of fundamental alterations to the basic tenets of Marxist theory. To be true to the spirit of Marxism it is necessary to depart from the letter of Marxism (Habermas 1976). The technical development of the forces of production undermines the labour theory of value and the deductions which have been drawn from this. In the stage of 'late capitalism' the economic crisis tendencies generated in the market are regulated by the state, but the price of this is that these tendencies are translated into the structure and operations of the state itself. In order to finance the required expenditure, the state has to borrow or raise taxation and so experiences 'fiscal problems' which cannot be resolved. The state also experiences an internal structural dislocation between its various constituent parts which makes it incapable of successfully pursuing policies aimed at coping with its own fiscal problems and its regulatory activities in the economy. Habermas argues that

Rationality deficits are the unavoidable result of a snare of relations into which the advanced-capitalist state fumbles and in which its contradictory activities must become more and more muddled [Habermas 1973, p. 63. See also Offe 1972].[13]

Like the theory of industrial society, the theory of capitalist society contains many important and useful ideas. Nevertheless, the contrary positions proposed from within Marxism by the Althusserians, the Marxist managerialists, and the critical theorists show that the theory is not without its internal difficulties. Any alternative explanation of the role of the business enterprise must build on its real, though flawed, achievements.

The corporation in modern society: an overview

The two major theories discussed in this chapter have been the most influential perspectives on the business enterprise. Each offers a relatively coherent account of the main developments in industrial capitalism, and each has a certain superficial credibility. Much of the empirical research carried out, and the main theoretical alternatives which have been proposed, can be seen as products of attempts to grapple with the implications of these two contending theories. Many of the most sophisticated researchers have been led by the results of their research to push beyond the limits of their initial theoretical formulations. Especially since Zeitlin's (1974) codification of the anti-managerialist position, empirical research and theoretical innovation have been able to advance together. The arguments presented in the rest of this book draw upon this work in an attempt to present an alternative explanation of the development of the business enterprise in industrial capitalism which has the scope of its two predecessors as well as having the capacity to generate further empirical advances. In order to clarify the distinctive features of this alternative, it is necessary to summarize its main elements before entering into the systematic investigations necessary to document it in detail.

Shareholders, those who have the legal entitlement to a dividend income from the activities of business enterprises, have no authority to participate in company affairs over and above their right to vote in the appointment of directors. It will be argued, however, that those shareholders who can mobilize votes in sufficient numbers, by owning large percentage blocks of shares or by acquiring voting control over shares held by others, have the power to intervene in corporate affairs and to ensure that their views are influential. Effective control rests with those who can benefit from the *de facto* disenfranchisement of the small shareholder. Although individuals and families have often been able to maintain or achieve this power, it is increasingly the case that the dominant owners of company shares are other companies and financial intermediaries. Banks, insurance companies, pension funds, and investment companies, have become the most important agents in the capital markets. These share-owning enterprises are, in their turn, subject to the same form of ownership, resulting in the formation of a network of intercorporate capital relations in each of the advanced capitalist economies. This structure of 'impersonal possession' is a common feature of all these economies, though the concrete forms which it takes depends upon the varying national patterns of industrialization. Banks, for example, play an important role in the reproduction of the system of impersonal possession, but this role may take a variety of forms. In some economies they exercise a generalized dominance in capital markets along with other intermediaries, while in other economies they are parts of cohesive groupings of industrial and financial interests. These variations in the role played by banks mean that the rise of impersonal possession cannot be equated with the rise of bank control.

These emerging features of impersonal possession are associated with a number of other features of the business enterprise and its relationship to the state. Internally, the enterprise has undergone not simply an expansion of its managerial hierarchy, but also a structural alteration in its mode of administration. Instead of personal systems of supervision, the modern enterprise relies on impersonal mechanisms such as the budgetary constraints imposed on corporate divisions, the bureaucratic constraints imposed on career executives, and the technical constraints imposed on factory and office work. Externally, the rising level of concentration in economic activity means that the enterprise operates in oligopolistic markets rather than under conditions of atomistic competition. A small number of large enterprises control the bulk of all corporate assets, and these enterprises are surrounded by a fringe of small and medium-sized firms in which some of the features of atomistic competition are still to be found. The large enterprises have a greater autonomy within their markets and possess considerable market power. In oligopolistic markets the commercial relations between enterprises are power relations, and are entwined with intercorporate shareholdings and interlocking directorships. Corporate policies are constrained by market relations and by the 'non-market' factors of power and influence.

At the international level oligopolistic competition is translated into the worldwide activities of the multinational enterprise. The foreign investments of the advanced capitalist economies involve the direct ownership of overseas subsidiaries which are constituent elements of large integrated enterprises. The pattern of capital accumulation within each national economy is determined by the particular mixture of domestic and foreign enterprises that operate within its boundaries. At the same time, the multinational enterprises of each of the advanced economies have increasingly turned their attention to other advanced economies. This is expressed in an increase in the number of capital relations, commercial relations, and interlocking directorships which connect enterprises of varying nationalities. National economies are formed into a world economic system through a network of international, intercorporate links.

The state in all of the advanced capitalist societies has taken an increasingly interventionist role, rather than simply facilitating private production. States have expanded their budgets to finance new areas of expenditure, and they have become involved in economic planning and the restructuring of economic activity. The modes and intensities of state intervention vary from one country to another and reflect not only the structures of their economies, but also the policies and practices of their upper classes. Class structure, in turn, reflects the economic transformations that that society has undergone. A propertied upper class can still be identified; the impersonal structure of possession has not resulted in the loss of power by wealthy, propertied persons. Yet the capitalist upper class is no longer merely a collection of individually powerful families. Wealthy families spread their shareholdings across a large number of companies rather than holding controlling blocks in particular companies, and they form a pool from which many top corporate managers are recruited. The propertied upper class has interests throughout the corporate system and is able to ensure its continuity over time through its monopolization of the educational system as well as its monopolization of wealth.

In the remainder of this book details of this alternative interpretation will be presented. It will be argued that the theories of industrial society and of capitalist society, although they have generated much relevant empirical data, must now be buried and that further advance requires their transcendence. Chapter 2 sets out the model of corporate control which is used in Chapters 3, 4, and 5 to explain the alternative patterns of capitalist development found in the advanced societies. In Chapter 6 the model is extended into a more detailed account of the internal administration of the enterprise. The national and international economies and the role of the state are discussed in Chapter 7, and in Chapter 8 the development of corporate capital is related to transformations in class structure.

Notes

1   In Britain the legal form is the joint stock company, while American law speaks of corporations. French and German equivalents are the *société anonyme* and the *Aktiengesellschaft*. Although there are numerous legal differences, all these forms may be referred to as companies or corporations. Strictly speaking there are both voting and non-voting

shares, but these technicalities can be ignored in the present discussion.

2 A parent company is one which owns a majority of the shares in another, subsidiary, company.

3 Giddens (1976, p. 727) claims that this theory is the substantive correlate of structural functionalism and of a positivist philosophy of science. See also Fay (1975, p. 55ff.).

4 See the important critiques in Goldthorpe (1964; 1972; 1974).

5 This has spawned a mass of work in the sociology of development according to which 'underdeveloped' societies develop on the basis of the transfer of technology from the already 'developed' societies. See Hoselitz (1960), Hoselitz and Moore (1966), McClelland (1961), and Rostow (1960). These approaches are criticized in Hoogvelt (1976). In political sociology the approach is associated with the 'pluralism' found in Lipset (1960), Aron (1960), and other sources. Pluralism is criticized in Parry (1969) and Keller (1963).

6 This viewpoint underlies much of the so-called 'functionalist' theory of stratification. See Davis and Moore (1945) and Parsons (1954a).

7 Variants of this non-sectional managerialism are also found in Dahrendorf (1959) and Crosland (1962; 1956).

8 See also Baumol (1959) and the contributions in Mason (1959). These arguments are discussed in Jackson (1982).

9 The concept of finance capital originated in the works of Kautsky (1902), Hilferding (1910), and Luxemburg (1913). For a general review see Kiernan (1974).

10 Machinery is referred to as 'constant capital' while labour, the source of a variable amount of value, is termed 'variable capital'. Strictly, the organic composition of capital is the ratio of constant to variable capital.

11 See also Gollan (1956), Harvey and Hood (1958), Frankel (1970), Rochester (1936, ch. 8), and Perlo (1957, ch. 15). Similar arguments can be found in Lenin (1917b), though the argument there is more complex. For critical discussions see Jessop (1978) and Wirth (1973).

12 The term 'late capitalism' is that used by Habermas (1973) and Mandel (1972), but others have written of 'contemporary capitalism', 'modern capitalism', and so on.

13   Habermas terms this the 'rationality crisis' and relates it to broader sociocultural problems of legitimation which cannot be discussed here. On the displacement of economic crisis tendencies see Wirth (1973), Gerstenberger (1976), Meier (1976). On legitimation problems see Habermas (1976, part 4) and Offe (1970). Habermas's general approach to sociology is discussed in Scott (1978).

2 Corporate capital and corporate control

The theoretical debates which were reviewed in the previous chapter centred around the social transformations which are presumed to follow from the emergence of the joint stock company. In order to pursue the research problems generated in those debates it is necessary to establish a conceptual framework which can be used to interpret the available evidence. No such framework can be theoretically neutral, but it is possible to construct a framework which does not contradict the basic tenets of the specific theories under consideration. Though they may differ as to whether 'management control' is the most appropriate description of the largest enterprises in the world today, the protagonists should be able to agree on what is meant by the concept of 'management control'. In fact it can be shown that Marxist writers such as Renner and Hilferding have a similar view of corporate capital to liberal writers such as Berle and Means, and that this is true also of a range of other concepts which they and their followers have formulated. Where they differ, of course, is in their application of these concepts in their interpretations of the development of industrial capitalism; and these differences are expressed in the polarization between the theory of capitalist society and the theory of industrial society. If these rival theories are to be transcended once and for all, it is necessary that the alternative interpretation which has been proposed should be constructed from concepts which are meaningful to supporters of the moribund theories. Only in this way can fruitful discussion take place and the basis be laid for future empirical research.

The corporation and finance capital

The most rigorous conceptualization of finance capital is to be found in the works of the 'Austro-Marxists' Renner and Hilferding, who based their analyses on Marx's scattered remarks on joint stock capital and the corporate form. Marx claimed that the relations of production which determined the effective possession of the means of production were to be distinguished from the legal property rights with which they were associated. Relations of production 'develop unevenly as legal relations' and so possession is always part of a 'more concrete substratum'. For this reason, 'The influence of laws in stabilizing relations of distribution, and hence their effect on production, requires to be determined in each specific instance' (Marx 1857, pp. 98, 102, 109). Study of law in the abstract is inadequate, since law must be related to its concrete historical context. In the legal form of the joint stock company, 'capital as property' was separated from 'capital as a function'. The function of capital in the process of production – which is to subordinate the labour process to the expansion of capital – is 'institutionalized' and so separated from the individual property owners who supply the capital. Those engaged in the 'work of management and supervision' which is inherent in the function of capital need not be those who are the legal owners of the corporation (Marx 1894, pp. 372, 376, 378–9, 428; see also Marx 1885). In joint stock companies the function of capital is divorced from capital ownership, but this 'divorce' develops gradually as part of the expansion of the credit system: 'Stock companies in general – developed with the credit system – have an increasing tendency to separate this work of management as a function from the ownership of capital, be it self-owned or borrowed' (Marx 1894, p. 380).

Renner (1904) and Hilferding (1910) developed closely related analyses of joint stock capital which went well beyond Marx's somewhat terse statements. Renner held that the legal institution of property is that set of legal imperatives which regulate the 'detention', or access to, social objects, and that a particularly important part of the law of property concerns detention of the objects involved in the production of goods and services (Renner 1904, pp. 53, 73–4). The institution of property defines legal relations of ownership, which comprise 'a person's all-embracing legal power over a tangible object' (ibid., p. 81). But the actual social relations which constitute a society rarely correspond exactly to such codified legal representations. To see social relations as consisting entirely of their legal expressions is to be subject to 'fetishism', to transform a social relation into a thing. Legal ownership differs from social ownership. While in legal theory 'ownership is reduced to a mere legal title' and is thereby fetishized (ibid., p. 147), legal forms are simply one of the conditions of actual social relations. In reality it is the 'social function' of legal forms which is crucial, and so a legal relation of ownership can have varying social meanings depending upon the social order of which it is a part. The social relation of ownership – the actually effective power of possession – may diverge from the legal relation of ownership, even though the latter is an essential condition of the former. Renner argues that it is possible for effective possession to be structured in a way which does not correspond to the prevailing legal forms, and that in such situations rights over objects become relations of social power:

Without any change in the norm, below the threshold of collective consciousness, a *de facto* right is added to the personal absolute domination over a corporeal thing. This right is not based upon a special legal provision. It is a power of control, the power to issue commands and to enforce them [ibid., pp. 107, 117].

Legal institutions, therefore, help to give rise to social relations, but are then themselves subject to transformation as these social relations develop. There will always be a greater or lesser lack of correspondence between property relations and the social relations of production.

In the individually-owned capitalist enterprise the scale of production is limited by the personal wealth of the capitalist, who invests his or her entire capital in this one particular enterprise. There is a long-term and active participation by 'working capitalists who must combine ownership with the entrepreneurial function' (Hilferding 1910, p. 121). The productive, functioning capitalist earns 'profit' on this invested capital. As the enterprise grows in size it begins to transcend the limits of the old legal forms in order to raise large amounts of credit. The joint stock company arose as a response to these altered social circumstances and opened-up new possibilities of social development. The individual capitalist now subscribes part of the capital jointly with others and so ceases to be an 'industrial capitalist'. Instead the capitalist is a creditor, an owner of money capital who has no necessary concern with the use to which the credit is put. The money capitalist, as a shareholder, earns 'interest' from profitable investments (Renner 1904, pp. 142–3), but no longer has effective possession of the means of production. Legal ownership of company stock gives the right to benefit from corporate activities,[1] but legal ownership of the corporate assets themselves is vested in the joint stock company as a corporate body.

Thus is created a problem of control: if the company is legal owner of the means of production, who has the actual power to determine the use of these means (ibid., pp. 198, 268, 275)? Renner's answer is that this power – the 'social power of command' (ibid., p. 283) – is vested in the organizational activities of salaried managers, who combine it with their technical expertise in the process of production. This social power, the 'capitalist function', becomes dissociated from the shareholding capitalists who retain the right to appropriate surplus value in the form of interest. In Hilferding's work this conclusion is allied with an analysis of the growing importance of banks and financial intermediaries in the ownership of money capital. The fusion of banking and industry into 'finance capital' removes most of the shareholding capitalists even further from actual production. But a small circle of shareholders who occupy key positions on the boards of directors of the major joint stock companies retain control over the money capital of the whole capitalist class. These finance capitalists are the leading edge of the class and are able to ensure that the power exercised by salaried managers is subordinate to the interests of the capitalist class (Hilferding 1910, pp. 119–20; Renner 1904, p. 114ff.). Capitalist development is the outcome of the interplay between finance capitalists and their subordinate managers, but both Hilferding and Renner draw the conclusion that the rise of the joint stock company points to the eventual demise of the capitalist class. Because capitalists no longer held the social power of command, they had become technically redundant to the actual process of production. The residual control of the finance capitalists no longer had any basis in the technical development of the forces of production.

The corporation and management control

The model of finance capital was developed in Germany and Austria, where late and rapid industrial development brought out forcefully the issues involved in the emergence of the joint stock company and the growth of monopolization. In Britain such problems were hardly apparent to contemporary observers before the

First World War, though Fabian writers and the liberal economist, Hobson, had outlined some of the consequences of the emergence of the joint stock company. Even Hobson, whose analyses were influential for Hilferding and Lenin, failed to see any major implications for the prevailing economic theory of the firm. Hobson recognized that the spate of company flotations after the 1870s involved an arrangement whereby a 'vendor' agreed with a 'promoter' to form a company and to sell a large block of shares to the general public, with the vendor ensuring that a large enough shareholding was retained to ensure continuing control. He concluded that 'Diffused ownership with concentrated control is the distinctive feature of the company' and that 'the monetary support of the public is wanted but not their direction' (Hobson 1906, p. 240). Hobson's argument raises to a central place a point which is subsidiary in the work of Hilferding and Renner. He argued that the individual shareholders who were separated from effective control were not capitalists but a large body of small shareholders. This point was central to the writings of the Fabian Socialists, who held that the bulk of the shareholders became purely passive and that the large shareholder adopted a 'rentier' orientation (Clarke 1889; Macrosty 1901). By the inter-war years, the Fabians felt, the leading role in business was played by the 'financiers and bankers who monopolise the art of collecting millions of spare money' (Shaw 1928, p. 181). Managers were employed as the subordinate 'brain workers', the 'intellectual proletariat' (Webb and Webb 1923, pp. 56–8), who served the capitalist rentiers. The post-war Fabian writings of Crosland (1956) show a reversal of this line of argument. Crosland claimed that *all* shareholders had become dissociated from control, and that the career managers had, in consequence, usurped the powers formerly exercised by the capitalist business class.

Neither Hobson nor the Fabians carried out any detailed empirical investigations in this area, many of their arguments drawing upon American debates. The late and rapid industrialization of the United States stimulated considerable discussion about the joint stock company and the power of the investment bankers who formed these companies into large, monopolistic enterprises. The most influential product of these debates was the work of Berle and Means (1932), which formulated the classic statement of the relationship between small shareholders and salaried managers in the modern corporation.

Berle and Means argued that the corporation involves a dissolution of 'the traditional logic of property', which assumed that the supplier of capital was able to determine the use of that capital. Before the rise of the corporation the owner of industrial property had full rights of both use and benefit over this property, but in the era of the corporation this has changed. The modern corporation involves 'the surrender and regrouping of the incidence of ownership, which formerly bracketed full power of manual disposition with complete right to enjoy the use, the fruits, and the proceeds of physical assets' (Berle and Means 1932, p. 8). Stocks and shares give their owners an interest in an enterprise, but they are not necessarily associated with control of the assets. There is a dissolution of these traditional property rights, since those who supply the capital of a joint stock company need not be identical with those who determine the uses to which it is put (ibid., p. 433ff.; Berle 1955, p. 17). When the two aspects of property are dissociated it is possible to distinguish 'nominal ownership', which is the right to receive revenue as a return for risking one's wealth by investing in a company, from 'effective ownership', which is the ability to control the corporate assets.[2] Thus, it is necessary to go beyond mere legal forms to the 'economic and social background of law' (Berle and Means 1932, p. 339). While the corporation emerged as a purely legal form, it rapidly became a 'social institution' to which the law had continually to be adapted. The corporate enterprise is not a mere creature of the law; it is 'not fictitious, but factual' (Berle 1955, p. 9).

In the corporate enterprise the shareholders are not the owners of the assets. The assets are legally owned by the corporation itself and are, therefore, subject to the effective control of whoever is able to determine corporate behaviour. As in Renner and Hilferding, Berle and Means see the problem of control at the heart of the modern corporation. Central to their argument was the claim that shareholders were gradually being forced to withdraw more and more from actual control. When there are few shareholders in a company they may, if they wish, continue to cooperate in the management of the corporation; but as they increase in number, this becomes more difficult. When shares are dispersed among a great number of individual investors, no one has sufficient shares to ensure them a decisive voice in the company's affairs. Under such circumstances owner control is weakened and other groups have enhanced opportunities for participation in control. 'Management control' is that situation where those who are able to dominate the composition of the board of directors – and Berle and Means see the internal executives as the main contenders – are almost totally divorced from legal owner-ship (Berle and Means 1932, pp. 80–4). This change in control status has definite consequences for corporate behaviour:

The separation of ownership and control produces a condition where the interests of owner and of ultimate manager may, and often do diverge, and where many of the checks which formerly operated to limit the use of power disappear [Berle and Means 1932, pp. 6, 121–2].

The emergence of the corporate form, of joint stock capital, creates a crucial condition for the dispersal of shareholdings among an anonymous mass of small shareholders. These share-holders can no longer be regarded as 'capitalists' as they have simply a beneficial, and often very small, interest in the affairs of the companies of which they are the nominal owners. The power of control becomes divorced from legal ownership, and it is no longer appropriate to regard the enterprise as a capitalist enter-prise at all. The managerial enterprise, subject to management-control, is effectively free from the constraints of capitalist prop-erty ownership. The 'democratization' of shareholdings means that if the system is capitalist, then it is 'People's Capitalism' (Berle 1960).

A model of corporate control

There are striking similarities between the analyses of the corpora-tion given by Renner, Hilferding, Berle and Means, though the important differences between them must not be underestimated. Berle and Means argued that a transition from owner control to management control was occurring. The Austro-Marxists recog-nized a similar transition, but held that share ownership, through the credit and banking system, remained a centrally important factor in the exercise of control. In order to explore the ramifica-tions of these differences and the wider issues raised in the con-frontation between the theory of industrial society and the theory of capitalist society, it is necessary to draw out and extend the areas of agreement in order to produce a coherent model of corporate control.

The emergence of the legal form of the joint stock company

involves the legal recognition of the corporation itself as the owner of its assets and the consequent separation of shareholders from control over that corporation and so from effective possession of the means of production. With nominal ownership of the means of production passing to the corporation itself, the question of *who* is able to control the corporation and determine its behaviour becomes all-important. Because the separation of shareholders from effective control is a legal separation and not an absolute divorce, it is possible that shareholders, or at least a portion of them, will be able to exercise control; but it is also possible that salaried managers or external finance capitalists may undertake this role. These three groups – shareholders, executives, and financiers – may be seen as the protagonists in a struggle for control in which the balance of power within and between the groups depends upon the social conditions which have been described in the works discussed above and in the debate which has gone on around these works.[3] The key questions which have arisen in this debate concern the interests of these groups, the nature of control and the mechanisms through which this control can be exercised.

The corporate form itself gives rise to the differentiation of shareholders, executives, and financiers because of the separation between the right to determine the *use* of the assets and the right to benefit from this use. The nominal legal owners 'become no more than creditors' (Westergaard and Resler 1975, p. 154) who can be treated 'as legitimate claimants to some fixed share of the profits' (Bell 1974, p. 295). This means that

individual investors of all sorts become rentiers and become aware that this is what they are. Their property consists less and less of their ownership of some part of the corporation's physical plant and stock of materials and products than of their right to a revenue from the ability of the corporation to manoeuvre profitably [MacPherson 1973, p. 154. See also Tawney 1920 and Levy 1950].

The property rights of individuals become mere financial claims upon the company, together with the right to transfer these entitlements to others (Jones 1982, pp. 86–92; Hadden 1977. See also Hollowell 1982; Causer 1982; Becker 1977). Property rights may be transferred through the sale of the shares in which they are embodied and are guaranteed in the constitutional rights of shareholders, as 'members' of the company, to attend the annual general meeting and vote on the selection of the directors who will be responsible for seeing that the legitimate interests of share-holders are protected. Shareholders, therefore, are rentiers who benefit from the use of corporate capital but may not participate in its control. It is possible, however, that a group within the body of shareholders may be able to exercise this control. As Poulantzas argued:

not every share or interest taken by a shareholder in a firm's capital corresponds to an equivalent or proportionate share in economic ownership and real control. This ownership is wielded as a whole by a few large shareholders, not necessarily a majority, who by various means . . . concentrate in their hands the powers that derive from it [Poulantzas 1974, p. 119].

That is to say, 'the relationship between ownership and control can be viewed as one consisting of several *degrees of separation* determined by the extent of the effective involvement of the owners in decision-making' (De Vroey 1976, p. 12). Large shareholders may 'retain real ownership through a partial legal ownership' (Carchedi 1975, p. 49).

The possibilities which shareholders have for participation in control are limited by the countervailing power of other contenders for control. Management have been depicted, especially by supporters of the theory of industrial society, as having their primary power base in the organizational hierarchy of the enterprise, and it has been claimed that this enables them to effectively subvert the residual powers of shareholders. Whatever the final judgement on this claim, it must be recognized that technical expertise and the ability of full-time executives to manipulate the flow of information does provide a power base for management. Managers have the potential to manipulate the passive shareholders and their representatives and so to pre-empt the decisions which are taken by the board of directors (Pahl and Winkler 1974). Those influenced by the theory of capitalist society have cast financiers in the role of main rival to passive shareholders. Those who control the availability of credit have the power to specify the conditions under which enterprises have access to this credit and so can determine the chances which they have to take up investment opportunities. Financiers have the power to subordinate managers and to displace those shareholders who are not themselves part of the system of finance capital (Soref 1980; Zeitlin 1980).

Shareholders, financiers, and executives are not, of course, always distinguishable as concrete groups. Those who provide loan capital may also be major shareholders, and shareholders may be members of the executive hierarchy. But as ideal types they are recognizable as distinct contenders for control. Influential work by Cutler, Hindess, Hirst, and Hussain, however, has suggested that the question of who controls the enterprise is unimportant. The important question concerns the social relations under which control is exercised. This radical position, if accepted, would lead to the conclusion that the bulk of the issues raised in this chapter and the last are irrelevant to an understanding of the capitalist enterprise. These writers claim that 'possession' of the means of production[4] refers to the power to control the functioning of the means of production and to exclude others from their use. Property and company law is the basis of the 'recognition' of the company as an agent capable of possession and of entering into contracts. While the 'corporation' is the legal agent, the 'enterprise' is the economic agent which unites possession with the performance of the function of capital within a unit of production (Cutler *et al.* 1977, pp. 249, 275). This function – direction and supervision of the labour process and the calculation of monetary costs and returns (ibid., p. 255) – is embodied in the enterprise which, like all agents, can be considered as a locus of decision and action in its own right. Its actions cannot be reduced to the actions and motives of individual managers. Rather, its actions are the outcome of definite modes and mechanisms of 'calculation' and 'supervision' through which decisions are made and implemented. The autonomy of the enterprise as a social organization depends upon a calculation which is 'effected by an organizational apparatus involving both individuals and machines (e.g. computers, tabulators, and sorters, etc.) so that the products of calculation can in no way be reduced to the work of any human individual' (Cutler *et al.* 1977, p. 277. See also Kitahara 1980, pp. 31–2). Managers are those who direct the operations of the enterprise as 'delegates' or 'supports' of the enterprise (ibid., p. 304); they do not themselves possess the means of production but are mere functionaries recruited through specialized labour markets to carry out the requirements of the capitalist enterprise itself (Hirst 1979, pp. 131–2; Tomlinson 1982; Kinsey 1983). Just as managers cannot be considered to be capitalists, neither can shareholders or financiers. The money of individuals only functions as capital when brought together in one unit of possession which is directed as a single agency of production. Shares are financial claims and only become capital if owned by financial intermediaries which use these shares as centralized money funds for credit as part of their own corporate behaviour. Insurance policies, bank deposits, and individually-owned shares are not capital, and so individual shareholders and beneficiaries are not capitalists (Hirst 1979, p. 135).

The conclusions which these writers draw from the idea of the enterprise as the personification of capital are not, however, compelling. The significance of the corporate form is that it creates the conditions under which various groups may struggle for the social power of command. The question of who is most active in determining the 'calculation' of the enterprise is an important matter because corporate behaviour cannot be considered as totally determined by market constraints. The 'dominant coalition' which comprises the active leadership of an enterprise may exercise a certain amount of choice within these constraints (Child 1972), and so researchers must investigate the interests of the various contenders for control, the conditions under which each may enter into the dominant coalition, and the consequences for corporate behaviour which follow from the social composition of the coalition. It can be accepted that nominal ownership is vested in the corporation and that, therefore, possession is expressed in and through the organizational structure of the business enterprise, but it must also be accepted that the direction in which this possession is expressed is neither given in advance nor derivable from an abstract model of the enterprise. Groups struggle for *control* over the direction which an enterprise is to follow, and so the question of control is fundamental to an understanding of corporate behaviour.

What, then, is meant by 'control' in this context? Berle and Means (1932, p. 69) define control as the ability to determine the composition of the board of directors,[5] but subsequent writers have seen it as 'the power of determining the broad policies guiding the corporation' (Goldsmith and Parmelee 1940, p. 99).[6] The common theme of these definitions is that control is the power to determine the fundamental features of corporate behaviour and that this power is institutionally located in the board of directors. The point of the Berle and Means formulation is that non-board members, such as bankers or family shareholders, may have the power of control because they are able to place their nominees on the board and so ensure a compliant directorate. Nevertheless, the important fact is that, however control may be secured, it is expressed in the ability to determine the behaviour of the enterprise. Control, then, is the power to decide upon the corporate strategy of an enterprise, where corporate strategy involves 'the determination of the basic long-term goals and objectives of the enterprise, and the adoption of courses of action and the allocation of resources necessary for carrying out these goals' (Chandler 1962, p. 13; Ansoff 1965). Effective possession of the means of production is expressed in the mechanisms of 'strategic control'.

Those who participate in the exercise of strategic control are those who make the strategic, structural decisions within the enterprise (De Vroey 1973, pp. 82–3; Eisenberg 1969, pp. 11–13). Strategic decisions are concerned with setting or altering the basic parameters within which the enterprise is to act. Strategic control involves deciding on the source and level of investment funds, the allocation of these funds to alternative uses, calculation of the rates of profit to be earned in different parts of the enterprise, the recruitment of the top executives, and the resolution of such constitutional issues as mergers, takeovers, and liquidation. Of course, relations of control are not restricted to the strategic level. Participants at all levels of the enterprise are involved in control relations, and the exercise of strategic control is an important constraint upon these subordinate relations. A particularly important level of control is that which may be termed 'operational control': the implementation of corporate strategy and thus the immediate day-to-day administration of corporate operations at plant level. Operational managers exercise their control within the general framework set out by those who control the corporate strategy,[7] and their work comprises the two dimensions of materials management and labour management. The acquisition and maintenance of raw materials, product research and development, and marketing and market research are all aspects of materials management, and have figured prominently in economic theories of the firm. By contrast, recent sociological discussions of operational management have focused on managerial control over those social relations that make up the labour process: work relations, employment relations, and industrial relations (Gospel 1983a, p. 12ff.). Labour management consists of the task structuring of work and the associated monitoring, disciplining, and rewarding of workers through such means as the division of labour in the work

place, integration of the various phases of production, recruitment, promotion, and dismissal of workers, determination of wage
levels, disputes machinery, and trades union recognition and nego-
tiation. The two aspects of operational control, the management
of materials and labour, are distinguishable only from an analytical
point of view, as concrete management roles will tend to involve
both sets of tasks. Such operational decisions as the choice and
implementation of technology, for example, involve both material
and labour implications, as forms of technology must be considered as specific combinations of these resources. At the higher
levels of operational administration managers are concerned with
financial rather than physical quantities, as the operational control
of a plant must be translated into monetary terms in order to
budget for the pursuit of the objectives specified in the corporate
strategy. For this reason the connection between strategic and
operational control is very close, with monetary calculation being
the intervening element between the two.

The problem of control was created by the emergence of the joint
stock company and thus strategic control is institutionally mediated through the legal forms of property relations (Giddens 1973,
p. 121; Clement 1975a, p. 13). It is important, therefore, to look at
the various modes of institutional mediation and the associated
mechanisms through which legal ownership is translated into strategic control. This has usually been approached in a formal and
ahistorical way, though most discussions are based around an
implicit historical interpretation of capitalist development. Berle
and Means, for example, saw a transition from those situations in
which strategic control rests upon the legal right to vote the majority of the shares through various intermediate forms which cul-
minate in dispersed shareholdings and management control. In
these intermediate modes of control are found situations where a
group of controllers have less than a majority of shares but are
able to maintain control on other bases. Berle and Means argue
that 'control is more often factual than legal, depending upon
strategic positions secured through a measure of ownership, a
share in management or an external circumstance important to the
conduct of the enterprise' (1932, p. 79). In particular, the situation
of 'minority control' is that where a small group with less than a
majority of the shares has 'working control' owing to the absence
of any other holdings large enough to oppose them. Clearly, the
level of shareholding at which minority control is possible depends

upon the distribution of the remaining shares. Unless the controlling group wishes, for whatever reason, to relinquish control, it can be assumed that they will endeavour to maintain sufficient shares to retain the controlling block. It can be argued that the degree of dispersal in share-ownership, and therefore the various modes of control, are consequences of the calculations made by those currently in control of the enterprise. In a growing enterprise, those who are in control will be willing to issue additional shares to raise capital so long as they feel that their chances of retaining control are still high. If they calculate that they are likely to lose control, they will be forced to withdraw their expansion plans or to try and maintain a controlling block of shares by forming an alliance with another group of shareholders. The essential point is that the calculation of the probability of retaining control is based on their knowledge of the existing distribution of shareholdings and their assumptions about the probable voting behaviour of other shareholders (Pitelis and Sugden 1983; Pitelis 1983).

Where control is based on almost complete ownership or on the holding of a majority of the shares by a single individual or group, the degree of dissociation between nominal ownership and effective possession is not very great and Berle and Means describe this as either 'majority ownership' or 'majority control'. As the controlling group reduces its percentage holding to below the majority level, majority control gives way to 'minority control'. The level of shareholding required for minority control is, of course, dependent upon the dispersal of the remaining shares, and the level will vary over time with trends in the general pattern of share distribution. In 1910, Hilferding had suggested that minority control required a third or a quarter of the shares (1910, pp. 118–19), but Berle and Means felt that the appropriate level for the 1920s was 20 per cent. Later writers have suggested that, with a wider dispersal of share ownership, minority control is possible with 10 per cent, 5 per cent, or even less (Larner 1970; Burch 1972; Scott and Hughes 1976). Clearly no absolute figure can be given, as the critical figure will vary not only over time and place, but also according to the unique circumstances of particular enterprises. Identification of minority control by a specific percentage cut-off point must inevitably be arbitrary, but if based on a realistic view of the prevailing distribution of shareholdings it may serve as an effective indicator of the significance of this particular form of strategic control.

Zeitlin *et al.* have argued that a situation of minority control is the most characteristic mode of control in modern industrial capitalism:

Minority control is one of the most important consequences of the development of the corporation as the decisive unit of productive property: the great majority of shareowners are stripped of control by a small segment of the capitalist class made up of the principal shareowners of the large corporations, who are thus able to extend their control of capital (and of the political economy) far beyond the limits of their ownership [Zeitlin *et al.* 1975, p. 92].

Whether they are correct in their assessment of the extent of minority control will be examined in later chapters, but the general import of their statement is clear. Minority control makes possible 'The simultaneous development of diffused ownership and of concentrated control' (Cole 1948, p. 124). But minority control is inherently unstable, since there is always the possibility that another shareholder may increase his or her holding and challenge the controlling group. The position of the minority controller is buttressed by factors such as control over the voting machinery, which is vested in the current members of the board of directors. This enables the directorate to solicit the right to vote on behalf of shareholders who are not present at the general meeting. This voting by 'proxy' is a powerful tool in the hands of the controlling group.[8] But an assertive rival group may engage in a 'proxy fight' by attempting to solicit the votes of the normally uninvolved shareholders.

Where a controlling group miscalculates the necessary size of a minority holding or deliberately reduces its holding below the critical level, there is no longer any possibility of minority control. It is this situation that Berle and Means describe as 'management control'. This mode of strategic control rests on the advantages of incumbency in a situation of dispersed share ownership. Management control is based on control of the proxy-voting machinery and a passive body of shareholders. No shareholding interest has sufficient shares for minority control and so the members of the board, who may have only minimal holdings in the company, will be a self-perpetuating control group. In such a situation, 'challenge to management comes only from the occasional shareholder or group of holders who together possess a relatively substantial minority position that can serve as a base to offset the advantages inherent in management's position' (Baum and Stiles 1965, pp. 12–13). If a proxy fight occurs, if a group of shareholders can form an alliance, or if a large holder increases its holding, the incumbent management may lose control.[9]

Management control, as has been shown, is often regarded as a precondition for changes in corporate strategy. Larner has claimed that 'the management, in the absence of gross incompetence or serious misfortune, has open to it a wide range of discretionary behaviour in which it can, without fear of punitive action by stockholders, pursue policies which serve its own interests at the expense of the owners' (1970, p. 3). Shareholders have an interest in the value of their shares and the dividend which they can earn, while non-owning managers have no such interest. The interests of the small shareholders, in a situation of management control, 'serve as a constraint rather than as the dominant motivating factor' (ibid., p. 4). This argument conflates two distinct claims: that the management acquires an autonomy from the *particular* ownership interests of its own shareholders, and that management acquires an independence from *any* ownership interest. To establish that managers may achieve a partial autonomy from the large mass of shareholders in the enterprise which they manage is not to establish that 'the managers' are a distinct social group from 'the owners'. Furthermore, the managers of a particular enterprise may not be unduly influenced by their own shareholders, but they may still be subject to influence from 'outside' interests such as financiers:

A powerful interest group, because it is powerful, possesses a certain degree of *influence* in the affairs of a corporation; that is, its desires, opinions, advice, remonstrances, or cajolings tend to be heeded by management. However, this sort of pressure is not decision-making if management itself . . . makes the final decision [Gordon 1945, p. 151].

This points to the limits of the concept of management control. Where managerial autonomy is reduced in this way, it is no longer sensible to speak of management control at all. Furthermore, Berle and Means have not shown the impossibility of shareholder influence in companies with no majority or minority controller. The Berle and Means classification is based on the assumption that, as share-ownership becomes more and more dispersed, control passes from majority to minority control and finally to management control. The achievement of management control is the final stage in corporate development, and occurs when the outstanding shares are so widely dispersed that no individual or group of associates holds sufficient shares to counterbalance the power of the incumbent management. But the assumption that any countervailing block of shares must be held by a small group of associates is questionable. The successful exercise of minority control requires that the major shareholders comprise a small compact grouping which is willing and able to intervene in pursuit of their interests and so it is true that such a coalition is unlikely where the major holders are not close associates of one another (Gordon 1945, pp. 36, 44). In such a situation, no one of the major holders will have sufficient shares to exercise minority control on its own, and any coalition of a subset of the major holders is likely to be countered by a coalition based on a different subset. Any coalition will be unstable since there is no community of interest among the large holders over and above certain minimal shareholder interests which are, in any case, shared with owners outside the group of major shareholders. However, it is possible to see the dispersal of share ownership as enhancing the power of those who have substantial holdings. If shares are more or less equally distributed among the major holders, then each of their shares has a greater power than it would in a situation of inequality since it competes on equal terms with all the other major holdings (De Alessi 1973, p. 844; Child 1969a, p. 45). Where this is the case, the way is open for 'behind-the-scenes alliances which can accumulate the necessary critical mass' (Blumberg 1975, p. 93). The relative equality which holds among the largest shareholders precludes the formation of stable coalitions, yet makes some sort of *modus vivendi* necessary. The largest shareholders may, collectively, hold a block of shares which is large enough to give minority, or even majority control, to a cohesive group, yet they lack the basis for a collective organization which would enable them to act as a controlling group. Therefore, in situations where the major shareholders are in a position of effective possession but do not constitute a coalition of associates, the mode of strategic control must differ from both minority and management control.

This form of control may be termed 'control through a constellation of interests'.[10] The origin of this concept is to be found in Weber's contrast between domination by authority and 'domination by a constellation of interests'. He argues that this latter situation is typical of monopolistic domination in the market, which is 'based upon influence derived exclusively from the possession of goods or marketable skills guaranteed in some way and acting upon the conduct of those dominated, who remain, however, formally free and are motivated simply by the pursuit of their own interests' (1921, p. 943). A large bank, for example, may have a dominating influence in the market and may be able to influence the behaviour of its potential debtors for the sake of its own financial interests. The mutual accommodation of interests between the bank and its customers places the bank in a dominant position.[11] If the bank is able to place some of its directors on the customer's board and these directors are given specific rights of command as a condition for the grant of credit, then the form of domination is transformed into 'authority' rather than a mere constellation of interests (ibid., pp. 943–4). Weber's concept accords closely with the situation described in the previous paragraph. No coalition can achieve a stable position of control, but the board cannot disregard the interests of those in effective possession. The major shareholders have effective possession, yet this constellation of ownership interests has no unity and little possibility of concerted action. The major shareholders may be able to co-operate in order to determine the composition of the board, this composition depending on the balance of power among them, but co-operation beyond this is unlikely. The board will reflect the 'congeries of intercorporate relationships' and the 'intricate interweaving of interests' among its major shareholders (Zeitlin *et al.* 1975, pp. 102, 106), though not necessarily in an immediate and direct manner, and so cannot achieve the autonomy from particular shareholder interests which is characteristic of management control. But, at the same time, the board is not the mere instrument of a cohesive controlling group.

An important question in the discussion of control through a constellation of interests must be the size of the controlling constellation. As in the case of minority control, no operational definition can encompass all the variations in individual circumstances. It can be assumed that the constellation must have a total shareholding equivalent to the size of a controlling minority holding, but this does not resolve the question of the number of holders who can participate in this controlling constellation. A group which is too large would be unable to co-operate at even the minimal level required for control, while a very small group is best seen as having or sharing in minority control. On the basis of probability theories of decision-making, Florence (1947) has argued that a group of size twenty is the maximum number of shareholders who could participate in control. The controlling group may be smaller than this, but it is unlikely to be bigger. Florence concludes that a procedure which investigates the block of shares held by the twenty largest shareholders is likely to result in a correct identification of the locus of control.[12] Control through a constellation of interests, therefore, can be operationally defined as the situation where the top twenty shareholders collectively hold a minority (or majority) block and no subset of these twenty constitutes a unified group of minority controllers.

The basis of management control is a distribution of shareholdings such that no individual or group of owners can be a serious threat to management. Control through a constellation of interests requires that a substantial block of shares be concentrated in a small but diffuse group of shareholders and that the remaining shares be widely dispersed. While minority and management control arise as share-ownership becomes 'democratized', control through a constellation of interests arises when 'democratization' is replaced by a movement of concentration. This is precisely what is involved in the growth of so-called 'institutional' share-ownership by credit-giving enterprises. The increasing importance of insurance companies, unit trusts, and pension funds in corporate capital since the 1950s has led to a new form of concentration in share-ownership. Individual persons tend to put their money in savings institutions or to invest in the financial intermediaries rather than investing directly in industrial enterprises themselves. As a result, the 'institutions' become the most important holders of company shares as well as the major financiers of enterprises through bank loans and other forms of credit (Berle 1960; Child 1969a, p. 46). As such, financial intermediaries are an extension of the principles of the joint-stock company and the stock exchange: the growth of a market for securities allows investors to attain 'independence of the fate of the particular enterprise in which he has invested his money' (Sweezy 1942, p. 258), and the growth of indirect investment is the completion of this process so far as the individual investor is concerned (Cole 1948, p. 125; Parsons 1958, p. 112; Hirst 1979, p. 135; Hilferding 1910).

Having discussed the modes of strategic control – majority, minority, management, and control through a constellation of interests – it is necessary to examine in more detail the mechanisms through which strategic control is exercised.[13] A fundamental distinction is that between 'passive' and 'active' mechanisms. Gordon has argued that passive control

usually implies approval rather than initiation of decisions, and may imply merely an indirect influence rather than direct approval or veto. The purpose of control is normally to further or protect particular interests of the controlling group, and this may be done without participating in the formation of many, perhaps most, policies [Gordon 1945, p. 173].

At its most general level, passive control is expressed in the power to sell shares or withdraw credit. All shareholders have an interest in the income and capital gains which their investments can yield, and corporate strategy is necessarily constrained by this interest (De Alessi 1973, p. 843; Peterson 1965, p. 18). The large share-holders will be a much greater constraint than the small share-holders, since any dissatisfaction that the former feel could lead to substantial share sales and so have considerable effect on the share price. A rapid and sustained decline in the share price will lead to considerable difficulties for an enterprise which is hoping to expand. The interests of the shareholders – and particularly the major holders – are a major influence on corporate strategy, and this 'does not require active participation in control. The power ... to sell a large block of capital can be enough – if clashes of policy between major shareholders and company directorate should occur' (Westergaard and Resler 1975, p. 160; Gordon 1945, p. 57).

Intermediate between these purely passive constraints and more active intervention are a number of mechanisms through which major shareholders are able to ensure that the management is responsive to their interests. The large shareholders tend to be better informed and to have greater access to the enterprise's management. Those making company policy will be influenced by the pressure and advice which major shareholders are able to offer:

Is it not likely that many of these major holders will own substantial blocks in particular corporations – substantial either in percentage or absolute dollar terms – and will either be skilled investors or under the guidance of investment professionals? Is it not likely, in other words, that while 'the average shareholder' may not be highly interested in structural changes, those shareholders who own the bulk of the shares held by individuals will consider such changes with some care and will expect to have a role in such changes [Eisenberg 1969, pp. 45–6].

Institutional shareholders, in particular, will be well informed and well placed to make their views known to management. As institutional holdings have grown in size, 'the predisposition to vote in management's favour seems to be breaking down' (ibid., p. 52). Financial intermediaries have the administrative apparatus to collect, analyse, and act upon business information, and so can ensure that management is more responsive to them than to the small shareholders (Baum and Stiles 1965, p. 165; Blumberg 1975, p. 94; Beed 1966, p. 13).

Active mechanisms of control are found when shareholders or financiers seek representation on the company's board. If some or all of the board members are direct appointees of the major shareholders, then their advice and opinions may be regarded as authoritative instructions: management feels it must obey their 'advice' (Weber 1921, p. 944; Gordon 1945, p. 151). Ultimately this power reflects the ability of the controlling shareholders to use their voting strength to alter the composition of the board, though this normally involves 'a milder sort of continuing pressure . . . plus reserve power to act when the occasion requires' (Peterson 1965, p. 20; Gordon 1945, pp. 57, 187; Monsen *et al.* 1968, p. 437). Intervention is especially likely when the enterprise has run into serious financial or legal difficulties. The rarity of intervention 'Indicates that such intervention is not often necessary because, in the generality of cases, such shareholders are satisfied that their interests are reasonably well-served' (Nichols 1969, p. 104). The more routinized are the decisions, the less likely are the controllers to wish to intervene. It is when strategic issues arise that the controllers will strive to influence the board and to see that its wishes are carried through (Zald 1969, p. 107). The rarity of intervention is exceeded only by the rarity of proxy fights. Generally, intervention can be handled without open conflict. As Peterson argues, 'Far from being an ordinary election, a proxy battle is a catastrophic event whose mere possibility is a threat, and one not remote when affairs are in conspicuous disarray' (1965, p. 21). Intervention, therefore, need not involve a dramatic struggle; it may consist in the gradual but firm imposition of the interests of the controlling group over the company's management. Where intervention does occur, however, it is likely that the composition of the board will come more and more to represent the controlling constellation or the minority controllers. Board members formerly in office under sufferance will tend to be replaced by others who are more representative of the controlling interests and the balance of power among them (Clement 1975a, p. 23).

It is important to emphasize that all these mechanisms are also available to non-shareholders with a substantial interest in the company, such as the holders of a company's loan stock and its bankers. This emphasizes that strategic control relates to the use of capital, and any groupings that are related to a particular corporation in the overall flow of capital may be able to exercise control over that corporation. Share-ownership is the most crucial form of capital, though its importance in relation to other forms of credit can never be merely asserted. The importance of this point is that, say, banking interests may be able to exercise considerable influence over minority- and management-controlled companies in which the control status would otherwise seem straightforward (Chevalier 1970, pp. 45–6; Morin 1974a, p. 35). Very often, however, those who are creditors of the company in this way are also owners of the share capital, either as direct beneficiaries or as trustees. This is particularly likely in companies controlled through a constellation of interests, where the major creditors will be represented among the constellation.

'Control' is by no means a straightforward self-evident concept. There are various modes of control and a number of mechanisms through which this control can be exercised. Some mechanisms of control are obvious and direct, while others are 'passive' and indirect. As Zeitlin has emphasized, the control status of a corporation can be decided only if it is examined in relation to 'the concrete situation within the corporation and the constellation of intercorporate relations in which it is involved' (1974, pp. 1091, 1107–8).[14] The boundaries between minority control, management control, and control through a constellation of interests are variable, depending, as Morin (1974a) emphasizes, on the changing pattern of share distribution which results from the constant restructuring of company capital. New issues, mergers, acquisitions, and so forth, create a complex and shifting pattern in the distribution of shareholdings. In the course of this restructuring, certain groups may be eliminated from positions of strategic control and new alliances may arise to positions of control. The joint stock company and the legal relations of property are crucial means through which these patterns of control are institutionally mediated.

The board of directors is not the *agency* of control, but the *arena* of .control. It is the institutional focus of the struggle for control between the various contenders for control. Overt or latent conflicts of interest result in the use of both passive and active mechanisms of control in order to secure an influence in the determination of corporate strategy (Scott 1982a, p. 230). Recruitment to the board reflects the struggle between shareholders, financiers, and executives, and this struggle is contained within a network of intercorporate commercial and capital relations. The high degree of interdependence between enterprises means that financial intermediaries, in particular, may have an interest in many separate enterprises. When one person is appointed to represent these interests on a number of different boards, a network of 'interlocking directorships' is created. The minimum inference which can be made about such interlocks is that they open channels of communication between enterprises (Scott 1985; Scott and Griff 1984). A person who sits on two boards, a multiple director, has access to the inside information of each enterprise and so has the power to 'transmit' information from one board to the other.

Interesting questions arise once the possibility of imbalance, or lack of reciprocity, in this communication is recognized. If a 'direction' can be attached to interlocks – information flowing predominantly one-way – then there is the possibility that they constitute institutionalized power relations between enterprises. Interlocks may express or reinforce capital relations, but they may also create new relations of power and influence. Not all interlocks can be regarded as power relations, but 'primary interlocks' – those created when an executive of one enterprise holds outside directorships in others – have often been regarded as being of particular significance, because it seems natural to assign a direction to the interlock and so to see it as a relation of control (Sweezy 1939). A bank executive, for example, may represent the bank on the boards of other enterprises and so effects a directed relation of 'bank control'. Many proponents of the model of finance capital have interpreted bank interlocks in this way (Fitch and Oppenheimer 1970a; 1970b; 1970c), but the temptation to draw such conclusions must be resisted as the direction which is to be assigned to a primary interlock is by no means obvious. It may be the case that a bank insists that one of its executives be placed on the board of an enterprise that it seeks to dominate, but it is equally possible that an enterprise might co-opt a bank executive on to its board in order to enhance its own power. All that can be concluded at this general level is that primary interlocks are more likely to be stable, institutionalized relations (Palmer 1983a; Ornstein 1982), and that they may, therefore, indicate deeper social relations. Primary interlocks are embedded in a more diffuse network of interlocks, the main significance of which lies in the creation of channels of communication between enterprises.

The model of corporate control which has been constructed in this chapter has been drawn from a wide range of sources in order to show the great deal of consensus that exists about the concepts necessary to study control in the large business enterprise. The major lines of theoretical contention, which were outlined in the previous chapter and at the beginning of this, centre upon the differing interpretations which have been placed on the available empirical material. Two observers may agree on the nature of management control, but disagree over its empirical application. The rest of this book is an attempt to marshall this evidence and to use the model of corporate control to illustrate the theoretical interpretation which was outlined in Chapter 1.

Notes

1   Renner terms this 'economic ownership', but this term has not been used in the present discussion because it has recently been employed by other writers in a very different sense. Renner's position is discussed in Kinsey (1983).

2   Berle and Means somewhat confusingly term these two aspects 'passive' and 'active', but these terms are rather unhelpful.

3   Some of the central themes in this debate have been raised in Zeitlin (1974), Kotz (1978), Useem (1980), and Glasberg and Schwartz (1983).

4   Their concept of 'possession' corresponds closely to Poulantzas's usage of 'economic ownership' which was discussed in Chapter 1. It follows that they depart from Poulantzas's concept of 'possession'.

5   Perhaps the earliest formulation of the position that control over the 'managerial function' was to be defined in terms of control over recruitment to top management was in Weber (1921). See the discussion in Zeitlin (1974, pp. 1091–2).

6 See also Larner (1970, p. 2), Villarejo (1961a, p. 49), Domhoff (1967, p. 50), Barratt Brown (1968a, pp. 53–4), and Francis (1980a).

7 The distinction between strategic and operational control has appeared, often implicitly, in many sources, although Pahl and Winkler (1974, p. 115) were the first to make the distinction an explicit point of reference in their work. For related views see: Parsons (1956, pp. 30–1), Peterson (1965, p. 2), Juran and Louden (1966), Lundberg (1969, p. 169), Jancovici (1972, p. 80), Burch (1972, p. 18), Poulantzas (1974, p. 119), Westergaard and Resler (1975, p. 163), Soref (1976, p. 362), Cutler *et al.* (1977, pp. 308–9), and Teulings (1984).

8 The term 'proxy' is used to refer to the form on which the shareholder who does not wish to attend a company meeting is invited to delegate a board member (or some other person) to vote on his or her behalf, normally in favour of management's own proposals.

9 One of the best-studied proxy fights between a management group and a minority shareholder is Rockefeller's battle over the control of Standard Oil of Indiana in 1929. See Baum and Stiles (1965, p. 13), Baran and Sweezy (1966, p. 32ff.), Fitch and Oppenheimer (1970a, p. 88), Blumberg (1975, p. 93).

10 Morin (1974a, p. 22) has a useful discussion of some aspects of this, but misleadingly calls it 'technocratic' control. See also Barratt Brown (1968, p. 43–4) on 'co-ordinating controllers'. Fennema, commenting on the first edition of this book, suggested that 'strong components' in the network of interlocking directorships are equivalent to constellations of interests. But this defines the concept as 'a financial group in which no definite locus of control can be distinguished' (Fennema 1982, p. 144). The argument of this book is that constellations of interests are not financial groups of this kind.

11 Weber goes on to say that for purposes of clarity it is best to restrict the word 'domination' to cases of authority (1921, p. 946), and this reinforces Mintz and Schwartz's (1985) description of the situation as 'bank hegemony'. This position is discussed in later chapters.

12 Florence was writing about minority control and its forms at a time when institutional ownership (see below) had not progressed very far. His conclusions on voting behaviour,

however, are germane to the discussion of control through a constellation of interests.

13 This discussion concentrates on mechanisms for *maintaining* control rather than the mechanisms which outsiders may use to *attain* control. On the latter see Chevalier (1970, p. 42) and Blumberg (1975, pp. 92, 145).

14 See also Zeitlin's paradigm for studying corporate control (Zeitlin *et al.* 1975, p. 110ff.) and also Marris (1964, p. 15) and Mace (1971).

3 Corporate control in America and Britain

The heartland of the model of the managerial enterprise, and its associated theory of industrial society, is the USA. It was there that Berle and Means undertook their classic study, and it is there that the debate has continued to rage in both the academic and the political world. If the arguments of this theory have any application, they should certainly apply to corporate development in America. The size of the American economy and the rapid growth of massive enterprises operating on a national scale created a need to mobilize capital from outside the immediate circle of the entrepreneurs who founded the enterprises. Joint stock organization was the basis for the expansion of American capital within the American economy itself and then in the international arena. Indeed, it was reflections such as this that led Berle and Means to carry out their study of the modern corporation. In Britain the formation of 'big business' was somewhat slower, and the smaller size of the British economy meant that founding entrepreneurs and their heirs came under less pressure to dilute their controlling shareholdings. Britain's pre-eminence as the 'workshop of the world' was achieved on the basis of small entrepreneurial firms which had not taken the step of joint stock organization. The growth of American competition was a major factor in forging these enterprises into larger units, and British capital was increasingly subject to the same pressure to mobilize capital from a mass of individual shareholders. Britain and the USA must, therefore, constitute the testing grounds for the theory of industrial society and any alternatives which might be proposed. The relationship between share-ownership and strategic control in these societies is central to an evaluation of the theories outlined in the previous chapters.

Families, managers, and financials in the USA

The debate over ownership and control in the USA has been dominated by the ideas and methods of Berle and Means (1932), who claimed that the dispersal of shareholdings in large enterprises destroyed owner control and created the conditions for management control. Table 1 shows that the number of shareholders in the largest corporations was very great in 1929, when Berle and Means began their investigations, and had increased substantially by 1974. Almost a half of those corporations which could be classified in 1929 had more than 20,000 shareholders, and by 1974 this proportion had risen to over 90 per cent. The number of large corporations with over 100,000 shareholders increased during this period from ten to seventy. This trend towards greater dispersal is not a recent phenomenon, but continued throughout the period. A Senate Committee of 1940 reported that, by 1937, the overwhelming majority of the shareholders in the top 200 corporations owned fewer than 100 shares each, and that only 0.25 per cent of shareholders held more than 5000 shares each (Goldsmith and Parmelee 1940, pp. 27, 36; Anderson *et al.* 1941). Villarejo reported that the 'average' corporation of 1951 was characterized by a wide dispersal of shareholdings. The majority of shareholders owned an average of just over thirty shares each and accounted for only 10 per cent of the share capital (1961a, p. 49). It is clear, therefore, that one major plank of the Berle and Means thesis is confirmed: there has been a tendency for corporate capital to be spread among a very large number of shareholders, the majority of whom own very small amounts of shares.

This dispersal in shareholdings, felt Berle and Means, was a clear sign of the drift away from control by ownership interests. The turn of the century saw many owners squeezed-out by the New York financial interests which restructured capital and reorganized production. In the period between 1914 and 1928 this move from majority to minority control was pushed even further, and the 1930s saw a massive growth in the number of enterprises without dominant ownership interests (Berle and Means 1932, pp. 84–9; Berle 1960, ch. 2). Berle and Means concluded that the traditional capitalist forms of private and majority control were disappearing, surviving mainly in smaller enterprises. Minority shareholders and other large shareholders were able to dominate the boardrooms of the largest enterprises and so became the main

Table 1 *Shareholders in the top 200 US non-financial enterprises (1929 and 1974)*

	Number of enterprises	
Number of holders	*1929*	*1974*
Less than 5,000	41	1
5,000– 20,000	53	8
20,000– 50,000	39	52
50,000–100,000	22	69
100,000–200,000	7	43
200,000–500,000	3	27
Unclassified	35	—
Totals	200	200

Source: Adapted from Berle and Means (1932), p. 49, and Herman (1981), table 3.6.

Note: The unclassified companies of 1929 were mainly owned through legal devices such as voting trusts.

Table 2 *Ultimate strategic control in the top US non-financial enterprises (1900–75)*

	Number of companies			
Mode of control	*Top 40 of 1900–1*	*Top 200 of 1929*	*Top 200 of 1963*	*Top 200 of 1975*
Private control	—	10	—	1
Majority control	5	9	6	3
Minority control	13	65	18	21
No dominant interest	9.5	81	167	173
Financial control	12.5	23.5	—	1
Legal device	—	9.5	9	—
In receivership	—	2	—	1
Totals	40	200	200	200

Source: Adapted from Berle and Means (1932), p. 106, Herman (1981), tables 3.2, 3.4, 3.5, and p. 71, and Larner (1970), pp. 12–13, table 1.

Note: The figures for 1929 incorporate Herman's corrections and adjustments to the original Berle and Means data. The cut-off level for minority control in 1963 and 1975 was 10 per cent, in the earlier periods it was 20 per cent. 'Private control' refers to the situation where the majority block is 80 per cent or more. Those companies subject to joint control were split between the categories according to the control status of their joint controllers.

shapers of corporate strategy. Because most enterprises were still subject to the influence of their largest shareholders, 'the separation of ownership and control has not yet become complete. While a large body of stockholders are not in a position to exercise any degree of control over the affairs of their corporation, those actually in control are usually stockholders though in many cases owning but a very small proportion of the total stock' (Berle and Means 1932, p. 343). As share-ownership became more dispersed, they argued, the proportion of shares represented on the board would fall even further and the separation of ownership and control would approach completion. As this situation was approached, so the opportunities open to career executives would increase and they would become a major force in strategic control. Enterprises lacking a dominant ownership interest would become subject to management control. These expectations are apparently confirmed by the data presented in Table 2. On the basis of his research on 1963, Larner claimed that 'it would appear that Berle and Means in 1929 were observing a "managerial revolution" in process. Now, thirty years later, that revolution seems close to complete' (Larner 1966, pp. 786–7). Larner recognized, however, that owner control was more persistent in smaller enterprises, and this was confirmed in research on the 500 largest enterprises of 1965 (see Table 3). Enterprises believed to be subject to management control were heavily concentrated in the top 125 and owner control remained important outside the top 200.

Table 3   *Strategic control in the top 500 US industrial enterprises (1965)*

| Mode of control | *Rank by sales* | | | | |
	1–125	*126–250*	*251–375*	*376–500*	*Totals*
Owner-controlled	24	45	48	44	161
Management-controlled	101	75	73	78	327
Unknown	0	5	4	3	12
Totals	125	125	125	125	500

Source: Adapted from Palmer (1972), p. 57, table 1.

Note: The cut-off point for owner control is 10 per cent.

It would appear, therefore, that owner control has gradually given way to management control, especially in the very large enterprises, and that internal career executives have become the dominant element in the corporate directorate. Herman's investigation suggests that management-control was characteristic of more than four-fifths of the top 200 enterprises of 1975.[1] But a number of serious reservations must be made about this conclusion. Apart from technical and methodological criticisms which can be made against these studies, it has been argued that the researchers have underestimated the importance of both family control and financial influence.

The technical and methodological difficulties of this research are so great that De Vroey has gone so far as to claim that 'procedural choices are almost shaping the very nature of the conclusion' (1976, p. 29). One particular problem concerns the cut-off level for minority control: Berle and Means took 20 per cent, while Larner and later writers have taken 10 per cent or even less. As was argued in the previous chapter, any such criterion is arbitrary but particular cut-off points can be justified in terms of the prevailing distribution of shareholdings. On these grounds Herman (1981, pp. 24–5) comes to the sensible conclusion that holdings of 5 per cent or less are unrealistic bases for control and that owners of 5 to 10 per cent may, at best, exercise a limited form of minority control. This conclusion applies most firmly to the post-war period and there are, in fact, good reasons for accepting Berle and Means' more restrictive cut-off point of 20 per cent for the inter-war years when shareholdings were less dispersed. The choice of a cut-off point, therefore, is not an insuperable problem. So long as it is recognized that the precise cut-off level is arbitrary, it can be assumed that the broad trends shown in Table 2 are an accurate reflection of the developments in control over the period. A more important technical problem concerns the treatment accorded to 'legal devices' and intercorporate shareholdings. Berle and Means use the category of control through a legal device to describe situations where majority or minority holdings are organized into a voting trust or into a pyramidal structure of intercorporate holdings. Herman's adjustments to the Berle and Means data involved a reclassification of many of these companies into the appropriate category of minority control or financial control (see also Zeitlin *et al.* 1975, p. 97). Pyramiding of company shares by financial enterprises was widespread in the 1920s with the expansion in the number of investment trusts and investment holding companies, most of which were affiliated to the big banks (Carosso 1970, ch. 14). This problem is related to the distinction between 'ultimate' and 'immediate' control. Where one enterprise was controlled by another, Berle and Means allocated it to the control category of its ultimate parent. Thus, an enterprise subject to immediate minority control by a management-controlled enterprise was itself regarded as subject to ultimate management-control. This does, of course, bring out certain important features of corporate control, but the neglect of patterns of immediate control can lead to the drawing of unwarranted conclusions about the autonomy of the internal managers in such enterprises. The implications of this are brought out in Table 4, which presents the results of the 1940 Senate Committee. The number of majority-controlled enterprises in 1937 appears to be considerably greater than in 1929 (Table 2), because the analysis is based on immediate control and includes numerous subsidiary companies. Where one enterprise was majority-controlled by another, Berle and Means did not include it in their 'top 200'. The Senate Committee, however, included all these subsidiaries and so inflated the figure for majority control.[2] Neither approach can be regarded as preferable to the other; the approach chosen must depend upon the questions to be investigated. It can be concluded, however, that researchers who include subsidiaries and classify them by their immediate control should make this clear in the presentation of their results. A final technical problem in this research is the lack of complete information on corporate ownership. Until recently, investigators had to rely on estimation and guesswork from newspaper sources and inside information. Half of the corporations classified as management-controlled by Berle and Means were simply 'presumed' to fall into this category on the basis of little or no information at all (Zeitlin 1974, p. 1081; De Vroey 1976, p. 16ff.). The figures for 1929 in Table 2 incorporate Herman's corrections on the basis of information unavailable to Berle and Means. The technical problems, therefore, do not necessarily undermine the general trend shown. The underestimation of family control and financial influence may, however, throw into doubt the conclusion that modern American capitalism is dominated by managerial enterprises.

   In a re-analysis of the 1929 data of Berle and Means, Burch estimated that the true figure for family control in the top 200 was

Table 4 *Immediate strategic control in the 200 largest US non-financial enterprises (1937)*

Mode of control	Number of corporations	% of corporations
Majority ownership	42	21.0
Predominant minority	37	18.5
Substantial minority	47	23.5
Small minority	13	6.5
No dominant shareholders	61	30.5
Totals	200	100.0

Source: Calculated from Goldsmith and Parmelee (1940), Appendix XI, p. 1486.

Note: Control is measured by proportion of voting stock held and by representation in the company's management. The dividing line between 'predominant' and 'substantial' minority is set at 30 per cent and that between 'substantial' and 'small' is set at 10 per cent.

between 37 and 45 per cent. Burch makes this claim on the grounds that enterprises could still be subject to control by particular families where these families had only a small block of shares (1972, pp. 114–15). In a similar vein the Senate Committee argued that single families held control in forty enterprises in the top 200 of 1937, with groups of families controlling a further thirty-five. Taking into account those subsidiaries which were ultimately controlled by families, the Committee's researchers concluded that family control was present in about two-fifths of the enterprises. Thirteen family groups were identified – including Ford, Du Pont, Mellon, and Rockefeller – and Burch's re-analysis of the data supports their conclusions on the extent of family control and the prominence of family groups (Anderson *et al.* 1941, pp. 172–3). Despite his argument that the Committee overstated their case, Gordon has produced evidence on family holdings which supports the general picture. Table 5 shows that family groups held majority or minority control in forty-two of the ninety-three largest manufacturers of 1937–9 and held smaller blocks in a further nine, though Gordon rightly points out that it should not be assumed that the largest shareholding families in an enterprise constitute a 'compact and unified group' (1945, p. 42). Work carried out in the 1950s suggested that family control has persisted into the post-war period. Villarejo estimated that almost two-thirds of the 232 enterprises which he studied in 1951 had a controlling block of shares held by their directors or other major interests (1961a, Appendices I and II), while Kolko found that seventy-two of the top 100 of 1937 still had the same dominant shareholders in 1957. In twenty-two of these enterprises the same families were dominant, though the size of their shareholding had generally fallen (1962, p. 62). Larner's study discovered that 14 per cent of the top 200 of 1963 were subject to family control, a conclusion that was confirmed by Sheehan (1967). Commenting on this finding, Burch claimed that the true figure for family control in 1965 was 40 per cent and that a further 18 per cent were 'possibly' family-controlled. Burch recognized, however, that family-control was less widespread in the top fifty (1972, p. 68). Family shareholdings were invariably associated with family representation on the board of directors, and Burch discovered that this situation had generally persisted over much of the post-war period (ibid., pp. 96, 101).

What conclusions can be drawn about family control? There can

Table 5   *Family control in the ninety-three largest US manufacturers (1937–9)*

| Size of shareholding block (%) | Number of enterprises in which block held by | | | | |
	Single family	Two or more families	Family and enterprise	No family	Totals
More than 50	4	3	0	0	7
30–49	9	5	1	2	17
10–29	10	11	4	1	26
Less than 10	5	4	0	0	9
No dominant interest	—	—	—	34	34
Totals	28	23	5	37	93

Source: Gordon (1945), pp. 40–1, calculated from *Temporary National Economic Committee* data.

Note: The category for 'no family' includes three cases where another enterprise holds the controlling block.

be little doubt that a number of cases of family control through majority or large minority blocks can be found in each period studied, but it is doubtful whether family holdings of less than 5 per cent can be taken as cases of family 'control'. Holdings between 5 and 10 per cent may be possible bases for control, but such control will necessarily be limited and restricted. It is possible to go much of the way with Chandler's judgement that:

What Burch's data does show is that wealthy Americans invest in the securities of large corporations, that some families of the entrepreneurs who helped to found a company still retained as much as five per cent of the stock in those companies, and that members of those families often have jobs in that enterprise. Burch helps to document the fact that wealthy families, particularly those of the founders of modern business enterprises, are the beneficiaries of managerial capitalism, but gives little evidence that these families make basic decisions concerning the operations of modern capitalistic enterprises and of the economy in which they operate [Chandler 1977, p. 584].

It remains true, however, that the presence of family shareholdings and their representation on the board, significantly qualifies the conventional view of the undisputed rise to power of internal executives. Family influence may be an important factor even in those enterprises not subject to family control.

It is now necessary to turn to the question of financial control. The large figures in Table 2 for financial control in the first half of the twentieth century reflect the role played by the big banks in amalgamation and 'rationalization'. Although this role has declined since the 1930s, Table 6 shows a massive growth in shareholdings by financial intermediaries. The possibility must be investigated that enterprises with no dominant shareholding interest are in fact subject to influence from their largest financial shareholders. They may be cases of control through a constellation of interests rather than cases of management control. Table 6 shows that the proportion of shares owned by financial enterprises rose from 6.7 per cent in 1900 to 34.7 per cent in 1978. This replacement of personal shareholders by 'institutional' shareholders was most rapid in the post-war period, and the most important type of financial shareholder is now the pension fund. By the 1970s the pension funds had become the largest single source of new investment capital and, because the majority of the funds were managed by banks, the banks increased their significance in the mobilization of capital (Drucker 1976, p. 1; Rifkin and Barber 1978, pp. 10, 234; see also Goldsmith 1958; Cox 1963, p. 52; Baum and Stiles 1965, pp. 31ff., 54–5). Although individuals are the ultimate beneficiaries of pension and insurance investment, 'the great bulk of financial institution stockholdings are of a character that cannot by any stretch of the imagination be regarded as representing ownership by masses of the population' (Perlo 1958, p. 30). Institutional shareholding reflects a move towards greater concentration in corporate capital, a fact which led a Congressional Committee to report in 1968 that 'the trend of the last 30 or 40 years toward a separation of ownership from control because of the fragmentation of stock ownership has been radically changed towards a concentration of voting power in the hands of a relatively few financial institutions, while the fragmentation in the distribution of cash payments has been continued' (Patman Report 1968, p. 13).

If holdings by financial enterprises are to be seen as evidence for control through a constellation of interests, this should be apparent from data on holdings by the twenty largest shareholders. Table 7 presents some figures which give considerable support to this view. The large number of 1937 enterprises in which the top twenty holders owned more than 30 per cent of the shares reflects the importance of majority and minority control at that time. In fact, thirty-two of the fifty-seven with more than 50 per cent held by the top twenty holders were majority-controlled by a single shareholder (Goldsmith and Parmelee 1940, pp. 89–91). The

Table 6   *Beneficial ownership of US company shares (1900–78)*

Type of holder	% of corporate stock held by each category			
	1900	1939	1974	1978
Bank-managed trusts	4.3	12.9	11.1	8.9
Pension funds	—	0.2	9.9	13.6
Investment companies	—	1.2	5.4	3.5
Life insurance companies	0.5	0.6	3.5	3.4
Other financials	1.9	2.1	3.3	5.3
Totals	6.7	17.0	33.3	34.7

Source: Kotz (1978), table 1, and Herman (1981), table 4.4.

Table 7   *Holdings by the twenty largest shareholders in largest US non-financial enterprises (1937 and 1976)*

% of shares held by top 20 holders	1937: 208 share issues Number	%	1976: 122 corporations Number	%
More than 50	57	28	7	6
40–49	} 36	17	4	3
30–39			9	7
20–29	} 69	33	31	25
10–19			47	39
5–10			11	9
1– 5	} 46	22	12	10
Less than 1			1	1
Totals	208	100	122	100

Source: Goldsmith and Parmelee (1940), p. 81, and Herman (1981), p. 102.

Note: The 1937 figures are based on 208 share issues for the 200 largest corporations.

changing patterns of share distribution can best be illustrated through a particular example. Union Pacific was classified in 1929 as management-controlled, at which time its twenty largest share-holders owned 10.4 per cent of its share capital (Berle and Means 1932, p. 99). By 1938 their collective holding had increased to 14.47 per cent, and Table 8 shows the top twenty holders included four family groups. Most of the large shareholders at that time were bank and trust companies holding shares on behalf of indi-viduals and having only limited voting rights for these shares. Perlo has argued that the proportion of shares held by the twenty largest holders in large enterprises increased between 1937 and 1954, and Eisenberg showed that the block held by the ten largest holders had become even greater by 1961 (Perlo 1958, pp. 29–30; Eisenberg 1969, pp. 43–4). Claims such as these led to a Congres-sional Committee on bank shareholdings, the evidence from which led Blumberg to claim that financial enterprises held at least 10 per cent of the shares in each of the top ten US enterprises of 1969, the holding lying between 30 and 40 per cent in eight of them. All except one of these ten companies had been classified by Larner

(1970) as 'management-controlled' (Blumberg 1975, pp. 98-9). Table 7 shows that by 1976 there had been a large increase in the number of enterprises in which the top twenty holders owned between 10 and 30 per cent. This can again be illustrated from the Union Pacific shareholder list in Table 8. In 1980 Union Pacific's twenty largest shareholders owned 22.43 per cent and most of the bank holdings were on behalf of pension funds. What is remarkable is the appearance of five family groups on the 1980 list, one of which had been the largest holder in 1937. There appears, therefore, to be considerable support for Burch's claim that family influence has persisted, and also support for the claim that a larger proportion of shares have come into the hands of institutional shareholders. This is by no means an isolated example. Exxon, in which the Rockefeller family were the second largest holder with 1.68 per cent, had 16.89 per cent of its shares held by its top twenty shareholders, and eighteen of these were financial enterprises (CDE 1981).[3]

It would seem, therefore, that control through a constellation of interests has become more widespread in the USA, and that it may be more typical of large enterprises than is management control. The extent of this was glimpsed in a study by Chevalier in the 1960s. Chevalier showed that the top fifty enterprises were most marked by management control in the strict sense. At other levels of the top 200 he discovered the importance of minority holdings of 5 per cent and 'predominant interests' of slightly less than 5 per cent (see Tables 9 and 10). In twenty-eight of the enterprises that would conventionally be classified as management-controlled, banks exercised a significant influence through shareholding and board representation. Altogether the six largest banks had minority participations or significant influence in forty enterprises (Chevalier 1970, pp. 115, 166).

Kotz has taken this analysis a step further, arguing that it is indicative of a growth in bank control. Table 11 shows that Kotz estimated that financials had minority control in thirteen enterprises and 'partial control', with a holding of between 5 and 10 per cent, in a further ninety-three. This appears to be impressive evidence for financial control in almost a third of the top 200 enterprises, a finding in stark contrast to Herman's discovery of just one case (see Table 2). These discrepant conclusions can more readily be reconciled if it is recognized that Kotz has produced evidence not for financial control but for control through a

(1970, p. 115). In 1966 almost all of the top 210 banks held some of their own shares, over a half held more than 5 per cent, and over a quarter held more than 10 per cent. Additionally, there were significant cross-holdings of bank shares: each of the top six New York banks had between 12 and 20 per cent of its shares held either by itself or by the other five banks (Patman Report 1966, p. 817, table VI; CDE 1980b, p. 13). A high proportion of bank shares was held by other financials. Almost a half of the top 275 banks of 1966 had 5 per cent or more of their shares held by other financials with full voting rights. The Patman Committee discovered that subsidiary banks held shares in their own parent and in the parent companies of other banks as well (Patman Report 1967, p. 918ff.). As Chevalier argues, 'the American banks are linked amongst themselves by an extremely dense network of financial participations' (1970, p. 117). Many banks are controlled through constellations of interests and are themselves members of the constellations controlling other enterprises. J P Morgan, which with Morgan Guaranty held substantial shareholdings in many of the largest enterprises, had 27.60 per cent of its capital held by its twenty largest shareholders (CDE 1980a).[4]

The American evidence suggests that there has been a transition from personal possession by particular families and interests to impersonal possession through an interweaving of ownership interests. But this transition was not a simple unilinear movement. Family ownership and family influence persist in many areas of the economy, and the initial move towards greater dispersal of share ownership produced a large number of management-controlled enterprises in the 1930s and after. By the 1950s, management control had become characteristic of many large enterprises (Useem 1984, pp. 175–9). Since the 1950s, managerial enterprises and the surviving family enterprises have been joined by enterprises in which intercorporate 'institutional' shareholdings are the dominant form of ownership. Even Herman, who has presented the most sophisticated statement of the managerial position, recognizes that enterprises with no dominant ownership interest are subject to considerable influence from institutional shareholders. He shows that many of these enterprises had significant share stakes held by financial intermediaries and that many of these shareholding interests were represented on the boards (Herman 1981, pp. 58–9). This situation is characterized as 'constrained managerial control' (ibid., p. 15), though the evidence

Table 8   *Top twenty shareholders in Union Pacific (1937 and 1980)*

	1937		1980	
	Shareholder	%	Shareholder	%
1	Harriman interests	2.99	Prudential Insurance	2.14
2	NV ... Administratie-kantoor	2.66	Harriman family	2.09
3	Central Hanover Bank & Trust	1.18	Equitable Life Assurance	1.76
4	City Bank Farmers Trust	1.12	Mellon National Bank	1.50
5	Harkness interests	0.92	Citicorp	1.48
6	Kuhn Loeb	0.78	Rothschild family	1.45
7	Chase National Bank	0.75	J P Morgan & Co	1.33
8	United States Trust	0.60	University of California	1.20
9	Chemical Bank & Trust	0.49	Bankamerica	1.15
10	J W Davis & Co	0.45	Manufacturers Hanover	1.13
11	Vanderbilt family	0.45	Rowe Price & Associates	0.86
12	Goelet family	0.43	Chemical New York	0.85
13	Dominick and Dominick	0.38	New York State Pension Fund	0.78
14	Bankers Trust	0.35	New Jersey Division of Investments	0.74
15	Home Insurance	0.34	Kirby family	0.74
16	Massachusetts Investment Trust	0.34	Hospital Trust	0.68
17	—		Bank of New York	0.67
18	—		Kemper family	0.60
19	—		DuPont family	0.59
20	—		Donaldson Lufkin & Jenrette	0.59
	Totals of top 20	14.47		22.43

Source: 1938 list from Goldsmith and Parmelee (1940), 1980 list from CDE (1981).

Note: The original 1938 list was based on registered shareholders and included a number of obviously connected holdings. After combining these holdings only sixteen large shareholders remained.

constellation of interests. The major financial intermediaries have become central agents in the mobilization of capital and have, in consequence, become central to the exercise of strategic control. Internal executives cannot ignore the interests of the financial constellations which comprise their major shareholders.

Table 9   *Strategic control in the top 200 US non-financial enterprises (1965)*

Mode of control	Rank by size 1–50	51–100	101–150	151–200	Totals
Majority ownership	1	3	3	4	11
Minority control	14	24	25	30	93
Predominant influence	5	6	4	1	16
Management control	30	17	18	15	80
Totals	50	50	50	50	200

Source: Chevalier (1970), p. 67.

Note: Minority control involves more than 5 per cent of shares as well as representation on the board. 'Predominant influence' is the situation where there is strong influence on the board, even if there is no evidence of a 5 per cent holding.

The analysis cannot, however, stop at this point. If financial intermediaries control the large non-financials, who owns and controls the financials? In a study carried out in the 1960s, Vernon analysed strategic control in the big commercial banks. Table 12 shows that most of these banks had no dominant shareholder, and

Table 10   *Identity of controllers in the top 200 US non-financial enterprises (1965)*

Mode of control	Type of controller Families	Banks	Other financials	Board	Other	Totals
Majority ownership	7	0	0	0	4	11
Minority control	58	14	5	16	0	93
Predominant influence	4	12	0	0	0	16
Management control	—	—	—	—	80	80
Totals	69	26	5	16	84	200

Source: Chevalier (1970), p. 67.

Table 11   *Financial control in the top 200 US non-financial enterprises (1969)*

Type of control	Number of corporations	% of corporations
Full financial control	13	6.5
Full owner control	31	15.5
Partial financial control	46	23.0
Partial owner control	2	1.0
Partial financial and owner	10	5.0
No centre of control	93	46.5
Other	5	2.5
Totals	200	100.0

Source: Kotz (1978), table 3 on p. 97.

Note: 'Full' control refers to control on the basis of 10 per cent of more of the shares, while 'partial' control is based on 5–10 per cent.

Vernon discovered that the larger the bank, the more likely was this to be the case (1970, p. 654). The main source on shareholdings within these banks is the series of reports produced by the Patman Committee, which found, in Chevalier's words, that 'the most important shareholders of the banks are the banks themselves'

Table 12   *Strategic control in the 200 largest US commercial banks (1962)*

Mode of control	Number of banks	% of banks	% of assets
Private ownership	1	0.5	0.1
Majority control	4	2.0	0.6
Minority control:			
(a) 20–50%	22	11.0	6.2
(b) 10–20%	17	8.5	3.1
No dominant interest	149	74.5	87.5
Not known	7	3.5	2.5
Totals	200	100.0	100.0

Source: Adapted from Vernon (1970), table 1.

Note: The analysis refers to those banks which are members of the Federal Reserve System, i.e. all the major commercial banks.

presented in this chapter suggests that it can more appropriately be termed 'control through a constellation of interests'. Internal executive managers have the power to make decisions, but this power is constrained by the power which banks and other financials have to limit the choices open to management. This 'negative' constraint (ibid., p. 19) is a latent base for active intervention in decision-making by representatives of the institutions, should this be necessary. Control through a constellation of interests is the dominant form of strategic control in the largest enterprises, but management control and personal control survive to varying degrees alongside this.

Corporations and the controlling constellations in Britain

The question of ownership and control has been far less intensively researched in Britain than is the case in the USA. Indeed, from the 1930s to the 1950s, apart from one or two pieces by financial journalists, there was only the work of Florence (1947; 1953; 1961). Despite the arguments of Hall *et al.* (1957) and Crosland (1956; 1962), and the work of a group of researchers at Cambridge on a continuing review of aggregate trends in share-ownership (Stone *et al.* 1966), no real debate took place until Nichols (1969) and Child (1969a) published their reviews of the American debates and outlined their relevance to the British situation. Even then, the debate was subdued until the mid-1970s, when a number of empirical studies by economists and sociologists began to appear.

An initial view of trends in family ownership can be gained from studies of family representation on corporate boards. Hannah (1980, p. 53) has shown that the proportion of the top 200 enterprises with family representatives on their boards increased from 55 per cent in 1919 to 70 per cent in 1930, but subsequently fell to 60 per cent in 1948. In the top 120 enterprises, the proportion remained constant at just over a third between 1954 and 1966 (see Table 13). The high figure for 1930 can perhaps be accounted for by the changing composition of the top 200 following the amalgamation of the numerous non-family railway companies into four large enterprises and the consequent entry into the top 200 of a large number of family manufacturers. From the 1930s to the Second World War the number of family firms fell, but the figure seems unlikely to have fallen to any great extent between the war and 1966. The data shown in Table 13 are based on only the largest 120 and so might be expected to have a lower proportion of family enterprises. The increase in the number of enterprises shown in the table as dominated by their internal managers is due to the expansion in the number of foreign subsidiaries operating in Britain, as Barratt Brown (1968a) unrealistically treated such subsidiaries as management-controlled.

The first person to approach the question of the supposed decline in owner control in a direct way was Florence, who carried out a series of investigations of share-ownership in England. Florence discovered that wholly-owned subsidiaries formed a larger part of the list of large enterprises in England than in the USA, and that shareholdings generally were less dispersed in England (Florence 1953, p. 189). Table 14 shows that, after excluding wholly-owned subsidiaries, there was a trend towards greater share dispersal between 1936 and 1951. The average percentage held by the major shareholders fell from 30 to 19 per cent, and personal holders were increasingly replaced by corporate holders. In 1936, twenty-one enterprises had been majority or minority-controlled by personal shareholders, and a further sixteen of the 'other owner' enterprises were, in fact, controlled by families or family groups. By 1951, just seventeen enterprises had personal majority or minority controllers and only nine of the 'other owner' enterprises were subject to personal control. Conversely, there was a great increase in the number of enterprises in which the twenty largest shareholders owned between 10 and 20 per cent of the capital. Florence's data suggest an overall decline in personal owner control, together with a shift from majority to

Table 13 *Board representation in the top 120 British enterprises (1954 and 1966)*

Dominant interest on board	1954	1966
Family or tycoon	36	38
External interests	53	47
Internal management	31	35
Totals	120	120

Source: Adapted from Barratt Brown (1968a), p. 45, table 7.

Table 14 *Strategic control in large English non-financial enterprises (1936 and 1951)*

	Number of companies	
Mode of control	*1936*	*1951*
Majority control	9	6
Minority control	13	11
Other owner control, 20% cut-off	47	36
Other owner control, 10–19%	15	28
No dominant interest	10	17
Totals	94	98

Source: Calculated from Florence (1961), pp. 112–15, tables Va and Vb.

Note: 'Other owner control' refers to holdings of twenty largest registered shareholders.

Table 15 *Mode of control in the top 250 British enterprises (1976)*

| | *Type of controller* | | | | | | |
| | | *Corporate* | | | | | |
Mode of control	*Personal*	*British*	*Foreign*	*State*	*Mixed*	*Other*	*Totals*
Public corporations	—	—	—	13	—	—	13
Wholly-owned	7	1	28	2	0	0	38
Exclusive majority	14	1	9	1	0	0	25
Shared majority	0	12		1	2	0	15
Exclusive minority	19	12	5	0	0	0	36
Shared minority	0	2	0	1	8	0	11
Limited minority	3	1	0	0	0	0	4
Mutual	—	—	—	—	—	8	8
Constellation of interests	—	—	—	—	100	0	100
	43	71		18	110	8	250

Source: Data collected by the author; see Scott and Griff (1984), Appendix.

Note: One company classified as 'exclusively minority' had its own pension fund as controller, and one classified as 'constellation of interests' had restrictions on voting rights which resulted in an extreme dispersal of votes.

minority control among those enterprises remaining under personal control. In the other enterprises there was a move towards control through a constellation of interests.

This move towards control through a constellation of interests was confirmed in a study for 1975, which found 39 per cent of the top 250 British non-financials to have no holder with 5 per cent of the capital and a further 10 per cent of enterprises in which no holder had more than 10 per cent. Almost a half of the enterprises, however, were found to be majority- or minority-controlled by a cohesive group (Nyman and Silberston 1978, table 1; Francis 1980a). The data presented in Table 15 confirm this picture. About a third of the top 250 of 1976 were subject to some form of majority control, and a further 20 per cent were minority-controlled. Personal control was evenly divided between the majority and minority forms, while foreign ownership was concentrated in the wholly-owned enterprises. 40 per cent of all the enterprises were controlled through a constellation of interests; in each of these, the twenty largest shareholders owned between 10 and 50 per cent of the capital.[5]

Table 16   *Beneficial share-ownership in British enterprises (1957–81)*

Category of owner	% of market value held				
	1957	1963	1969	1975	1981
Persons	65.8	54.0	47.4	37.5	28.2
Banks	0.9	1.3	1.7	0.7	0.3
Insurance companies	8.8	10.0	12.2	15.9	20.5
Pension funds	3.4	6.4	9.0	16.8	26.7
Other financials	8.2	12.6	13.0	14.6	10.4
Public sector	3.9	1.5	2.6	3.6	3.0
Overseas	4.4	7.0	6.6	5.6	3.6
Other	4.6	7.2	7.5	5.3	7.3
Totals	100	100	100	100	100

Source: From Stock Exchange (1983), table 2.16.

Note: Data relate to stratified samples of quoted companies carried out by the Stock Exchange and by Stone *et al.* (1966), Moyle (1971), and Department of Industry (1979). Figures for 1957 involve an estimate for 'other financial', which may account for the apparent rise between 1957 and 1963.

Underlying this move towards control through a constellation of interests was the growth of 'institutional' shareholdings. Parkinson (1951, pp. 45–6) discovered that over a half of the major shareholders in thirty large companies in 1942 were persons, but that financial intermediaries were already a significant force in many enterprises. Table 16 shows that these financials have extended their shareholdings throughout the corporate sector over the post-war period. The proportion of shares held by individuals and families, as measured by the market value of these shares, declined consistently from 65.8 per cent in 1957 to 28.2 per cent in 1981. Conversely, holdings by financials increased from 21.3 to 57.9 per cent over the same period. The main growth was in insurance and pension funds, related to the extension of occupational pension schemes in the 1970s (Diamond Report 1975b, pp. 11–12; Erritt and Alexander 1977; Wilson Report 1977; Briston and Dobbins 1978; Westergaard and Resler 1975, p. 160). Despite an increase in the number of shareholders in each large company, the controlling intercorporate holdings have become more concentrated. In 1942, most shareholders in the thirty large companies analysed by Parkinson held less than £100, and companies such as the London, Midland and Scottish Railway had over 200,000 registered shareholders (1951, pp. 51, 122, 125, 128–9). At this time, Imperial Tobacco had 94,690 shareholders, but in 1982 it had 154,837 shareholders.[6] By the 1970s the growth in 'institutional' shareholdings had become so great that the total number of shareholders in the largest companies had even begun to fall. This growth in institutional holdings has been matched by an enhanced role for the banks which manage the institutional funds. Minns (1980; 1982) has shown that the bulk of the shares owned by pension funds are actually managed by banks together with insurance companies and big stockbrokers. Although banks held only 0.7 per cent of shares in 1975, they had voting control over 17.6 per cent. Hence, banks (and especially the big merchant banks) and insurance companies dominate the mobilization of capital and having voting rights to about one-third of all corporate capital. Reflecting on trends such as these, Barratt Brown (1968a) argued that the 'external interests' on company boards (see Table 13) could be seen as 'co-ordinating controllers' representing the major corporate shareholders and creditors, and Florence (1947) had earlier described this as a situation of 'oligarchic minority owners control'. It should be clear that this is precisely the situation which has been described above as 'control through a constellation of interests'.

The way in which this has come about is illustrated in Table 17. Florence believed that his studies of 1936 and 1951 showed that there was no sign of a managerial 'revolution', but that there were definite indications of a managerial 'evolution' (1961, p. 187). The facts which led him to this conclusion were the decline in the percentage holding by the board of directors and a decline in the percentage holding by the twenty largest shareholders. It can be seen from Table 17 that the total shareholding by the directorate did indeed decline continuously from 1936 to 1976 in the four largest enterprises studied by Florence. By 1976, the directors held less than two in a thousand shares in each of the enterprises. It can also be seen that in three of the enterprises the holding of the twenty largest shareholders fell between 1936 and 1951; in the fourth case it increased from a very low level. In 1951, the holding of the top twenty shareholders exceeded 10 per cent only in the case of Imperial Group. Even Nichols (1969, p. 77) concluded that these figures show Dunlop to be 'the epitomy (*sic*) of the "management-controlled" company'. But a comparison of the figures for 1951 and 1976 shows that these judgements were premature; during the period of growth in institutional holdings, the proportion held by the top twenty increased to the point at which they held more than 10 per cent in all four of the large enterprises. In a detailed investigation of ICI in 1957, Hall *et al.* (1957) showed

Table 17   *Development of control in Britain (1936–76)*

Enterprise	% held by board			% held by top 20		
	1936	1951	1976	1936	1951	1976
Courtaulds	3.3	1.2	0.011	21.0	7.1	18.49
ICI	0.2	0.1	0.006	10.1	9.3	13.60
Imperial Group	10.4	4.2	0.038	19.0	15.8	17.39
Dunlop	0.09	0.03	0.015	5.1	9.6	20.14

Source: Florence (1961), Appendix, and data collected by author; see also Nichols (1969), p. 76, table 6.3.

Note: In a similar comparison by Nichols, British American Tobacco and Unilever were included. These have been excluded because both were special cases of high vote concentration.

the progress of this growth. This enterprise, classified by Barratt Brown (1968a) as controlled by external co-ordinators, had 9 per cent of its shares held by the eleven largest shareholders, and a number of these holders were represented on the board. The fragmentation of small and medium holdings among a large number of individuals gave effective control to the major shareholders.

Cubbin and Leech (1983) constructed a model of voting behaviour analogous to that discussed in Chapter 2, and they applied this to data collected by Collett and Yarrow (1976). The latter had discovered none of their selection of eighty-five large industrials of 1970–1 to have less than 10 per cent held by their twenty largest registered shareholders. Cubbin and Leech showed that these twenty always had more than the critical block necessary to ensure control.[7] The holdings of the top twenty holders in those enterprises subject to control through a constellation of interests in 1976, can be seen in Table 18. In most cases the top twenty held between 20 and 30 per cent of the capital, and in no case did the block fall below 10 per cent. The enterprise with the most dispersed voting distribution was British Home Stores, where the top twenty held 10.27 per cent. By contrast, the top twenty held over 40 per cent in four enterprises, the greatest concentration being in Steetley, where the top twenty held 41.57 per cent. Table 19

Table 18 *Holdings by the twenty largest shareholders in large British enterprises (1976)*

% of shares held by top 20 holders	Number of companies
More than 50	0
40–49	4
30–39	13
20–29	61
10–19	22
Less than 10	0
Total	100

Source: See Table 15.

Note: Data based on the 100 enterprises in Table 15 which were controlled through a constellation of interests.

Table 19   *Top twenty shareholders in ICI and Prudential Assurance (1976)*

	Imperial Chemical Industries Shareholder	%	Prudential Assurance Shareholder	%
1	Prudential Assurance	3.36	Britannic Assurance	3.09
2	Imperial Chemical Industries	1.84	EMI	2.19
3	Commercial Union	0.78	Legal and General Assurance	1.71
4	Mercury Securities	0.71	Electricity Council	1.58
5	Royal Insurance	0.69	Prudential Assurance	1.36
6	Legal and General Assurance	0.63	Mercury Securities	1.18
7	Kuwait Investment Office	0.59	Midland Bank	1.17
8	Oil Transport and Trading	0.54	Hill Samuel	0.94
9	Electricity Council	0.47	Standard Life Assurance	0.91
10	Britannic Assurance	0.47	Barclays Bank	0.79
11	National Westminster Bank	0.40	Oil Transport and Trading	0.76
12	Baring Brothers	0.39	Baring Brothers	0.48
13	Norwich Union	0.37	British Airways	0.47
14	Robert Fleming	0.37	British Gas	0.47
15	Hill Samuel	0.36	Lucas Industries	0.46
16	Standard Life Assurance	0.34	Eagle Star Insurance	0.44
17	Hambros	0.34	Scottish Provident Institution	0.44
18	Equity and Law Life Assurance	0.31	Philip Hill Trusts	0.43
19	Barclays Bank	0.31	Morgan Grenfell	0.42
20	Co-operative group	0.31	National Coal Board	0.42
	Totals of top 20	13.60		19.72

Source: See Table 15.

Note: Listings for 100 enterprises controlled through constellations of interests are contained in J. Scott, 'The Controlling Constellations', booklet available through BLL and the national copyright libraries. 'Oil Transport and Trading' in the above lists is the pseudonym of a large British oil company. All holdings in the names of non-financial enterprises were, in fact, holdings by pension funds.

illustrates this from two of Britain's largest enterprises, and it can be seen that in neither case did the largest holder have sufficient votes for minority control. The large holders comprised a mixture of corporate shareholders, predominantly bank and insurance companies, and the extent of the overlap among the controlling constellations of Britain's largest enterprises is illustrated by the fact that the two enterprises had nine of their top twenty holders in common.

In both the United States and Britain the prevailing form of strategic control is control through a constellation of interests. A comparison of Table 7 with Table 18 shows that dispersed share-holdings, and therefore forms of 'constrained management control', remain more significant in the USA than in Britain. Management control emerged in America on a large scale in the 1930s and persisted as the dominant characteristic of the largest enterprises until the 1950s. The growth of 'institutional' holdings, which began earlier and progressed more rapidly in Britain (compare Tables 6 and 16), has increasingly supplanted this by control through a constellation of interests. This pattern holds for all large British enterprises without a dominant ownership interest, and it is likely to spread in America as well. Although control through a constellation of interests is characteristic of the majority of large enterprises in the USA and Britain, family control remains important in both countries and is especially important in the 'smaller' of the large enterprises. In Britain there is also an important category of enterprises controlled by foreign parents, especially American parents, reflecting the increasing internationalization of capital. By contrast, Herman's study found only one foreign-controlled enterprise in the American top 200 of 1976. It may be concluded, however, that the largest enterprises are increasingly subject to control through a constellation of interests, and that this form of control has come to dominate the British and American economies.

Notes

1 Eight of the 173 companies listed in Table 2 as having no dominant interest were separated-out by Herman as having minority controllers with 5–9 per cent of their shares. This qualification is discussed later in this chapter.

2   Herman has shown that exclusion of these subsidiaries from the figures in Table 4 leaves fifteen majority-controlled and fifty-two minority-controlled, which is much more consistent with the trend in Table 2 (Herman 1981, p. 72).

3   In addition to the Rockefellers, the DuPont family held 0.60 per cent.

4   The exceptions to this rule are the mutual insurance companies which are, strictly, controlled by their policy-holders. The only study of control in mutuals (Gessell and Howe 1941) concluded that financial interests controlled the companies through proxy voting and complex electoral arrangements. See also Perlo (1957), p. 82, and O'Hara (1981).

5   Florence's analysis was based on the largest registered share-holders, termed shareholders of record in the USA. The data presented in Table 15 is based on an identification of the beneficiaries or vote-holders and involved grouping shares subject to a common management. An analysis limited to regis-tered shareholdings underestimates the concentration of votes.

6   By this time it had been renamed Imperial Group.

7   Cubbin and Leech attempted to show that minority control could be exercised by one of the twenty largest holders in some of these enterprises. They claimed this as a possibility in twenty-five of the seventy-one without a dominant interest. In fact, these are best seen as, at most, cases of limited minority control, as they conclude that a holding of less than 10 per cent by an institution is a less secure base of control than a similar holding by an internal family executive (1983, p. 366). Their analysis, therefore, confirms the picture of control through a constellation of interests.

4 Finance capital in America and Britain

The theory of industrial society and the associated managerialist position have been shown to involve a misreading of the evidence on corporate development in America and Britain; but does the model of finance capital fare any better as an explanation of the development of industrial capitalism? The growth of 'institutional' shareholdings and the consequent realignment of money capital and industrial production which have led to the dominance of control through a constellation of interests might be expected also to have produced the kinds of changes depicted in Hilferding's (1910) analysis. 'Finance capital' as the fusion of 'banking capital' and 'industrial capital' was held to involve the emergence of alliances and coalitions between enterprises in various economic sectors and the formation of extensive networks of intercorporate linkages. A small inner circle of financiers occupy a central position in this system of relations and ensure a degree of coordination and intercorporate unity by virtue of their occupancy of key directorships on the banks which determine the availability of capital. Such ideas have their repercussions in debates about the 'Money Trust' in the USA and the 'City' in Britain. The common theme in such debates is the claim that banks and other enterprises involved in the granting of credit have interests which are opposed to those of manufacturing enterprises. On the basis of their divergent interests and their differential power, the two types of enterprise are seen as forced into antagonistic relations in which banks are able to assert their dominance by coercing manufacturers to act under conditions which will serve the interests of the providers of credit.

A number of confusions run through these debates. Although Hilferding was clear that finance capital was to be seen as a *fusion* of banking and industrial capital, his emphasis on the organizational centrality of banks has led later commentators to interpret this as a theory of bank control. This gloss on Hilferding's position is obscured by a tendency to equate 'finance capital' with the 'financial sector'. The latter, consisting of all those enterprises operating in the monetary sphere, is distinguished from the non-financial sectors of commerce, services, manufacturing, and so on, and this distinction is translated into a contrast between 'financial capital' and mere 'industrial capital'. Hilferding, however, was concerned to show that manufacturers, for example, were increasingly forced to adopt joint stock organization and so were forced to enter into the monetary sphere and, through such mechanisms as stock exchange dealing and currency trading, so to become 'financial' as well as 'industrial' enterprises (see also Sweezy 1971, p. 31; De Vroey 1975a, pp. 8–9). Financials in the narrow sense, those enterprises involved primarily in monetary processes, come into closer contact with the joint stock industrials, traders, and so on. Thus, large enterprises are increasingly likely to be involved in both 'financial' and 'non-financial' activities, and within the financial sector they are likely to enter into various forms of organizational alignment and co-operation. This is the situation described by Hilferding as finance capitalism.

The question remains, however, whether the model of finance capital – or perhaps the derived model of bank control – is at all accurate as a description of the reality of modern capitalism. It is necessary to investigate the organization of the 'financial' sectors in Britain and America and to explore their relations to other sectors of those economies. If institutional shareholdings have brought about a closer alignment of financial intermediaries and 'non-financial' enterprises, has this resulted in an enhanced role for these intermediaries in strategic control? Do the financials actually intervene in corporate decision-making in an attempt to assert their own interests in the face of those concerned with actual production?

The Money Trust and interlocking directorships in the USA

For most of the nineteenth century manufacturing industry was of marginal importance, and those few firms that did undertake manufacturing activity were family firms operating in local markets. The main growth area in the economy was railway development, and the railways were the basis for the wealth and power of a group of private and commercial bankers who undertook the promotion and financing of the emerging railway systems. From the 1890s, however, the economy underwent a process of rapid industrialization, and the period up to the First World War marked the establishment of big business in America. The bankers who financed the railways were able to use their position of dominance to apply the same techniques of business finance to the new industrials. It was not generally possible for a single bank to raise all the capital required by a large enterprise, and so banks had developed the practice of joining together into loose underwriting syndicates which undertook the issue and sale of shares. Each bank, therefore, was involved in a number of overlapping syndicates, and the biggest of the banks were also able to act as lead banks in their syndicates and were in a position to offer 'advice' to the leadership of the new enterprises and even to place their representatives on the corporate boards (Carosso 1970, ch. 3; Sweezy 1940; 1941). The ability of these 'investment bankers' to mobilize the savings of individuals and to make them available to industry was the basis of their power to intervene in the formation, merger, and expansion of enterprises and to engineer a number of 'trusts' and 'cartels' in important markets.

Considerable public disquiet was expressed about the emerging 'Money Trust' or 'financial oligarchy' which many saw as undermining the competitive market economy (Veblen 1904; Pratt 1905). John Moody, a financial writer, countered with an apologia for their business practices, arguing that the big trusts created by Morgan, Rockefeller, Vanderbilt, and Harriman were responsible for America's economic success (Moody 1904). Public concern about the 'Money Kings', 'Masters of Capital', and 'Captains of Industry' continued to grow, and by 1910 had crystallized into a debate about the powers and responsibilities of the 'Money Trust' (Bunting 1976, pp. 7-8; Andrews 1982). A Congressional committee of investigation was set up in 1912 and its report made the first published reference to the phenomenon of the 'interlocking directorate' in the USA (Pujo Report 1913).[1] Louis Brandeis, a lawyer and anti-trust campaigner, popularized the Report's findings on the Money Trust, asserting that 'The practice of interlocking directorates is the root of many evils. It offends laws human and divine' (1914, p. 35). Brandeis was critical of the bankers' use of other people's money to enhance the economic power of large enterprises and to engage in anti-competitive actions. The large enterprises, he argued, were tied together through a chain of interlocks, a 'vicious circle of control', in which 'each controlled corporation is entwined with many others' (Brandeis 1914, p. 38). Such attacks were instrumental in securing legislation and regulation, though the Clayton Anti-trust Act was virtually unenforced and there was little effect on business practice. After the First World War, however, the climate of public opinion altered, and Moody restated his defence, arguing that the war had eliminated business unpopularity (Moody 1919). Only in the 1930s, in the wake of the Great Crash, was critical debate once more prominent in government circles. Brandeis's book on the Pujo investigations was re-issued in 1933, at a time when Berle and Means (1932) had extended the scope of the debate to a concern with the inner workings of the large corporation. Brandeis and Means were associated closely with one another, and Means's work on the *National Resources Committee* drew on specially commissioned reports by Sweezy on the economic significance of financial groups (Means *et al.* 1939). At the same time, the *Temporary National Economic Committee* (Goldsmith and Parmelee 1940) was set up at the instigation of 'New Deal' liberals influenced by Brandeis and concerned about the responsibility of big business for the economic problems of the 1930s. The debate over ownership and control, which was reviewed in Chapter 3, was the outcome of a long series of practical political debates.

What is the reality behind this public debate, which stretched across the first forty years of the century? All those involved in the debates regarded the existence and number of interlocking directorships as a crucial diagnostic tool for assessing the concentration of economic power, and Table 20 presents an overview of interlocking in the period 1899–1974. It can be seen that the top 167 enterprises experienced a continuous increase in the total size of their directorate up to 1969, but that the proportion of directors who held more than one directorship in the top 167 (the 'multiple directors') reached its peak in the years 1905–19. In the latter period multiple directors comprised between 15 and 16 per cent of the total directorate, in the following years they made up a constant 13–14 per cent. The peak period was also the high point for the prominent multiple directors with six or more directorships: twenty-seven directors held this number of directorships in 1912, but by 1935 the figure had fallen to three. More detailed figures show that the proportion of multiple directors with four or five directorships also declined after 1935, and that the solid core of multiple directors has been those with two or three top directorships. Analyses of the top 200 and top 250 enterprises confirm this picture, though it is clear that the average number of directorships held by each director increases with the number of enterprises analysed. Directors of large enterprises were more likely to accumulate directorships in the lower ranks of the corporate system than in the upper levels, indicating a hierarchical character to interlocking (Bunting and Barbour 1971; Dooley 1969).[2]

Recent work has shown that these trends can be explained in terms of the rapid formation of 'big business' around the turn of the century. Interlocks developed early in the nineteenth century among banking, insurance and railway enterprises, as the bankers sought to monopolize corporate finance and the emerging railway systems sought to monitor their rivals and suppliers. This resulted in the creation of an extensive community of interest into which the expanding enterprises in other sectors of the economy were gradually incorporated (Bunting 1983). By the 1880s banking, insurance, railways, coalmining, and telegraphs were all tightly linked together, and by the 1890s the biggest manufacturers had become part of the community of interest (Roy 1983a and b; Kotz 1978).[3] Thus the data for 1905 in Table 20 shows a situation where most enterprises in the big business sector of the American economy were part of a massive web of interlocks. Until the end of the century the railways had been the central enterprises in this network. The railways were the first site of the fusion of banking and industry, and so the intermediaries which had grown to meet their needs – the Wall Street banks and stockbrokers – provided the institutional structure that administered this fusion. The Wall Street enterprises, however, gradually enhanced their power and by the end of the century had become the dominant element in the intercorporate network (Roy 1983b; Mizruchi 1982; 1983).

The argument that a 'Money Trust' existed in the period from the 1890s to the First World War seems, therefore, to be confirmed. Wall Street bankers had become the central agents in an extensive intercorporate network with a large number of these bankers holding six or more directorships. Most commentators at the time pointed to the overwhelming power of J P Morgan, and the research evidence does indeed confirm that Morgan and his bank were at the heart of the community of interest. The contemporary Pujo Report demonstrated that six banks and their dependent trust companies made up the heart of the corporate

Table 20 *The distribution of directorships in the top 167 US enterprises (1899–1974)*

Number of directorships per person	Number of people								
	1899	1905	1912	1919	1935	1964	1969	1974
1	1530	1632	1786	1915	2040	2437	2527	2402
2–5	244	292	297	333	306	371	403	371
6 or more	16	20	27	14	3	4	2	0
Totals	1790	1944	2110	2262	2349	2812	2932	2773

Source: Bunting (1976), part 1 (table 3), part 2 (table 3). See also Dooley (1969), p. 315; Bunting and Barbour (1971), p. 324; Herman (1981), p. 199.

system: the private banks of Morgan, Kuhn Loeb, Lee Higginson, and Kidder Peabody, together with the commercial banks First National Bank and National City Bank. Morgan and the two commercial banks,[4] in which Morgan had shareholdings, were the 'inner group' to which the others were affiliated, and all six were surrounded by their numerous associates and clients (Pujo Report 1913, II, pp. 1102–3). By 1914 the commercial banks had already come to challenge the private bankers as the sources of investment banking capital, and this opening-up of the capital market was reflected in the loosening-up of the interlock network shown in Table 20. Investment banking remained a prominent feature of the American economy throughout the 1920s, with the big banks playing an active role in the formation of many general investment companies and utility holding companies[5] which controlled numerous enterprises through minority participations and the legal device of pyramiding. This activity fuelled the stock market boom which culminated in the 'Great Crash' of 1929 (Carosso 1970; Galbraith 1954). The crash finally broke the power of the investment bankers, but this merely confirmed a decline which resulted from deeper causes. The big industrials had established their positions in their markets, and their ability to secure internal resources for expansion enabled them to dispense with the services of the investment bankers. At the same time, the growth of institutional investment and the associated private placement of corporate shares undermined the role of the investment banker as the crucial intermediary (Gordon 1945, pp. 214–16; Sweezy 1941, pp. 190–3; 1942, p. 267).

The model of finance capital holds that the intercorporate network should be structured into distinct 'financial empires', groups of enterprises subject to some degree of central co-ordination (Pastré 1979). Research in America has produced some support for this idea, but has shown there to be a high degree of overlap among the groups. Mizruchi (1982) demonstrates that the period up to 1919 was characterized by the unification of a number of powerful financial groups under the leadership of Morgan. A number of bank-centred groups could be identified, but they had numerous commercial relations as members of overlapping syndicates and they were tied together through a web of interlocks in which directors of the Morgan bank had such extensive contacts that they brought about a high level of cohesion between the various groups. Sweezy's study for the *National Resources*

Committee analysed data for 1935 and found evidence for the existence of eight 'interest groups' among the top 200 enterprises, these groups being tied together through a mixture of family majority and minority holdings, bank credit, and interlocks. Morgan, Rockefeller, and Mellon were the most prominent groups identified (Sweezy 1939, p. 168; Poland 1939; Means *et al.* 1939).[6] Sweezy found, however, a considerable overlap of membership between the groups, and a re-examination of data for 1935 by Mizruchi (1982) showed clearly that there were not eight distinct and competing 'empires' but an extensive intercorporate network which had become rather more fragmented as a result of the declining power of the Morgan bank to hold the system together.[7] By the 1960s investment banking power had declined even further. Villarejo argued that interest groups could be identified, but they were loose communities of interest rather than financial empires (1961b, p. 60). Dooley's study of the top 250 enterprises of 1965 claimed to have discovered fifteen such interest groups, including the eight identified by Sweezy thirty years earlier, but he showed that they tended to be regional in character and to be less compact than those of the 1930s (1969, pp. 320–1). The fact that groups were loose and overlapping was also recognized by Marxist commentators: financial groups are seen as alliances of banks and other enterprises, often based around one or more families, which do not eliminate the differing interests of the constituent enterprises

Table 21   *The distribution of interlocks in the top 250 US enterprises (1975)*

| Number of interlocks per enterprise | Number of enterprises | | |
	200 non-financials	50 financials	Top 250
0	15	1	16
1–4	54	7	61
5–9	62	13	75
10–14	44	12	56
15 or more	25	17	42
Totals	200	50	250

Source: Calculated from Herman (1981), p. 201, table 6.5.

and which do not prevent joint ventures and financial associations being established between groups (Menshikov 1969, pp. 216–21, 229; Chevalier 1970, p. 123ff.). A study by Allen on data for 1970 produced a similar picture: the groups of 1970 were smaller and less cohesive than those of 1935, they were regional in character, and they were likely to be based on interlocks alone rather than on capital and commercial relations together with interlocks (1978a). Similarly, Sonquist *et al.* (1976) discovered thirty-two regional groups ranging in size from three to fifteen, with banks having central positions in over a half of the groups.

The intercorporate network, therefore, had become less dense and cohesive since the First World War, but the groups which could be identified were loose, overlapping regional groups rather than sharply divided financial empires. New York and its Wall Street financials remained the dominant region within this network, and so the system was structured into 'a giant national wheel of interlocking directorates with the New York hub dominating the many spokes that spread out from and back to it' (Warner and Unwalla 1967, p. 146). Within this network the financial and non-financial sectors had come closer together. More industrials were incorporated into the network as the century proceeded, despite the overall decline in the level of interlocks. At the height of the Money Trust interlocking tended to be particularly intense, with enterprises linked through two or three common directors. In the post-war period each link became less intense and enterprises were linked mainly through single common directors. In this way, a smaller proportion of multiple directors with fewer directorships could spread their influence over a larger number of enterprises. The 'endless chain' identified by Brandeis had grown to encompass more and more enterprises in an extensive national network (Dooley 1969, p. 315, table 2; Allen 1974, p. 404; Bunting and Barbour 1971, pp. 330–4).[8] The extent of this network in 1975 is shown in Table 21, which presents the number of interlocks carried by each of the top 250 enterprises. Only sixteen of these enterprises had no interlocks within the top 250, and, though a large number had more than fifteen each, most interlocked enterprises had fewer than ten interlocks. Financials were considerably more likely to be interlocked, and to be interlocked at a high level, than were the non-financials, and most of the interlocks within the network ran between the two sectors. The most influential, and most accurate, account of this network has been produced by the

Stony Brook group of researchers.[9] Reflecting on the growth of connections between financials and industry, the discovery of loose regional groups, and the fact that banks invariably appear at the centre of such groups, these researchers have constructed a powerful and persuasive model of the American intercorporate network. When all interlocks among top enterprises are studied an extensive network with little sign of grouping is discovered. If, however, only those interlocks involving executive officers (termed primary interlocks by Sweezy) are examined, regional groupings become a prominent feature of the network. There is an overall national network which is extensive but loosely connected, and which contains denser regional groups built from intercorporate shareholdings, indebtedness, and primary interlocks (Bearden *et al.* 1975, p. 50; Mariolis 1975, pp. 433–5). These financial interest groups tend to be found among the smaller enterprises and are tied together in an overall structure of intercorporate unity (Mintz and Schwartz 1981a and b; 1983; Bearden and Mintz 1985).[10] The interest groups are loose, bank-centred, and regional groups of small and medium-sized enterprises which are tied into an extensive national network through the banks. The Stony Brook researchers argue that

the integration of New York, Boston, Philadelphia and California centers of business into a national and even international network of corporations has occurred simultaneously with the maintenance and further development of interest groups which continue to organize and coordinate intercorporate cooperation and control [Bearden *et al.* 1975, p. 50].

Clearly, bank centrality is an important feature of the American intercorporate network. The twenty enterprises with the largest number of interlocks in 1969 included eight banks and three insurance companies, and three banks (Morgan Guaranty, Chase Manhattan, First National City Bank) had more interlocks than any other enterprises. It is noticeable that there was a degree of continuity from the days of the Money Trust, as the successor banks of Morgan and the two commercial banks highlighted by the Pujo investigators as the 'inner group' were among the three most interlocked banks – the third is widely regarded as a surviving member of the Rockefeller interests. The Stony Brook group discovered that this continuity was greater for banks than for industrials. While large industrials showed year-to-year variations in the level of their interlocking, four-fifths of the heavily interlocked banks in 1962 held a similar position in the network of 1969. The researchers conclude that

banks are the foundation of intercorporate networks. While other firms may rise into momentary prominence and a few remain there for some years, the major commercial banks persist from year to year [ibid., p. 59].

The model of the contemporary intercorporate network proposed by the Stony Brook group posits that the main New York commercial banks are the peaks of the national network, and that each is also the hub of numerous connections to major insurance companies and large industrials (such as AT & T and United States Steel). A number of regional banks based in areas such as Chicago, Pennsylvania, Boston, and California, are linked to the national hubs through the insurance companies and through big regional industrials, and, at the same time, those regional banks are hubs for connections to the smaller financial and non-financial enterprises in their own region. Inter-bank conflict at the national level and conflicts between New York and the regions are contained within an extensive network of intercorporate unity.

The City and interlocking directorships in Britain

Early industrial development in Britain was based around the small entrepreneurial firms of the North and the Midlands, which were able to raise additional capital from the small 'country banks' which were scattered through the regions. The individual entreprencurial family provided capital for investment and the local banks supplied short-term working capital (Mathias 1969; Payne 1967 and 1974; Hobsbawm 1968; Kindleberger 1984, pp. 92–4). The City of London, where all the large financial enterprises were to be found, was virtually uninvolved in long-term industrial finance, concentrating instead on government loans and foreign investment. The City merchants had grown alongside the expansion of agrarian and mercantile capitalism and were especially involved in Imperial trade. As a result, the City financiers and the provincial manufacturers were sharply separated from one another (Scott 1982b; Rubinstein 1976). The expansion of the banking system in the late nineteenth century sharpened this separation into a division between 'banking' and 'industry', as the majority of the country banks were incorporated into the large City banks and so were forced to withdraw from industrial finance. A number of regional joint stock banks remained, however, and played a limited role in the finance of regional industrials, but the predominant feature of the British economy at the turn of the century was a separation between City capital and provincial capital (Scott and Griff 1984, ch. 6; Ingham 1982).

The City banks were, however, associated through capital relations and interlocks with enterprises involved in credit, commerce, and transport: insurance, railways, and shipping being especially important. To this extent there was a superficial similarity with the American intercorporate network of the middle of the nineteenth century. But under these surface similarities were certain crucial differences. In the USA, railway finance had involved investment bankers and the whole Wall Street system, and so the development of the railways led to the development of a banking system capable of responding to the turn of the century industrial amalgamations and of incorporating the new giant enterprises into its existing network of connections. In Britain, railway finance was more decentralized, with few of the private banks taking an active role in promotion and finance. The clearing banks and most of the private and merchant banks, continued to regard commerce as their major area of involvement. Merchants, merchant banks, and discount houses were the key agents in the financing of international trade, with the clearing banks acting as providers of funds to the active dealers in the money market. At the hub of this system were the Bank of England, for a long time owned and controlled by City merchants, and the Stock Exchange.

There was little public discussion of this as a problem until the 1960s and 1970s. Marxist writers of both the orthodox and 'new left' wings began to regard the separation of 'City' and 'industry' as an endemic feature of British capitalism, arguing that the City fraction dominated the flow of capital and diverted it abroad at the expense of domestic industry. Britain's economic decline, it was argued, is due to the starving of manufacturing industry by a City fraction which dominates the state machinery (Anderson 1964; Nairn 1972 and 1977; see also Longstreth 1979). Among writers before the First World War, only Hobson and the Fabians had anything to say on the relations between City and industry. Drawing on the debates which were current in America, Hobson suggested that the industrial amalgamations of the turn of the century in Britain were created by a 'financial class' whose members had become involved as promoters, bankers, and brokers and who operated as intermediaries between the investors and those who actually ran the enterprises (1906, p. 242). Hobson recognized, however, that the big banks were not the leading agents in this process and that financiers did not generally become involved in the management of the enterprises.[11] Smaller, marginal banks did become involved in the American way, but their scope of action was limited by the scale of their funds (Hannah 1980, p. 55). The period before the First World War was not, therefore, dominated by a Money Trust of the kind found in the USA, but was dominated by a City of London group centred around banking, insurance, commerce, and transport.

Table 22 shows that 197 of the top 250 enterprises of 1904 were interlocked, reflecting the extremely large number of railway companies included in the top 250 at that time. The proportion of directors who held two or more directorships was somewhat lower than in the USA (see Table 20), and the proportion with six or more was considerably lower – just one British director held this many directorships. Table 23 shows that the interlocked enterprises at this time tended to have relatively few interlocks, only a

Table 22 *The distribution of directorships in the top 250 British enterprises (1904–76)*

Number of directorships per person	Number of people		
	1904	*1938*	*1976*
1	1901	1844	2400
2	234	218	195
3–5	68	102	85
6 or more	1	9	2
Totals	2204	2173	2682
Inclusiveness	197	201	189
Density	0.013	0.019	0.017

Source: Scott and Griff (1984), table 2.7.

Note: 'Inclusiveness' is simply the number of companies with interlocks. 'Density' is the ratio of the actual to the possible number of interlocks. The enterprises analysed are those discussed in Table 15.

98   *Corporations, Classes and Capitalism*

Table 23   *The distribution of interlocks in the top 250 British enterprises (1904–76)*

Number of interlocks per enterprise	1904	Number of enterprises 1938	1976
0	53	49	61
1–5	148	116	112
6–10	39	63	54
11 or more	10	22	23
Totals	250	250	250

Source: Scott and Griff (1984), table 6.3.
Note: The enterprises analysed are those discussed in Table 15.

quarter of the interlocked enterprises having six or more connections to others in the top 250. The ten enterprises with the largest number of interlocks comprised two banks, two insurers, four railways, and just two industrials (a mine and a steel producer). The enterprise with the largest number of interlocks, an insurance company, had just eighteen interlocks, compared with the finding that sixteen of the top 167 American enterprises of 1905 had more than fifty interlocks each (Bunting 1976). It is clear, therefore, that the level of interlocking in Britain before the First World War was considerably lower than in the USA, the banks were far less prominent, and the network included fewer industrials (Scott and Griff 1984).

In the inter-war years this situation was altered. For much of the period the City faced declining opportunities for profitable foreign investment and so was forced to look more closely at domestic outlets for its funds, and these funds were being swollen by the spread of life insurance and the consequent growth in 'institutional' funds. Perhaps more important in bringing about the re-alignment of City and provinces were the economic problems of the 1920s and 1930s. Economic recession led to many of the largest enterprises reaching, or passing, the brink of bankruptcy, and the big clearing banks were forced to become concerned in their affairs. Although involved only as the providers of short-term overdrafts, the clearing banks had to become actively involved in the long-term future of enterprises in difficulties in case the sheer scale of industrial collapse should affect them also. In 'normal' circumstances a bank may have been able to withstand the bankruptcy of one of its customers, but the banks were faced with the possible bankruptcy of many of their largest customers and so could not afford to be so sanguine (Pollard 1962; Hannah 1976c, chs. 3 and 5; Payne 1978; W. Thomas 1978; Clarke 1967). Banks became the reluctant holders of industrial shares and loan stock, and the Bank of England set up a number of finance agencies to aid the activities of the banks in industrial reconstruction. Banks were active in involving insurance companies in long-term industrial finance, and the boards of industrial enterprises came to include a number of representatives of the financial intermediaries. This is apparent from Tables 22 and 23, which show an increase between 1904 and 1938 in the average number of directorships held by each director, an increase in the density of the network, and a substantial increase in the proportion of enterprises with six or more interlocks. Of the ninety-eight large enterprises studied by Florence in 1936 fifty-six were interlocked with one another, indicating the extent to which interlocking had become the norm for the largest enterprises (Florence 1961, p. 88). By the Second World War the intercorporate network had extended to a national scale and, though structured around the City financials, incorporated both financial and non-financial enterprises. The inter-war period saw the birth of 'finance capital' in Britain.

The post-war expansion in economic activity further consolidated the coalescence of banking and industry in Britain, though the clearing banks withdrew as soon as possible from long-term finance. It was in the 1960s, in the wake of an official report on the involvement of City bankers in a leakage of secret information (Radcliffe Report 1959), that these trends first came under critical scrutiny and Marxist writers began to discuss the existence of financial interest groups in Britain. Aaronovitch (1961, p. 78ff.) and Barratt Brown (1968a, pp. 58–60) suggested that ten or more interest groups had been formed around the major banks and insurers. Central positions in these groups were claimed for the big five clearing banks (Barclays, Lloyds, Midland, National Provincial, and Westminster) and for merchant banks such as Rothschild, Lazard, and Morgan Grenfell (part-owned by the American Morgan bank), and it was held that these banks were responsible for a loose degree of co-ordination and the avoidance of competition within groups. This work was based on *ad hoc* procedures and tended to involve circular reasoning, and later research has not confirmed the existence of such sharply divided groups. Research for 1971 showed that all the major financials of the City were closely tied together and had close links to the large industrials. Although the banks had more interlocks than other enterprises, conforming to the picture of bank centrality found in America, they did not maintain exclusive connections with particular interest groups. Rather, they were part of a unified intercorporate network (Whitley 1973 and 1974; Stanworth and Giddens 1975).

By 1976 the British economy had come to resemble that of the USA very closely. Table 24 shows that the number of multiple directors in America was considerably larger, but that the distribution of directorships which they held was very similar. The densities of the two networks were also comparable, and in both Britain and America there is strong evidence for bank centrality. The ten British enterprises with the largest number of interlocks included the Bank of England, all four big clearing banks, a specialist industrial credit bank, and a merchant bank.[12] Banks were especially important in the network of executive officer interlocks, though there was little evidence of regionalism in this network.[13] Banks were associated with loose and overlapping groups of enterprises through primary interlocks, but these were even less financial interest groups than those found in the USA. The major difference between the two economies lay in the number of uninterlocked enterprises. Over 90 per cent of the American top 250 of 1976 were interlocked, compared with a figure of three-quarters in Britain. The reasons for this difference are twofold. First, the British network includes a number of foreign subsidiaries which tended not to interlock within Britain, while the American network included few such subsidiaries. In Britain, thirty-seven of the sixty-one isolated enterprises were foreign subsidiaries. Second, family ownership remained stronger in Britain than the USA, and family enterprises in both countries were less likely to interlock. Of the top 250 enterprises in Britain thirty-nine had families or individuals with majority or minority control, and a further thirty-six had family participants in their controlling constellations. The stronger the family influence, the less likely was the enterprise to interlock within the top 250 (Scott and Griff 1984, table 4.3; A. B. Thomas 1978).

Since the 1930s, and especially since the late 1950s, the 'City'

Table 24 *Multiple directorships in the top 250 British and US enterprises (1976)*

Number of directorships per person	% of directorships held Britain	USA
2	69	64
3	21	24
4	6	8
5	3	3
6–10	1	1
11 or more	0	0
Totals	100 (N=282)	100 (N=564)

Source: Stokman and Wasseur (1985), table 2.2 and figure 2.1.

Note: Tables 22 and 23 relate to the same group of British directors. The US data is based on 3108 directors in total.

has moved away from an exclusive reliance upon its commercial activities. The growth of institutional shareholdings and the property and take-over booms of the post-war period brought all sectors of the economy into closer alignment with the financial intermediaries. At the same time, the City enterprises were them- selves undergoing a transformation. 'Merchant' banks became more active in industrial investment and fund management, and the clearing banks (no longer controlled by the City merchants) became involved in these same areas as well as entering into consumer credit, domestic mortgages, industrial leasing, and so on. The clearing banks and some of the big merchant banks be- came massive conglomerates of finance capital (Channon 1977) and were later followed by some of the larger insurers. In the 1970s and 1980s these enterprises, and similar enterprises from the USA, extended their activities into the heart of the old City opera- tions by buying stakes in stockbrokers and jobbers, Lloyds insur- ance syndicates, and discount houses. Thus, the City has been subject to two interrelated processes: a concentration of activity into large and diverse enterprises rather than small, specialist partnerships and 'houses'; and a shift from commercial capital *per se* to finance capital with a well-developed commercial arm. The heart of the British economy consisted of an intercorporate network in which these 'City' enterprises were closely integrated with 'non-financial' enterprises. There was no real separation of 'City' and 'industry': the intercorporate network formed and connected units of finance capital.[14]

Corporate interlocking and bank power

Both Britain and the USA have moved away from the nineteenth-century economy of small-scale businesses providing their own investment funds to a modern economy of large-scale enterprises which draw a considerable part of their funds from outside sources. Whereas investment funds in the small entrepreneurial firm derived from the entrepreneur and from his family and associates, the large enterprise acquires its investment funds through the credit system as 'finance' in the form of share capital, loan stock, or bank credit. To this extent, the concept of finance capital captures an important dimension of the transformation which industry has experienced in Britain and the USA (Edwards 1938; Hussain 1976). This transition from entrepreneurial capital to finance capital has involved the emergence of a close relationship between the 'financial' and the 'non-financial' sectors. The integration of the two sectors, and the consequent conversion of all big business into units of finance capital, has in each country been accelerated during periods of industrial change when company formation and amalgamation brought about higher levels of concentration. In the USA, the Morgan-dominated community of interest which emerged at the turn of the century gradually dissolved into a more extensive network which, until the 1930s, was organized around the overlapping remnants of the groupings built up by the invest-ment bankers. Already by the 1930s regionalism had become an important aspect of the intercorporate network, due partly to the territorial scale of the USA and partly to legal restrictions on banks operating in more than one state. By the 1970s regional groupings were the most obvious feature of the network of primary interlocks, though these groups were contained within a framework of intercorporate unity in which the New York banks held central positions. In Britain the move from entrepreneurial capital to finance capital was slower and followed a different route. The City of London interests fused with provincial manufacturers only slowly, and they required a deep recession to bring them to

the point at which a national network could be said to have
emerged. During the 1950s and 1960s the British intercorporate
network was forged into its present state of an extensive national
network structured around the big clearing banks. The latter were
associated with loose and overlapping groups of enterprises, but
these groups were not regional in character. Both Britain and
America, therefore, had diffuse bank-centred intercorporate networks of low density.

It is important, therefore, to arrive at a satisfactory interpretation of the role which banks play in the two economies. Are they
centres of control which can coerce other enterprises to act in their
interests, or has their power been overemphasized by proponents
of the theory of capitalist society? It is important to emphasize that
there are two distinct variants of the model of bank control. The
best-known variant holds that banks exercise control over particular groups of enterprises which constitute their 'empires' or
'interest groups', but it has been suggested above that there is little
evidence for the existence of such groups (see also Glasberg and
Schwartz 1983, pp. 316–17). The other variant of the model is not
undermined by this lack of evidence as it simply holds that banks
are more powerful than any industrials with which they come into
contact and that banks may be expected to exercise this power
whenever it suits their interests. Particular industrials may be
subject to continued dependence on a particular bank, but it is
equally possible that industrials will be subject to pressure from a
number of banks. For this reason, proponents of this variant of the
bank control model have tended to stress the possibilities which
banks have for co-operation and collusion in order to collectively
pursue their interests *vis-à-vis* the industrial sector. An especially
prominent advocate of this variant of the model has been Fitch,
who claims that interlocks express 'the exercise of raw economic
power' and are one of the means through which banks can force
industrials into 'buying and selling goods on the basis of considera-
tions other than price, quality, and service' (Fitch 1972, p. 107).
That is to say, banks can coerce industrials to take decisions which
may run counter to the profit calculation which would be taken on
pure 'market' criteria: the banks become the dominant force in the
determination of corporate strategy.

The bases on which banks may be able to exercise such power
are capital relations and interlocking directorships[15] and through
capital relations, banks have the ability to grant or withhold credit,

to vary the rate of interest, to buy and sell large blocks of shares, and to exercise the voting rights attached to these shares. Through interlocking directorships, banks can not only give effect to underlying capital relations to ensure a monitoring of the behaviour of enterprises which they seek to control, they are also able to garner knowledge and information about business conditions which they can then dispense to other enterprises as they choose (Baum and Stiles 1965, p. 36; Patman Report 1968, pp. 19, 23ff.; Mintz and Schwartz 1981b). Undoubtedly the ultimate source for any power which a bank can exercise will be the capital relations in which it is involved, as an interlocking directorship without such an institutional base is unlikely to be strong enough to serve as a source of bank control. For this reason, an assessment of the model of bank control must begin with an analysis of the lending and shareholder relations of banks and other financial intermediaries.

While 'internal' funding refers to the use of retained earnings as sources of investment capital, loans and shareholdings are both forms of 'external' funding. Advocates of the managerialist thesis have seen internal funding as reducing the power of shareholders and financiers. For this reason, the ability of large industrials to fund their investments from internally generated resources has often been taken as evidence against the notion of bank control. Indeed, it is widely believed by managerialists that 'only a minor proportion of corporate capital today is raised through the sale of equity capital. A more significant portion of capital comes through self-financing' (Bell 1974, p. 294); and Sweezy (1941) has claimed that the decline of the investment banker in America was associated with an increase in the level of internal funding in the 1930s. In the most extensive factual study carried out, Lintner (1959) has shown that 'the proportion of funds from external sources in American non-financials stood at 40–42 per cent throughout the period 1900–25, fell to 37 per cent in the late 1920s, and varied between 37 and 42 per cent in the period 1930–49' (see also Kuznets 1961). This evidence gives some support for Sweezy's claim, though the drop in external funding in the 1920s was not as substantial as might have been expected if it had been directly associated with the power of investment bankers. In the period 1949–57, the level of external funding increased to a level of about 44 per cent, a return to the level that existed around the turn of the century. These figures, argues Lintner, suggest a high level of stability in the sources of funds over the course of the century, the only discernible long-term trend being a slight rise in the level external funding (ibid., p. 181). Lintner concludes that the evidence runs counter to the managerialist thesis. Large enterprises are constrained by the capital market, and the relative balance between share issues and bank loans depends upon market circumstances rather than the power of bankers. Berle himself arrived at a slightly lower estimate for the level of external funding in the immediate post-war period, though his findings must be seen as confirmation of Lintner's claim (Berle 1960, pp. 25–6). More recent estimates are in line with these conclusions, though Fitch and Oppenheimer suggest that the level of external funding increased during the 1960s. Their estimates show that the level varied from 30 per cent in 1964 to 39 per cent in 1966 and 43 per cent in 1968, and Fitch claims that the increase was sustained into the 1970s (Fitch and Oppenheimer 1970b, p. 74; Fitch 1971, p. 156). If Fitch is correct in positing a trend for this seven-year period, it may best be seen as a continuation and slight acceleration of the trend identified by Lintner. Fitch and Oppenheimer (1970b, p. 75) suggest that, since the availability of internal funds is dependent on the profitability of enterprises, the level will vary with the profit rate. Where there are cash flow problems, enterprises will be forced to borrow externally and under terms decided by the banks. Observed trends in external funding, therefore, may best be seen as the counter trend to corporate profitability: a long-term rise in external funding signifies a long-term decline in profitability. External funding and bank power will vary with general economic circumstances, and Fitch and Oppenheimer conclude that the rise in external funding in the 1960s was a sign of worsened profitability and was associated with an enhancement of the power of bankers.

There are no comparable long-term figures for Britain, but the proportion of funds from external sources between 1950 and 1970 has been shown to be around 30 per cent – though Thompson (1977, pp. 254–5) estimates that the figure was as low as 23 per cent in 1950. It has been suggested that external funding is mainly used for expansion, and Barratt Brown (1968b) has estimated that the fastest growing enterprises in the early 1950s obtained a half of their funds from external sources (see also Williams *et al.* 1968, pp. 111–12). A study by the Stock Exchange during the 1970s confirms this idea, showing higher rates of external funding when growth was at its highest (Stock Exchange 1977, p. 14, table 3).

The figures on internal and external funding are complex to compile and to assess, and any general conclusions must be treated with care. It is clear, however, that a significant proportion of investment funding has come from external sources in both Britain and America, and that this proportion is higher when enterprises are seeking to expand or where earnings are insufficient to sustain internal funding. A crucial finding for the model of bank control, however, is that external funding in Britain and America has tended to come more through shares and loan stock than through bank loans (Thompson 1977). Fitch and Oppenheimer (1970a, b, and c) suggest that the extent of bank power increases as external funding increases; but if the evidence for an increase in external funding is to be taken at its face value, then this signifies not so much an enhanced role for bankers as providers of credit as an enhanced role for the institutional shareholders who have taken up the bulk of the shares issued in the post-war period. But before turning to examine bank shareholdings, it is important to point out that banks are not necessarily interested in increasing the indebtedness of the enterprises which they may control. An enterprise with a good cash flow is regarded as a good customer by the banks, and if such an enterprise decides to fund its investments from external sources it is in a good position to choose which bank to give its business. Cash flow, regardless of indebtedness, is a source of autonomy from dependence on banks (Sweezy 1971, p. 13; Beed 1966, p. 39). Cash flow depends upon profitability, and poor profitability may lead to increased dependence on banks; but the evidence on external funding is not as compelling as Fitch and Oppenheimer suggest (Herman 1973, p. 26).

The evidence on internal and external funding, therefore, supports neither the managerialist nor the bank control argument. The major finding is the importance of share issues and loan stock and the lesser importance of bank loans. If external funding strengthens the position of any of the contenders for control, it is that of the big institutional shareholders. But, as was shown in Chapter 3, banks play a major role in the management of institutional funds through their trust and investment departments. It is necessary to examine the extent to which institutional shareholdings can buttress bank power. Institutional power has most recently been discussed in relation to the massive expansion of pension funds. A pension fund is a trust fund, financed by employer and employee contributions, which invests in shares, bonds, property, and other income-producing assets in order to generate a stable income from which to pay the pensions of its retired members. Some pension funds are run 'in-house' by the employer, while others have their management delegated to external agencies such as banks, insurance companies, and stockbrokers. Pension funds, like bank deposits and insurance policies, are controlled by people other than the beneficiaries. Those currently in employment contribute part of their salary to ensure a future pension benefit for themselves, but they play little part in determining the uses to which the investment funds are put. Radical writers have claimed that the question of control is raised in an especially acute form, because employees do not make individual decisions to hand over money to professional managers: pension contributions are generally part of their union-negotiated conditions of employment, and decisions on the management of the fund are taken or supervised by the employer. Thus, pension fund capital is a form of socialized capital which has been institutionalized under private control. Where funds are managed by banks they are 'captive funds' (Rifkin and Barber 1978, p. 95), which can be used by the banks as part of their investment and corporate finance dealings rather than simply being treated as trustee holdings. Banks can use institutional funds to bolster the position of their clients by, for example, voting on their side in a takeover struggle or using them to take-up a share issue (Minns 1980; Schuller and Hyman 1984). Drucker drew rather different conclusions from the usurpation of control by fund managers. He argued that adoption of the trustee role is undesirable as it encourages a 'play safe' attitude towards industrial investment, and so concluded that bankers should more actively use the captive funds to engage in long-term investment banking (Drucker 1976, pp. 72–3).[16] Rifkin and Barber, therefore, advocated an extension of trades union control over pension funds to counter the power of bankers, while Drucker argued for an extension of the investment power, but not the controlling power, of bankers.

The growth of pension fund capital does not, in itself, strengthen the case for bank control. A number of pension funds are, in any case, managed 'in-house' by the employing enterprise rather than by banks,[17] and a wide range of other institutional funds are outside the direct control of banks. But even allowing for this, it has to be shown that banks and other institutional shareholders are actually willing to use the power inherent in their shareholdings to intervene in strategic decision-making. Financial intermediaries are not always able to use the remedy of 'exit', of selling their shares when they are dissatisfied with a corporate policy. The size of a holding may be so great that it could not be sold without a massive drop in the share price, which would be financially damaging to the shareholder. Institutions become locked-in to the enterprises in which they invest (Baum and Stiles 1965, p. 11). For this reason, argue Fitch and Oppenheimer (1970b, pp. 62–3), they must adopt a strategy of 'voice', of direct intervention. Only by making their views known can they safeguard their investments. Thus, the growth of bank and other institutional shareholding has led to a progressive move away from passive and neutral orientations and towards more active involvement:

In spite of the banks' apparent reluctance to intervene in the administration of corporations, it appears likely that they will be progressively impelled to give up their neutrality, in so far as the volume of stock they hold obliges them to shed the simple role of institutional investor [Chevalier 1969, p. 168].

At a minimal level this will involve placing their nominees on the boards of enterprises in which they invest, or at least ensuring that the board includes the 'right' kind of outside influence (Parry 1969, p. 79; Allen 1976, pp. 889–90; Blumberg 1975, p. 168). In a stronger strategy this will involve constant monitoring of an enterprise's affairs through regular visits to examine the accounts, and, ultimately, by voting against the management or by attempting to alter the composition of the board. Baum and Stiles have shown that the large institutional shareholders have access to business information on plans and markets, and have the expertise and means to make the best use of this (Baum and Stiles 1965, pp. 34–6; Wilson Report 1977, p. 26):

institutional investors are in a position to obtain corporate information not available to other shareholders. This position springs from the power of large holdings and from the ability as a day-to-day matter to send competent men into the field to question management, not to mention the fact that institutions are themselves big business and, thus, their executives are the natural associates of industrial executives [Baum and Stiles, 1965, pp. 65, 162–3; Chevalier 1970, p. 202].

It has been argued that cases of extreme intervention are rare (Herman 1973, pp. 20–1; O'Connor 1971, pp. 139, 143), and the reason for this is perhaps that direct public intervention reflects a failure of the normal processes of institutional 'intervention' through constant surveillance and persistent pressure. There is growing evidence that surveillance and pressure are important aspects of strategic decision-making and that covert intervention by institutional shareholders has increased:

There is occasionally therefore some intervention by the institutions, normally on a collective basis through Investment Protection Committees, when a company gets into difficulties. It takes place in an informal and confidential manner, since publicity about a company's problems can easily precipitate the crisis which it is the purpose of intervening to avoid [Wilson Report 1977, p. 26].

Direct, public intervention is rare because it is limited to times of crisis. When the crisis is on its way to resolution, institutions wish to return to the 'normal' processes of covert supervision (Glasberg 1981; see also Gogel and Koenig 1981). It is from this standpoint that the significance of interlocking directorships may be assessed. The financial enterprises that participate in the controlling constellations are able to put their representatives on company boards, and the latter will seek out the directors of financial enterprises as a way of enhancing their access to capital. From this perspective, the composition of corporate boards can be seen as 'reflecting the organisation's perceived need to deal differentially with various important sectors or organisations in the environment' (Pfeffer 1972, p. 220; Aaronovitch and Sawyer 1975, p. 261). Recruitment through co-optation ensures that the board is adapted to the interests of its constellation of major shareholders, its sources of credit, and its suppliers and competitors (Pennings 1980, ch. 6; Allen 1974). Over and above this, financials will recruit leading industrial executives to their boards in order to increase their knowledge of business conditions, and industrial executives will seek out such financial directorships so as to obtain access to the accumulated expertise and knowledge. The relationships which bring credit, partners for mergers, and opportunities for successful share issues, also bring access to the expertise and information which permits a more rational and planned strategy (Herman 1973, pp. 25–6). Banks and the large institutional shareholders have access to business information about the financial markets and the activities of the enterprises in which they invest, and this makes their directors 'the most important carriers of information and opinion from one sector of the business establishment to another' (Domhoff 1967, p. 53; Smith 1970, p. 49). The flow of information is a base of power and influence over and above the power inherent in the flow of capital.

Of all the financial intermediaries, banks are the main institutional arenas for these mechanisms. Banks are not only managers of institutional funds and providers of credit, they are continually involved in corporate advice and corporate finance; it is on this basis that bank centrality in intercorporate networks may be explained. But the studies reviewed above have suggested that banks do enter into capital, commercial, and personal relations with specific groups of enterprises, though not on the scale required by the concept of 'interest groups'. The reason for this must be sought in the tendency of banks to recruit outside directors from among their own clients and associates, and the tendency for industrials to recruit directors from their primary bank. In this way, banks appear as the centres of loose spheres of enterprises, while the fact that large enterprises have credit relations with more than one bank will mean that these spheres will overlap within a larger intercorporate network. Where there is regionalism in bank operations, the spheres will have a regional character also.

The banks are the 'nerve centres of the communication network' between enterprises (Mokken and Stokman 1974, p. 30); they are the foci through which information flows from one part of the network to another. This ability to control the flow of information, whether used intentionally or unintentionally, is a way of influencing corporate strategy. The influence which banks can exercise over enterprises with which they interlock is greatest when these interlocks express capital and commercial relations between banker and client. Capital and commercial relations are fundamental to the structure of the intercorporate network, but these may be expressed in and reinforced by interlocks carried by bank and industrial executives (Fennema 1982, p. 140). It is investigations of these primary interlocks which have shown the existence of loose and overlapping bank-centred spheres, and it is now possible to give an interpretation to this structure. Such spheres are not financial interest groups. They are bank-centred spheres of influence, groups of enterprises which have a common orientation to a particular bank whose boardroom provides an arena in which the interests of the enterprises may be mutually pursued. The bank is central not because it is an agency of control, but because it is an arena of influence.

The structure of intercorporate capital relations and primary, executive officer interlocks is overlain by a structure of interlocking directorships which have no direct institutional base. Retired business leaders, retired civil servants and military officers, politicians, landowners, and even trades unionists are recruited to corporate boards in large numbers, and those who are recruited to more than one board are those who create interlocking directorships. It was this network of relations which observers in Britain and America have found to be diffuse and national in scope. These weaker interlocks consolidate the outlines of the bank-centred spheres of influence and determine the overall shape and cohesion of the observed network of interlocking directorships. The structure of this network is the outcome of a myriad of individual recruitment decisions, but its structure is nevertheless reproduced, or transformed, over time (Levine and Roy 1977; Warner and Unwalla 1967, pp. 124–5). Its reproduction and transformation is not, however, a consciously intended result of the actions of those who recruit directors. The structure of the system of interlocks and its development over time are the largely unintended consequences of these actions (Scott and Griff 1984, ch. 1). The recruitment of directors is constrained by the system of interlocks which that recruitment generates. The strong ties created by primary interlocks are overlain by weaker ties, which, nevertheless, act as important channels of communication between enterprises (Granovetter 1973). Banks are central in this structure of weak ties as well as in the structure of primary interlocks, and this enhances their role as centres of communication within the intercorporate network (Mokken and Stokman 1976). From this it follows that the reach of a bank's influence may be far greater than the reach of its direct control (Allen 1976, pp. 889–90). The structure of the system of directorships, the opportunities for communication which it opens and closes, is a determinant of the limits and possibilities of corporate behaviour. This may not be intended by the banks which stand at the centre of the system, but it is none the less real.

If 'finance capital' is taken to designate the situation in which the availability of monetary advances determines when and where production will take place (Thompson 1977, p. 247; Hussain 1976, p. 11ff.), then Britain and America can be seen as societies in which finance capital dominates the operations of big business. Manufacturing and commercial activity are dependent upon the availability of share and loan capital for their investment funding. Even where enterprises employ internal funding, they are dependent upon stock market valuations and the necessity of maintaining a satisfactory cash flow. In most big enterprises, internal funding is no longer a deduction from the income of an entrepreneur; it is a deduction from the income of shareholders, banks, and others who advance capital. The growth of institutional shareholdings, reflected in the spread of control through a constellation of interests, has produced a system of business finance in which each individual enterprise is embedded in an extensive network of intercorporate shareholdings and interlocking directorships. The rise of the large corporate enterprise led to the supplementing of the invisible hand of the market by the 'visible hand' of corporate planning; the rise of finance capital has resulted in the emergence of a new invisible hand of intercorporate relations.[18]

The form of intercorporate structure found in Britain and America can best be described as a system of polyarchic financial hegemony.[19] A number of large financial intermediaries hold powerful positions within the business world, but they do not exercise direct control over particular dependent enterprises. Their collective control over the availability of capital, however, gives them the power to determine the broad conditions under which other enterprises must decide their corporate strategies. Those enterprises which are involved in the provision of credit through the granting of loans and the purchasing of shares are those in which is institutionalized the collective power to constrain corporate decision-making. This power of constraint is exercised without deliberate and overt intervention:

bank and insurance company decisions regarding the most promising locales for capital investment lead to the nurturance of some industries or firms and the decline of others. Since most companies are dependent upon outside funds, they will adapt to conditions placed upon available funding, thus allowing financial suppliers to influence and coordinate the activities of industrial companies without necessarily intruding on their decision-making processes or tampering with executive autonomy [Glasberg and Schwartz 1983, p. 318].

Within this structure of polyarchic financial hegemony, banks play a key role by virtue of their role in the management of institutional funds and in corporate advice. They are the dominant agents within the hegemonic system. An extensive group of credit intermediaries have control over access to capital, but bank boards are the institutional arenas in which the major credit givers and credit recipients come together to determine the constraints under which that credit will be used. Banks have considerable power and influence in the business world, even though they may not deliberately seek out such a role. Bank dominance in the hegemonic system is the basis of bank centrality in the network of interlocking directorships. The fusion of banking and industry is expressed in the structure of property ownership, the mode of corporate control, and the structure of intercorporate relations.

Notes

1 Strictly, a 'directorate' is a board of directors and, by extension, the whole body of directors. In many American studies, however, the word has been used interchangeably with 'directorship', which refers to the occupancy of the role of director. In this book, 'directorate' and 'directorship' are used in their strict senses.

2 The two sources cited disagree as to whether the proportion of multiple directors in the period 1935–65 declined very slightly or remained constant. The disagreement is partly because of different data selection criteria. The figures in Table 20 in fact show an increase from 13.2 to 13.3 per cent over the same period, but the figures for 1969 and 1974 show clearly that the period since 1935 can be characterized by a long-term constancy in the proportion of multiple directors, with particular years showing minor fluctuations around this constant figure.

3 This is discussed further in Scott and Griff (1984), ch. 5.

4 Commercial banks are those involved in 'retail' deposit banking through national branch systems. In Britain they are normally termed clearing banks.

5 The 'utility' sector refers to electricity, water, and gas companies.

6 See also Anderson *et al.* (1941), p. 25, and Goldsmith and Parmelee (1940), pp. 129–30. The evidence produced by Sweezy was similar to the more speculative suggestions of Rochester (1936), chs. 2–5.

7   A general review of various attempts to identify interest groups and a comparison of their allocation of enterprises to groups can be found in Fennema (1982), pp. 26–9. Herman (1981), p. 217ff., discusses the concept of interest group, and Allen (1978a) discusses various methods for identifying groups.

8   See also Baran and Sweezy (1966), p. 31; Fennema and Schijf (1978), pp. 11–12; Smith (1970), pp. 48–9; Smith and Desfosses (1972), p. 66; Patman Report (1967), p. 965; Antitrust Committee (1965).

9   The label 'Stony Brook' is used for convenience to describe the work of Michael Schwartz, his students and colleagues, though members of the group are now to be found in many universities and colleges. The group is unified by its orientation towards a massive data set, described in Mariolis (1975), and common procedures of analysis. Its most active leaders include Schwartz, Mintz, and Mizruchi, and the group has close links with the work of Bunting. The group is an offshoot of the productive network of 'structural analysts' trained by Harrison White at Harvard, the larger network including Levine and Berkowitz in the field of interlocks. The origins of the group at Harvard are described in Mullins (1973) and its present influence has spread through the creation of INSNA and its journal *Connections*, based at Toronto under the leadership of Barry Wellman.

10 Palmer (1983a and b) raises serious doubts about the strong variants of the interest group theory proposed by writers such as Kotz (1978) and Knowles (1973). Levine (1978) criticizes Mariolis (1975) and attempts to re-assert a strong case for bank control. See also the reply in Mariolis (1978). The overall research strategy of the Stony Brook group has been criticized in Andrews (1982). On regional structuring see Galaskiewicz and Wasserman (1981) and Ratcliff (1980).

11 Hobson presents an analysis of interlocks between City financiers and South African mining, the first analysis of interlocks to be carried out in Britain (1906, p. 265ff.). The operation of mines in Imperial territories was not, however, incompatible with the City's traditional role. The 1906 edition of Hobson's book, which included this analysis, was seen as the definitive statement of his position, and the 1926 edition is identical except for a supplementary chapter.

12 The others were an oil company, an insurance company, and a metal producer.

13 The Scottish economy retained a regional distinctiveness. This is discussed in Chapter 5 below and in Scott and Griff (1984), ch. 4.

14 This argument runs counter to that developed in Ingham's (1984) book on finance capital, but this was, unfortunately, not available to me at the time of writing. I have, therefore, relied on Ingham (1982).

15 In Scott (1982a) a distinction is made between capital, commercial, and personal relations. In the case of banks, their commercial relations with other enterprises mainly involve the granting or withholding of credit and thus are indistinguishable from capital relations.

16 Drucker argues, however, that bankers should act simply as investors and not as controllers, and that the investments should be supervised through a socially responsible board (Drucker 1976, p. 91).

17 Control over the funds is still a problem as they may be used as an adjunct to normal business operations or as a way of manipulating the share price rather than as a trustee investment.

18 This formulation was suggested to me by Michael Mann. I have subsequently come across Useem's similar idea of the 'collective hand' (1984), p. 181. See also Herman (1981), p. 297.

19 The notion of hegemony reflects the usage of Mintz and Schwartz in their recent works. As will be argued in Chapter 5, the system is 'polyarchic' by contrast with the 'oligarchic' bank hegemony found in some other economies.

5 Alternative patterns of capitalist development

The joint stock company is the institutional form through which strategic control is mediated, and variations in the form of the joint stock company from one country to another will both reflect and influence their variant patterns of capitalist development. The mechanisms of capital mobilization, and especially the organization of the banking system and the differing roles of persons and intermediaries in the provision of investment funds, will be mediated through the prevailing form of corporate organization. All modern legal systems involve a similar conception of the property rights of shareholders, but there are important variations in the legal constitution of the board of directors. In countries that follow the practices of English law – the USA, Australia, Canada, and Britain itself – the law prescribes one and only one board, its rights and obligations being indivisible and inalienable. All directors, executives and non-executives, are appointed by the controlling shareholders and, through their monthly meetings, are responsible to the annual shareholders' meeting (Bacon and Brown 1977; Bank of England 1979). By contrast with this 'Anglo-American' system, the legal codes of West Germany, Austria, Switzerland,[1] and the Netherlands prescribe a two-board system in which an executive board is responsible for overseeing the operational managers and a supervisory board of non-executives is responsible for corporate strategy and for monitoring the activities of the executive board (Grossfeld and Ebke 1978).[2] A mixed system is found in Japan, where corporate law is based on both American and German principles and a single board system is prescribed. In France, Belgium, and Italy, a 'Latin' variant of the two board system is found. An administrative board combines both supervisory and executive responsibilities as in the Anglo-American system, but there is also an auditing board which functions in a similar, but more formal, way to the accounting auditors in Britain and the USA. Members of the administrative board in the Latin system and of both boards in the German system operate as 'directors' of the type found on the single board of the Anglo-American system (Bacon and Brown 1977).

Capitalist development in Britain and the USA has involved a transition from a system of entrepreneurial capital to a system of finance capital in which control through a constellation of interests and polyarchic financial hegemony prevail. In this chapter it will be shown that a similar transition has taken place in other countries where the Anglo-American system prevails. In Germany, on the other hand, a weak entrepreneurial system gave way very early on to a system of oligarchic bank hegemony which has subsequently developed in a direction closer to the Anglo-American pattern. France and Belgium had a rather stronger entrepreneurial sector, but developed a system of holding companies which subsequently evolved into a tighter system of industrial and financial combines. Japan, like Germany, had a weak entrepreneurial sector, but this was transformed through the emergence of a number of powerful interest groups and combines rather than through an oligarchic banking system. Although capitalist industrialism has involved a generic transition from entrepreneurial capital to finance capital, and from personal to more impersonal forms of possession, the mechanisms involved, the route followed, and the current stage reached have varied from one country to another. This chapter will document those variations.

Anglo-American variations

Though societies other than Britain and the USA have been less intensively studied, evidence on Australia, Canada, and Scotland shows the existence of an 'Anglo-American' pattern of development in which the transition from personal to impersonal possession involved the supplementing of family ownership by control through a constellation of interests and the rise of polyarchic financial hegemony. In Canada, the academic and political debates have concerned the implications for ownership of Canada's status as a 'satellite' economy. First Britain and later the USA, it is argued, have dominated Canadian trade and industry and determined its pattern of development. Discussion has centred on the unity or division to be found among the corporate directors who run the major Canadian enterprises: are they oriented primarily towards the Canadian national economy or towards the 'metropolitan' economies of Britain and the USA? Clement (1975a) and Niosi (1981) have argued that the Canadian directorate can be divided into an 'indigenous' group which controls the Canadian-owned enterprises, and a 'comprador' group which acts as the executive managers of foreign-owned subsidiaries. Carroll (1982) has argued against this, claiming that the multiple directors should be seen as a unified group of finance capitalists with interests in both the domestic and the overseas sectors of the economy.

Evidence for and against the model of finance capital has been drawn from the history of banking in Canada. The big four chartered[3] commercial banks (Bank of Montreal, Bank of Nova Scotia, Royal Bank, Canadian National Bank) and the large insurance companies such as Sun Life and Manufacturer's Life stand at the heart of a highly concentrated financial system which has followed the British practice of avoiding long-term industrial finance. A number of shareholding trust companies, however, were set up on the American pattern and, though ostensibly independent of the chartered banks, were for a long time tied to them through numerous interlocking directorships. The close association between commercial banks and trust companies became greater in the 1960s, until interlocks of this kind were made illegal under the 1967 Bank Act. Separate from these dominant enterprises were investment banks which, like their American counterparts, were involved in company promotions and mergers in the first part of the century but declined in importance from the 1930s. Thus, the argument over the nature of the Canadian corporate directorate resolves itself into the question of whether the financial intermediaries have close relations with non-financial enterprises, and, in particular, whether they are allied with foreign-owned non-financials.

Carroll (1982) supports his position from a study of the 'top 100' enterprises[4] over the period 1946–76. He shows that the proportion of enterprises that could be classified as Canadian-owned declined from 68 per cent in 1946 to 56 per cent in 1966, though the figure had risen to 61 per cent by 1976 (Carroll 1982, pp. 97–8). He concludes that these figures evidence fluctuations rather than a trend; the basic fact is one of consistency. The domestic sector has been a major part of the economy and is concentrated among the very largest enterprises. The 61 per cent of large enterprises that were Canadian-owned accounted for 86 per cent of the assets of the top 100 enterprises. On this basis, Carroll concludes that it is difficult to see the 'indigenous' group as subordinate to foreign interests.

Table 25 *Strategic control in Australian and Canadian enterprises (1955 and 1960)*

	Number of enterprises	
Mode of control	Australia (1955)	Canada (1960)
Private ownership	2	11
Majority control	6	16
Minority control	33	23
No dominant interest	32	3
Not known	0	11
Totals	73	64

Source: Wheelwright (1957) and Porter (1965), p. 589, table 12.

Table 26 *Strategic control in large Canadian enterprises (1975)*

	Type of controller					
Mode of control	Personal	Corporate	Foreign	Mixed	None	Totals
Majority control at 80%	10	0	61	0	—	71
Majority control 50–79%	14	1	51	3	—	69
Minority control	24	0	18	1	—	43
Limited minority control	2	—	—	—	—	2
No dominant interest	—	—	—	—	20	20
Totals	50	1	130	4	20	205

Source: Calculated from Niosi (1978), table II, pp. 113–16, and Niosi (1981), table 5.1, p. 124.

Note: The cut-off point for minority control is 10 per cent, and limited minority control is based on holdings by directors of 5–9 per cent. The figures above are calculated from the raw data given by Niosi, and there seem to be certain discrepancies, with the various summaries calculated by Niosi himself. The corporate holdings in the 'Corporate' and 'Mixed' categories are mainly by investment and holding companies. It is impossible to assess how many of these were, in fact, family holdings.

Table 25 shows the data on ownership and control which was collected by Porter in the first such study in Canada. The sixty-four large enterprises accounted for the greater proportion of Canadian industrial output, and almost a half were subject to some form of majority control. Many more were subject to minority control and relatively few of those on which there was information had no dominant shareholder. Table 26 provides a more detailed break-down for 205 large enterprises in 1975.[5] The small proportion with no dominant interest is confirmed by these data, and it is also apparent that there is an important distinction to be made between those enterprises where families or other personal shareholders had majority control and those where foreign interests were the majority shareholders. Families such as Molson, Eaton, Weston, Bronfman, Desmarais, Webster, and Irving are important as con-trollers of a large proportion of the 'indigenous' Canadian enter-prises. Those enterprises in which there was no dominant interest seem to be subject to control through a constellation of interests; Niosi observes that financial intermediaries have accumulated large shareholdings and that, for this reason, the category of 'management control' becomes 'a residual category where, through lack of information, one classifies the companies which could not be placed elsewhere' (1978, pp. 83, 100, 168). For ex-ample, Abitibi Paper had no dominant shareholding interest, but the eleven largest registered shareholders held 34 per cent of its shares – making it a clear case of control through a constellation of interests (ibid., p. 82).

The consequences of this pattern are clear in the structure of the network of interlocking directorships. Canadian ownership has been dominant in the financial sector and substantial in the indus-trial sector, and the two sectors have been closely interlocked over the whole post-war period. Carroll's study of the 'top 100' enter-prises discovered that the density of the network of interlocks increased between 1946 and 1966 and then remained constant until 1976 (Carroll 1982, table 4, p. 105). It appears that the Canadian network was much more dense than those in Britain and the USA.[6] This was confirmed by Porter's finding that 22 per cent of directors in 1951 held two or more directorships in the top 170 enterprises; the corresponding figure for the top 113 of 1972 being 30 per cent (see Table 27). The figures for Britain and the USA never reached such high levels, even at the height of the Money Trust. The explanation for this high level of interlocking seems to

Table 27 *Interlocking directorships in Canadian industrial enterprises (1951 and 1972)*

Number of directorships per person	1951		1972	
	Number of people	Number of directorships	Number of people	Number of directorships
1	704	704	672	672
2	112	224	155	310
3	43	129	58	174
4	21	84	28	112
5	13	65	20	100
6	7	42	6	36
7	3	21	6	42
8	2	16	1	8
9	1	9		
10	1	10		
Totals	907	1304	946	1454
Number of companies	170		113	

Source: Adapted from Porter (1965), p. 589, table 12; Clement (1975), p. 166, table 18.

be the large number of foreign subsidiaries operating in Canada and a strong tendency for such subsidiaries to recruit Canadian directors to sit alongside their own executives (Safarian 1966, p. 64; Gonick 1970, p. 51). The Canadian economy is not such a dependent 'branch plant' economy as it is sometimes seen, and the foreign-owned enterprises adopt a strategy of co-optation which ties them into the domestic economy and, in particular, to the banking sector. Porter has shown that directors of the largest banks held nearly a quarter of all directorships in the top industrial enterprises of 1951, and that a further 14 per cent of industrial directorships were held by directors of large insurance companies (Porter 1965, pp. 579, 234). Carroll concluded that there has been a fusion of banking and industry to form 'finance capital', albeit a form of finance capital in which foreign ownership plays a considerable part. Even Clement (1975a, p. 159) argues that the banking establishment has gradually moved into association with those industrial sectors which have been developed and made profitable by foreign capital. There is no evidence for any significant separation of indigenous and comprador groups within the corporate directorate. Porter concludes that

It is not . . . the role of directors as the overseers of individual corporations taken separately that makes them an economic elite. Rather it is the fact that collectively they preside over all major segments of the corporate world in an extensive interlocking network. They are the ultimate decision-makers and co-ordinators within the private sector of the economy. It is they who at the frontiers of the economic and political systems represent the interests of corporate power. They are the real planners of the economy. . . . Planning, co-ordination, developing, taking up options, giving the shape to the economy and setting its pace, and creating the general climate within which economic decisions are made constitute economic power in the broad sense [Porter 1965, p. 255].

Those who sit on the boards of the large Canadian enterprises are predominantly the finance capitalists who express the fusion of banking and industry and the importance of the controlling constellations. They are the co-ordinating controllers who are able to secure a degree of intercorporate unity in the face of competitive diversity.

Ownership and interlocking have been less extensively researched in Australia than in Canada, though the pattern which emerges is, nevertheless, consistent with that described for the other Anglo-American economies. In a study of the large Australian enterprises of 1955 which were not subject to foreign ownership (see Table 25), Wheelwright (1957) discovered the overwhelming majority to be either minority-controlled or to have no dominant shareholding interest. A larger and more systematic investigation of the 299 largest manufacturers of 1963 found that foreign entgerprises had majority control in 127 and minority control in fifteen.[7] Almost a half of the enterprises, therefore, had dominant foreign controllers. In some of the cases of foreign minority control there were joint Australian participations, and it is clear that the predominant form of control in large Australian enterprises was control by foreign corporate interests, with or without the support of Australian enterprises (Wheelwright and Miskelly 1967).[8] Among those enterprises subject to purely Australian control, there were a large number in which particular personal owners had controlling interests. In almost a quarter of the top 299 enterprises, families or individuals held 10 per cent or more of the capital – and, as in the earlier study, most were cases of minority control. Forty-six enterprises had no dominant shareholding interest and were designated as 'management' or 'unclassified' by Wheelwright and Miskelly, though they observed that they were characterized by a high degree of institutional shareownership and that this might indicate a need for 'a new category of control by financial institutions' (ibid., p. 8; see also Wheelwright 1974, p. 131; Connell 1976). In fact, closer examination of the original data confirms that they were characterized by control through a constellation of interests. The holdings of the top twenty shareholders varied from 12.4 per cent in Broken Hill Proprietary to 47.1 per cent in Tom Piper. In the majority of cases, the top twenty held between 20 and 40 per cent. What distinguishes this from the British and American pattern is the large number of family and non-financial members of the controlling constellations.

Table 28 *Strategic control in large Australian enterprises (1975)*

| | | Type of controller | | | | |
Mode of control	Directors	Australian corpora-tions	Foreign corpora-tions	Joint corporate	None	Totals
Majority control	11	6	28	3	—	48
Minority 15%	—	22	11	1	—⎫	99
control 10%	65	—	—	—	—⎭	
No dominant interest	—	—	—	—	79	79
Totals	76	28	39	4	79	226

Source: Lawriwsky (1984), calculated from table 1.1 and figure 5.3.

Though not directly comparable, recent data produced by Lawriwsky (see Table 28) confirms the finding that a high proportion of Australian enterprises are subject to family minority control; though Lawriwsky did suggest that institutional holdings in the enterprises with no dominant interest are actually higher than in Britain (Lawriwsky 1984, p. 38). Almost three-quarters of the enterprises with dispersed ownership had financial intermediaries with aggregate holdings of 20 per cent or more among their top twenty shareholders, and in many of these the largest shareholder was an intermediary with 5 per cent or more. In most cases this was Australian Mutual Provident (ibid., pp. 108–9; Crough 1980). Of the seventy-nine enterprises with no dominant shareholder twenty-one had family participants dominant in their controlling constellations, these families holding between 4 per cent and 9 per cent of the capital and being represented on the board.[9] Family control by the major dynasties remained important, though being progressively supplemented by 'institutional' and foreign ownership (Encel 1970, pp. 338–9, 376ff.).

Evidence on interlocking directorships in Australia is very sparse, though a study by Rolfe (1967) showed that 12 per cent of the directors of the top fifty Australian enterprises of 1962 held a quarter of all directorships in these enterprises. The density would, therefore, seem to be lower than in Canada, perhaps reflecting the greater importance of family enterprise in Australia. Indeed, a large proportion of those directors who sat on financial boards were drawn from the wealthy families (Encel 1970, p. 396).

Scottish research again confirms the existence of an 'Anglo-American' pattern of development. The Scottish economy exists as a regional enclave within the British economy and, like Australia and Canada, has higher levels of both family and foreign ownership than in Britain as a whole or in the USA. Table 29 shows that the top sixty-two Scottish non-financials of 1973 included twenty-four cases of family or individual control, fifteen cases of 'foreign' control,[10] and seven cases of control through a constellation of interests. The spread of control through a constellation of interests has been inhibited partly by the continued vitality of family enterprise and partly by the expansion of English and American ownership in the post-war period. The Scottish enterprises tended to be closely interlocked into an intercorporate network with close relations to England, and the banks and insurance companies were central in this network (Scott and Hughes 1976; 1980a). Although the level of interlocking seems to have been lower than that found in Canada, just as British levels were lower than those in the USA, the general pattern is similar. Banks and industry are allied in a system of finance capital in which Scottish interests play an important role in linking Scottish to foreign enterprises (Scott and Griff 1984, ch. 2).

Table 29 *Strategic control in the sixty-two largest Scottish non-financials (1973)*

Mode of control	Personal	Corporate Scottish	Corporate Other	Mixed	None	Totals
Wholly-owned	0	0	7	0	—	7
Majority control	7	0	3	3	—	13
Exclusive minority control	14	1	4	0	—	19
Shared minority control	0	0	1	11	—	12
Limited minority control	3	0	0	1	—	4
Constellation of interests	—	—	—	—	7	7
Totals	24	1	15	15	7	62

Source: Calculated from Scott and Hughes (1980b), table 4.c, p. 244.

Note: The categories of control are similar to those in Table 15. Teith Holdings is misprinted in Scott and Hughes (1980b) list as 'shared minority', but it was in fact 'shared majority'; the remaining data and the textual discussion, however, are correct.

It would appear that in each of the three economies considered in this section – Australia, Canada, and Scotland – there was a trend towards control through a constellation of interests and polyarchic financial hegemony. But this trend was weakened by the fact that all three economies had a high level of external ownership. The major foreign owners in these economies were, of course, Britain and the USA, with the latter being an important foreign shareholder in Britain. The foreign subsidiaries in Australia, Canada, and Scotland are parts of multinational enterprises which are themselves increasingly subject to ultimate control through a constellation of interests. Foreign ownership creates a high degree of control by other enterprises at the level of immediate control, but the level of ultimate control shows the overwhelming significance of control through a constellation of interests.[11]

Oligarchic bank hegemony: the German pattern

German industrialization was slow and dependent on foreign capital until the 1870s, largely because of the restrictions on economic activity inherent in its political fragmentation and the archaic practices of the dominant Prussian state. Such development as took place, for example in the heavy industry of the Rhine and the Ruhr, was heavily dependent on foreign capital, as sufficient domestic funds could be generated by neither the entrepreneurs nor the banking system. 'Mobilier' type banks – banks which mobilize capital from small depositors for long-term investment in industrial and commercial activity – were established in the 1850s and began to invest in utility and transport companies as well as industrials, but their role was not of crucial importance until the 1860s and 1870s (Kindleberger 1984, pp. 123–5). The capital needs of rapid industrialization were so great that the new mechanisms of bank involvement seemed the only possible solution to these needs (Kocka 1980, p. 109). The 1870s saw a great concentration in both banking and industry, with the banks being especially prominent in industrial promotions and mergers (Kocka 1978, p. 542). The big Berlin banks emerged as 'universal' banks, combining mobilier business with the activities of commercial banking, and achieved a dominant position in the economy. Together with their affiliates and associates they formed large national banking chains which became involved in the underwriting of share issues, long-term loans, and share participations. A major basis of their power over industrial enterprises was their trustee holdings – shares held on behalf of their clients and in which the banks held the legal right of voting. Through their trustee holdings and their own participations, the banks built up large stakes in coal, iron, steel, engineering, and chemicals, and they became actively involved in the formation of the cartels which regulated those industries (Henderson 1961, p. 62ff.). The peak period of banking power was 1902, when the banks expanded their industrial participations by purchasing shares on a large scale during the depression of that year (Kocka 1978, pp. 565–70). From this peak bank power *per se* began to decline as the industrial enterprises grew in size, increasing their opportunities for internal funding and so increasing their autonomy. The largest enterprises had capital needs which required the co-operation of two or more banks, and so the relationship between the big banks and the big industrials became more of a two-way affair (Kocka 1980, p. 90; Gille 1970, pp. 285–7).

Large enterprises, therefore, operated in an economy dominated by the bank-controlled and bank-allied enterprises, a situation of oligarchic bank hegemony. The smaller enterprises remained 'entrepreneurial' in character, while many of the large enterprises were controlled by banks or by coalitions of banks and family shareholders; but all enterprises operated in an environment in which a small group of banks held a position of institutional dominance. Bank boards represented a union of bank executives and industrialists, this union of interests determining the corporate strategy which the banks would pursue in relation to their clients. Bankers did not control industry; bankers and industrialists united to effect co-ordinated policies on the bank boards. It was through this mechanism of oligarchy that bank hegemony was ensured: banking strategies determined the conditions under which other enterprises formulated and implemented their own strategies.

This close relationship between banks and industry was studied by Jeidels (1905), who investigated the number of directorships in large enterprises which were held by those who sat on the boards of the big Berlin banks, and whose analysis became the cornerstone of Hilferding's model of finance capital. Hilferding assumed, however, that the situation described by Jeidels was generic to all capitalist economies and that the effect of the credit system on industry would be the same everywhere. As was shown in the earlier parts of this book, however, the pattern of development in the Anglo-American economies has been very different from the model of bank control. It must be recognized that the effect of credit on industrial production varies with the form of organization of financial intermediaries and industrial enterprises and on the relations between them (Cutler *et al.* 1978, p. 93; Thompson 1977). The German system of the turn of the century represents simply one form of finance capital, not the only form.

The German economy was severely disrupted by the Second World War and the subsequent partition of Germany into East and West sectors. American support for the Federal Republic, however, made a major contribution to economic recovery and many enterprises were able to reorganize themselves rapidly for expansion in post-war Europe. The banks too were able to recover much of their pre-war power, and the big three – the Deutsche, Commerz, and Dresdner banks – came to dominate the regional

Table 30   *Strategic control in large German enterprises (1961–70)*

Mode of control	Number of companies		
	1961	*1966*	*1970*
Family ownership (25%+)	74	63	47
Other owner (25%+)	147	213	220
No dominant interest	22	18	15
Unknown	68	29	15
Totals	311	323	297

Source: Thonet and Poensgen (1979), p. 26, table 1.

and co-operative banks which had achieved some importance. Table 30 presents the structure of corporate ownership in the 1960s and 1970s, showing clearly the continuing importance of family ownership and, especially important, of ownership by banks, non-financials, and state enterprises. Minority control with a holding of 25 per cent or more was especially strong in Germany, as a legal requirement of 75 per cent support for certain corporate decisions gives an effective veto to these minority shareholders. Families such as Krupp, Thyssen, Flick, and Quandt survived from the pre-war period, and were joined by newer entrepreneurs such as Grundig and Springer (Krejci 1976; Dyas and Thanheiser 1976). Families had majority control in four of the top twenty-two non-financials of 1970 and held a minority veto in a further two (Jacquemin and De Jong 1977, p. 166, based on Vogl 1973). A study of the thirty-one largest manufacturers in the early 1970s showed family control or influence in nine (Francko 1976, p. 5), and in 1978 individuals, families, and foundations had substantial interests in thirty of the top 100 non-financials (E. O. Smith 1983, pp. 206–7).

Table 31 shows the continuing influence exercised by banks over non-financials. The big three banks directly owned 6.1 per cent of the capital of the top seventy-four enterprises, but they owned a further 28.8 per cent through their trust departments and so their total voting control came to over one-third of the issued capital of the enterprises.[12] Altogether, banks and investment companies owned almost two-thirds of the capital of the seventy-four enter-prises. These holdings were not, of course, spread evenly through

Table 31 *Bank shareholdings in seventy-four largest German enterprises (1974–5)*

	% directly owned	% as trustees	Total holding
Big three banks	6.1	28.8	34.9
Other banks and investment companies	3.0	24.8	27.8
Totals	9.1	53.6	62.7

Source: E. O. Smith (1983).

all enterprises; the big three banks, in particular, held substantial blocks in particular enterprises. In 1978 their holdings were concentrated in twenty-six of the top 100, and twenty-two of these holdings were in the range 25–50 per cent (E. O. Smith 1983, pp. 206–7). Other important controllers were the state, with majority control in six enterprises and minority participations in a further ten, and foreign enterprises and governments with minority holdings in thirteen of the top 100. The big three banks themselves had no dominant shareholders and, like non-financials without dominant holders, may best be regarded as controlled through a constellation of interests.

In Germany, banks dominate the availability of institutional funds and thus there are fewer rivals to them in the mobilization of capital. Insurance companies such as Allianz are important, but pensions have generally been paid out of the current income of enterprises rather than being formed into separate funds. Since the 1970s more pension schemes have been incorporated as funds, but the banks have been appointed as advisers and managers (Readman *et al.* 1973, ch. 5). Thus, most industrial share capital is closely held by banks and insurance companies and by a number of families and their foundations. The fact that banks hold their shares as long-term participations means that there is no significant secondary market in shares. Those who wish to buy or sell shares, and those enterprises that wish to issue shares must do so through the banks. But share capital is, in any case, of less importance in industrial funding than bank loans, giving German enterprises a very different capital structure to that found in the Anglo-

American economies. This has implications for economic growth because of the multiplier effect of the banking mechanism. When banks lend to a customer, the money is deposited in the customer's account and can be re-lent to another customer, and so on. In this way, a small amount of saving can generate a high level of industrial investment (Carrington and Edwards 1979, p. 192). By contrast, the Anglo-American reliance on the stock market involves no such multiplier effect: institutional funds are dissipated in the secondary stock market, buying shares that are already in issue, and so represent no addition to the capital stock of enterprises.

Table 32 shows the way in which this was reflected in the pattern of interlocking directorships in 1976. Multiple directors made up 10.7 per cent of the directorate of the top 250 enterprises, and tied over three-quarters of the enterprises into an extensive network. The density of this network was considerably higher than that found in any of the Anglo-American economies, reflecting the

Table 32   *Directorships held by multiple directors in Europe (1976)*

Number of directorships per person	% of directorships held in top 250 enterprises in						
	Austria	Germany	Switzer-land	Nether-lands	Belgium	France	Italy
2	65	60	67	64	57	60	63
3	17	20	19	17	19	19	17
4	9	9	6	8	9	9	7
5	4	5	2	6	6	6	5
6–10	4	5	5	5	6	6	7
11+	2	1	1	0	2	0	1
Totals	100	100	100	100	100	100	100
Number of multiple directors	271	420	405	357	373	378	322
Inclusive-ness (%)	62.7	76.1	82.4	77.6	70.4	88.0	77.6
Density of large component	0.08	0.07	0.05	0.05	0.07	0.04	0.06

Source: Stokman and Wasseur (1984), table 2.2 and figure 2.1.

high proportion of multiple directors who held four or more directorships. Bank directors were especially important in this network. Of all interlocks in 1976, 28 per cent were carried by executives, about a half of these being carried by executives in financials – most of them from the big three banks (Ziegler, Bender and Biehler 1985; Schönwitz and Weber 1980). In 1980 bank directors held almost one-fifth of the seats in the supervisory boards of the top seventy-four enterprises, and they provided the chairman in a half (E. O. Smith 1983, p. 227).

For much of its history Austria followed a route similar to that of Germany. In the nineteenth century there were parallel periods of bank formation and bank growth, though German and French banks provided the capital and leadership for a number of the Austrian banks. The Credit Anstalt, backed by the French Rothschilds, and the other big banks operated as universal banks on the German model and were greatly involved in industrial finance. This high level of foreign ownership continued into the inter-war years. During the inter-war period, however, the system of oligarchic bank hegemony was transformed by the failure and subsequent nationalization of the Credit Anstalt, together with its industrial participations. The role of the state was considerably expanded in the post-war period when the Austrian government nationalized many major financial and non-financial enterprises to prevent their confiscation by the Soviet Union as 'German' property. As a result, state and local government owned seventy-one of the top 250 enterprises in 1976. Despite some partial denationalization, the banking system is firmly under the control of the state and so the oligarchic system has virtually been replaced by a unitary system of state-bank hegemony. The state banks were the peaks of the intercorporate network (see Table 32) and, though they exercised considerable power over other enterprises, they were themselves subject to the control of the political authorities (Ziegler, Reissner, and Bender 1985). This 'corporatist' system will be discussed further in Chapter 7.

The holding system in France and Belgium

Industrialization in Belgium and France began earlier and proceeded more slowly than in Germany. In the 1830s, Belgium experienced the first industrial revolution outside Britain, but the political problems of France inhibited its economic development until the 1860s. The lesser capital requirements in these societies engendered different institutional forms of capital mobilization. The Société Générale de Belgique (SGB) was formed in 1822 as the fiscal agent of the Dutch imperial state in the area of Belgium. Until the 1830s, when Dutch political control ended, the SGB pursued a very conservative policy, but then became actively involved in industrial development through the provision of loans to industrial ventures in coal, iron, and steel. In addition to mobilizing loan capital through savings banks and providing overdraft finance, the SGB acted as underwriter for family firms which wanted to form joint stock companies and it protected its investments by taking share participations and placing its representatives on the corporate boards. A particularly important aspect of its industrial activity was the formation of subsidiary investment and holding companies which extended its role in capital mobilization by enabling other interests to participate in the holding companies that invested directly in industry. In this way the SGB built up a complex system of holdings, or share participations, in numerous enterprises. There was, however, considerable hostility to the SGB, which was seen as pro-Dutch, and the government was persuaded to sponsor the formation of the rival Banque de Belgique in 1835. The Banque was organized on the model of the SGB and used similar methods to promote industrial expansion; thus the credit monopoly became a credit duopoly. Rivalry intensified to the point at which, in 1838, the SGB initiated a run on the Banque to bring about the latter's collapse and re-establish its own monopoly (Morrison 1967; Dhondt and Bruwier 1970). Family enterprises which wished to expand without the support of the SGB, and the consequent complete or partial loss of control, were forced to accommodate to an economic environment in which the SGB and its methods were predominant. Industrialists such as Solvay formed small investment banks which participated in the capital of smaller family firms, so ensuring them access to outside capital while maximizing their autonomy from the SGB (Gille 1970, p. 285). There thus emerged a differentation between the holding system which predominated in the SGB sector and among the smaller investment banks, and the small capital sector of autonomous family-owned firms. Within the 'holding system', industrial development occurred under the aegis of loose interest groups which combined enterprises involved in a range of business activities and tied them together through reciprocal shareholdings and interlocking directorships.

The private banks of Paris – the *haute banques* such as Roths-child, Mallet, Mirabaud, and Vernes – were concerned principally with state finance and foreign trade, and the deposit banks formed in the 1850s and 1860s were unwilling to commit their funds to long-term industrial ventures. Such economic development as took place in France, therefore, was restricted to small, self-financing family firms. During the 1870s and 1880s, however, French banking was transformed by the rise of 'mobilier' invest-ment banks, which mobilized available savings for use as industrial capital. The *Credit Mobilier* was the prototype of the large-scale investment bank, though much of its investment had been in public works rather than private manufacturing (Kindleberger 1984, pp. 108–9). Other investment banks became increasingly important in French industrialization, and their use of the holding system of share participations and interlocks enabled their depen-dent enterprises to expand more easily than could other enter-prises. Nevertheless, the increasing power of investment banks meant that, as in Belgium, the autonomous enterprises had to imitate their methods, and the private banks began to counter the power of the mobilier banks by taking industrial participations and forming holding systems of their own. Old family firms wishing to expand allied themselves with existing bank groups or formed rival groups of their own. The mobilier and investment banks were, however, weaker than their Belgian counterparts, because of the smaller size of the Belgian economy and the earlier period in which investment banks arose in Belgium. There was not such great pressure on French manufacturers to expand, and many family firms could choose to protect family control by restricting the growth of the business. This 'entrepreneurial failure' slowed down French industrialization (Gille 1970, pp. 280–1; Palmade 1961; Fohlen 1978).

The holding system arose in France and Belgium because of the low level of development of the stock exchanges, the absence of state involvement in industrial investment, and, most important, the peculiarities of their banking systems (Chandler and Daems 1974, p. 10; Daems and van der Wee 1974). Where an enterprise seeks to expand beyond the resources of its family controllers it is forced to align itself with a bank or investment holding company which can ensure it access to the required capital, but the French and Belgian investment banks were separated from the deposit banks and so could not operate as German-style universal banks.

The holding system allows banks to be involved in industry without having to tie up deposit funds in long-term investments; the system is, therefore, compatible with conventional commercial banking operations. Capital is mobilized through investments from outsiders in the investment and holding companies rather than from mass savings deposits. The monetary base from which the system could draw was narrower than in Germany, and the funds which could be mobilized were correspondingly less. Co-operation among banks and alliances among enterprises were therefore necessary, and the complex holding systems arose as a consequence of this. The system was strongest in heavy industry, utilities, and transport, and outside these sectors small- and medium-sized entrepreneurial firms persisted because of their relative failure to pursue the strategy of growth.

In the massive industrial reconstruction which took place in Belgium after the First World War, the holding system extended its influence. A consequence of this close relationship between banks and industry was that the depression of the 1930s led to banking failures as industrial enterprises collapsed. A law of 1935 made direct bank investment in industry illegal and reinforced the trend towards an organizational separation of bank companies from investment holding companies, and the depressed level of share prices enabled the holding companies to buy up the devalued shares (Readman *et al.* 1973, p. 96). The interorganizational consequence of this was to reverse the relationship between banks and their holding companies: instead of banks controlling holding companies, the latter became the principal shareholders in the banks. In this way, the holding system was consolidated as the dominant feature of the Belgian economy, the major holding companies tying together the largest enterprises in the traditional sectors of mining, iron and steel, transport, and power (Daems 1978, pp. 10–12). In France also the investment banks and holding companies expanded their role in the raising of external funds (Lévy-Leboyer 1980, p. 124), but this occurred through industrialists taking the lead in building financial enterprises to compensate for the failings of the banking system. During the 1920s the number of joint ventures between enterprises grew in many areas of the economy, and this trend was reinforced by the practice of enterprises undertaking the joint finance of ventures, often through specialized credit and banking subsidiaries. The parent enterprises came more and more to resemble holding companies rather than operating companies, as more of their activities were hived-off to subsidiaries and joint ventures: 'The holding of securities was left with the parent firm, but the financing of their issue became a separate function carried on by different institutions' (Lévy-Leboyer 1980, p. 146). Within the resulting interest groups, the profits of one enterprise could be circulated in order to support the expansion of others. The group structure, however, did not completely squeeze-out the smaller family firms. The holding system was powerful in metallurgy, chemicals, coalmining, textiles, cars and electricity, but family enterprise remained a significant factor in most other industries.

What, then, is meant by the 'holding system' which crystallized in the inter-war years? Although the phrase 'holding company' is widely used to describe the parent company of any enterprise, it is used in discussions of Belgium and France to designate a specific type of company and its group of associated companies. Unlike an investment trust or investment company, a holding company is designed explicitly to control or influence other companies without taking full ownership of them. Such a holding company is structured through the pyramidding of majority and minority shareholdings in operating enterprises and sub-holding companies. Though linked through shareholdings, indebtedness, and interlocks, the companies brought together in this way are only loosely co-ordinated, they are not consolidated into a single set of accounts, they do not pursue a single corporate strategy, and only rarely do they have a common corporate identity (Daems 1978, pp. 2–3, 34–5; Allard *et al.* 1978, pp. 6–7). The constituent enterprises retain a measure of autonomy from the holding company, and thus the holding system is a means of loose co-ordination which is stronger than a mere community of interest but looser than a combine (Scott and Griff 1984, figure 1.1). The arena in which this co-ordination is effected may be the board of the main holding company, or it may be a central committee separate from any of the constituent enterprises. In Britain and the USA holding systems achieved some importance in transport and utilities in the first thirty years of the twentieth century, but were not widespread outside these sectors. Even where they were important, they were not dominant: the transport sector in Britain in the inter-war years, for example, was dominated by the big four railway companies, which participated in some of the holding systems which existed in road and air transport but which were themselves large, unified, and centralized enterprises. In France and Belgium the holding system resulted in a granular, group structuring of the economy: economic activity was concentrated into the hands of a number of rival groups, each of which had subsidiaries and associates operating in the leading sectors of the economy.

In the post-war years the holding system has undergone a partial transformation. Especially in France, the structure of the groups has tightened up and many have become combines or have amalgamated their constituent companies into a single enterprise (Lévy-Leboyer 1980, pp. 118–19). In both countries the groups have taken over many enterprises formerly subject to family control, while those small enterprises that survived have become increasingly dependent upon the big groups. The investment banks and holding companies dominate the flow of capital to other business enterprises. Over two-thirds of investment funding in France in the period 1967–71 was from internal sources, with most of the external funding coming through the banking system. Insurance companies and pension funds are unimportant in the capital market and, because shares tend to be closely held by the controlling groups, the stock exchange itself is unimportant in the mobilization of capital. Indeed, in Belgium about one-quarter of stock exchange transactions involve the shares of just one company (Petrofina). The role of the French state had expanded through its acquisition of the big three deposit banks in the 1950s (Banque Nationale de Paris, Crédit Lyonnais, Société Générale), and the role of the investment banks was enhanced after 1967 when changes in the banking laws allowed the investment banks to set up deposit networks in competition with the traditional deposit banks (Carrington and Edwards 1979, p. 149; Readman *et al.* 1973, chs. 4 and 7). A number of recent studies have shown the implications of these trends for patterns of ownership and control prior to the extension of the French public sector in 1981.

Table 33 shows that, in 1971, a half of the top 200 French enterprises were family-controlled, most families having majority or exclusive minority control. In those that are described as subject to 'relative minority control', the former family controllers are subject to challenge from outside industrial or financial interests – their control is limited by the countervailing power of other large shareholders. Thus, family control has tended to become diluted and to involve the sharing of power with outside interests (Bleton 1966, pp. 135–42). The top 500 enterprises of 1976 (see Table 34)

Table 33 *Strategic control in the 200 largest French industrial enterprises (1971)*

| | Type of controller | | | | | |
Mode of control	Family	Corporate	State	Foreign	Co-operative	Totals
Majority ownership	38	6	7	41	1	93
Exclusive minority control	43	13	1	9	0	66
Relative minority control	19	11	0	6	0	36
Internal control	—	5	—	—	—	5
Totals	100	35	8	56	1	200

Source: Adapted from Morin (1974a), p. 65, table 9.

Note: 'Relative minority control' refers to the situation where a minority controller is subjected to influence from other groups. Morin misleadingly allocates the five 'internal' (i.e. management) controlled companies to the column for corporate controllers.

Table 34 *Strategic control in the 500 largest French non-financial enterprises (1976)*

| | Type of controller | | | | |
Mode of control	Family	State	Techno-cratic	Foreign	Other	Totals
Exclusive majority	94	40	23	88	—	245
Exclusive minority	112	13	43	21	—	189
Predominant influence	6	0	4	0	—	10
Mutual	—	—	—	—	20	20
Joint	—	—	—	—	36	36
Totals	212	53	70	109	56	500

Source: Adapted from Morin (1977), p. 38, table 18.

Note: The heading 'other' refers to those situations where there is no single controller. All jointly controlled enterprises have been allocated to this category, and no distinction is made between majority and minority holdings.

show a similar pattern, suggesting that family enterprises were spread throughout the size hierarchy. Morin (1974a) classified just under one-fifth of the largest enterprises in his 1971 study as subject to control by corporate shareholders, and in a later work (1977) he classified these as subject to 'technocratic control'. Morin introduced this term to describe the situation where a number of large, predominantly corporate, shareholders prevent any one from achieving dominance, and where the board of directors is recruited from internal executives and from external groups such as retired civil servants (Morin 1974b, pp. 6–7).[13] Technocratic control, therefore, is

the situation in which it becomes impossible to determine control on the basis of economic property. Too dispersed and/or too heterogeneous in its nature (banks, state, insurance, family) and its strategies, economic property cannot confer control directly to any of the holders. Control is therefore delegated to the agents which exercise it without being holders themselves, in any significant sense, of economic property [Morin 1977, p. 33].

This situation of 'technocratic control' is clearly that which has been described in earlier chapters as control through a constellation of interests, though the shareholders which participate in the constellations include not only financial intermediaries but also the quasi-financial holding companies.[14] Similarly in Belgium (see Table 35) almost one-quarter of the forty-one large enterprises studied by De Vroey (1973) were controlled through intercorporate holdings. The constellations of interests which comprised these 'technocratic' corporate shareholders were the building blocks of the holding companies and combines which dominated the French and Belgian economies.

The contours of the intercorporate network of capital relations show how the major groups are tied together by the pattern of shareholdings. De Vroey discovered that the biggest corporate shareholder in Belgium was the SGB. In 1969 this holding company controlled twenty-five of the top 115 Belgian enterprises and shared control in a further eight. All eight of the enterprises classified as subject to corporate control in Table 35 were, in fact, controlled by the SGB, which also had minority participations in two of the family enterprises (De Vroey 1973, p. 112ff.; 1975b, pp. 7–8). The SGB, and its associated holding companies such as SOFINA, controlled about a half of Belgian industry, especially

Table 35   *Strategic control in forty-one large Belgian non-financial enterprises (1972)*

Proportion of shares held by principal owners	Type of controller				
	Family	Corporate	Foreign	Mixed	Totals
0–25%	0	0	0	1.5	1.5
25–49%	0	4	1	1	6
50–74%	2	2	1	3	8
75–99%	5	2	3	2	12
100%	0	0	11	0.5	11.5
Not known	—	—	—	—	2
Totals	7	8	16	8	41

Source: De Vroey (1973), pp. 119–20.
Note: The firm of Agfa-Gevaert was a union of a minority-controlled company and a wholly owned company, and so De Vroey allocated half to each category.

those enterprises in steel, metals, mining, and the financial sector. Other important holding companies, operating on a lesser scale, included Lambert, BRUFINA, Empain, Electrobel, and Cobepa, the Belgian subsidiary of the French Paribas group (CRISP 1962; Cuyvers and Meeusen 1976; 1978). De Vroey argues that 10 per cent of the shares in SGB are owned by enterprises under the control of the SGB itself (1973, pp. 145–6, 157; Daems 1980). While the SGB has influence and minority control in a number of other enterprises, it is itself controlled through a constellation of interests composed of these same enterprises together with such families as Solvay, Boel, and Janssen (Readman 1973, p. 98). Cuyvers and Meeusen (1985) designate this as 'managerialism within finance capitalism', a particularly tight form of control through a constellation of interests.

Morin (1974a; 1977) discovered that the largest French investment banks of 1971, Suez and Paribas, directly controlled twenty-three of the top 200 enterprises, and had a major influence in five others. The Banque d'Indochine, which was absorbed by Suez a year later, controlled two enterprises and influenced five others. In ten of the enterprises subject to relative minority control, family power was shared with one of these investment banks. Although a number of smaller investment banks, such as Worms, Lazard, Rothschild, Dreyfus, and Schlumberger, were controlled by families or other specific interests, the largest investment banks were subject to a similar pattern of circular control to that found in the SGB. In Suez, 'in-house' holdings of 17 per cent in 1974 were buttressed by holdings of 10 per cent by the nationalized savings banks and insurance companies, 9 per cent by an American insurance company, and 10 per cent by the British government (Bleton 1974, pp. 26–7).[15] In Paribas the circularity was more clear-cut, with fewer large blocks held by companies unconnected with the group (Allard *et al.* 1978).

SGB in Belgium, and Suez and Paribas in France, were at the heart of their national economies, and each of the three enterprises was at the centre not only of its own 'group' but also of a larger 'set' of allied groups. Allard *et al.* (1978, p. 9) employ the term 'set' (*ensemble*) to designate the extended interest groups which are federations of semi-autonomous groups centred on a dominant group.[16] Thus, Paribas is claimed to have been the basis of a set which incorporated the BSN-Gervais-Danone, SCOA, Poliet et Chausson, DNEL, and other groups. The emergence of these large sets in France has been seen as a phenomenon of the post-war period. In the 1950s and 1960s, banking was restructured around the investment and private banks which had escaped the nationalization of the deposit banks. Having been originally oriented towards overseas investment, Suez and Paribas took over a number of other banks and their holding companies and extended their links with the industrial sector. These two banks became the leading forces outside the state banking sector and became key agents in industrial reorganization. It was their role in corporate finance and corporate restructuring which led to the formation of their sets of associated enterprises. Paribas has been identified with the 'modernist' wing of finance capital, supporting state intervention and being involved in a number of large industrial mergers; while Suez has been identified as the 'traditionalist' wing, which has been more wary of state intervention and direction (Morin 1974b, pp. 9–10; Allard *et al.* 1978, p. 10). This extension of investment banking power and the holding system was partly encouraged by the threats of American competition and investment in France – the *défi américaine* of the 1950s and 1960s – though it is important to recognize that foreign enterprises have frequently entered the French economy in alliance with French enterprises. Alongside the two big 'sets' in France were to be found the large groups of Rothschild and Empain-Schneider,[17] and below these big four groupings were a number of large groups controlled by families (Willott, Dassault, Cartier-Bresson, Michelin, Chegaray, Bettencourt, and Peugeot), foreign enterprises (Chrysler, Honeywell, Hoechst, Fiat, IBM, ITT, and Nestlé), and the state (Allard *et al.* 1978; Bleton 1974; 1976a; Citoleux *et al.* 1977). Outside this whole holding system was the sphere of family capital, which remained strong as new entrepreneurial capitalists rose to replace those which disappeared (Bleton 1966, pp. 135–42).

The fact that the large 'sets' overlapped and incorporated a number of semi-autonomous groups points to the important fact that there were capital relations tying most of the large French enterprises into a single network. The formation of combines and the survival of the holding system did not result in an atomistic structuring of the economy as the various groups had cross-holdings which linked them together. Suez and its associates invested in enterprises within the Paribas set, for example, and the state enterprises were important investors in numerous large companies. The major sets appear as centres within this network, and the key banks held peak positions because they were more active than 'institutional' investors in the use of their holdings for purposes of control. Even within their sets, however, Suez and Paribas were frequently only minority holders, with equal or larger holdings held by family groups such as Gervais, Gillet, Hachette, and Fabre. The big groups and their associates were federations of interests with a higher density of linkages than the surrounding network of which they formed a part.

This pattern was reflected in the structure of interlocking directorships. Table 32 shows that the distribution of directorships in the top 250 enterprises of 1976 was very similar in the two countries. Enterprises in Belgium had slightly larger boards than those in France, but the number of multiple directors and the proportion of directorships which they hold were almost identical. The densities of the two networks, however, diverged sharply: in Belgium the density was similar to the high level found in Germany and Austria, but in France it was similar to the low levels found in Britain and the USA. The Belgian network, because of the dominance of a single group and its extended set, was highly centralized through a mass of interlocks which had their focus on

142   *Corporations, Classes and Capitalism*

the boards of the SGB and its associates (Cuyvers and Meeusen 1985; see also Daems 1978, pp. 69–84).[18] By contrast, the French network was polarized around the rivalry of the Suez and Paribas sets, with the density of the interlocks between the two sets being far lower than the density within each set. The state enterprises had few interlocks with any of the private groups, and remained marginal to the network as a whole (Swartz 1985).

The structure of ownership and control in France, however, was radically transformed in 1981. For a long time the parties of the left had discussed an extension of the nationalization initiated in the 1950s. The 'Common Programme' of the PCF and PS envisaged nationalization of the whole banking system and nine of the large private groups with strategic positions in the economy. The return of a socialist government in 1981 resulted in the implementation of such a policy. The whole of the banking system, including Suez and Paribas, was nationalized, giving the state control over the extensive share participations which the banks had built up, and state control was extended into all major industries through the acquisition of a number of other holding companies and combines. The whole structure of capital relations and interlocking directorships has been disrupted, but it remains uncertain what new patterns will emerge from this extension of the public sector.

Combines and aligned participations: the Japanese pattern

During the Tokugawa period of 1615 to 1868 there was little industrial development in Japan outside traditional small-scale handicraft production. The political rulers of the shogunate, hereditary nominees of the Tokugawa royal family, ensured that the country remained sealed-off from the outside world and so foreign trade was also unimportant. Merchants were extremely powerful by virtue of their role in the domestic market, but they held a lowly position in the hierarchy of social status. Dynastic merchant families such as Mitsui were organized as corporate bodies in the legal form of the 'house', in which there was a unity of the enterprise and the family household (Clark 1979, p. 14; Allen 1972). Restoration of the monarchy led to a greater encouragement of industrial development by the government of the emperor Meiji. The government became involved in strategic economic and military enterprises and supported private capital accumulation. The latter was considerably stimulated by the conscious and deliberate adoption of the German corporate form of the joint stock company in the 1890s (Westney 1979; Yazawa 1963; Clark 1979, pp. 29–31).[19] Key agents in this industrialization were the merchant houses, which formed and acquired enterprises in a wide range of industries and began to construct large business groups. These groups, and newer groups formed by industrial entrepreneurs, found joint stock organization an important support for their economic expansion. The joint stock form enabled each business to be formed as a separate corporation but, at the same time, enabled the various corporations to be subjected to a common control. The policy of divestment which was pursued by the government from the 1880s enabled the nascent groups to expand further through the acquisition of profitable state factories (Clark 1979, ch. 1). The banks, unlike those in Germany, were not generally willing to invest in industry, preferring to advance credit to agriculture and commerce. For this reason, banks were not a major source of funds for most enterprises. The exceptions to this – and they were major exceptions – were the banks associated with the big merchant houses which became heavily involved in the expansion of their groups (Yamamura 1978, pp. 241–2).

The largest business groups which emerged in the period leading up to the First World War came to be known by their opponents as *zaibatsu*, a word which means 'financial clique', 'estate of wealth', or, more colloquially, 'money trust'. Initially used as a critical term, the word was taken up by the wealthy controlling families themselves as a description of the form of business enterprise which produced their wealth. Minomura built up the old Mitsui family trading house into a major industrial group, and newer entrepreneurs such as Iwasaki (of Mitsubishi) and Yasuda founded similar *zaibatsu*. During the period 1910–20 the number of *zaibatsu* increased considerably as the founding generation of industrial entrepreneurs who were preparing to hand over to their successors began to consolidate their diverse interests into more unified groups under a parent holding company (Allen 1972, ch. 8; Lockwood 1968, pp. 214–22). In the 1930s, when their power in the economy was at its peak, there were ten major *zaibatsu*: the big four of Mitsui, Mitsubishi, Yasuda, and Sumitomo, and the smaller groups of Asano, Furukawa, Nakajima, Nissan (Ayukawa), Nomura, and Okura. A *zaibatsu* was organized as a

strict hierarchy, headed by a family-owned holding company
which owned a number of banking, commercial, and manufacturing subsidiaries which, in turn, owned smaller subsidiaries (Halliday 1975, pp. 53–60; Hadley 1970, pp. 20–4; Noguchi 1973,
p. 85). Non-*zaibatsu* enterprises were important in the economy,
but were generally dependent upon their commercial relations to
particular *zaibatsu*. In order to expand they had to raise funds on
the stock exchange, and a number of the smaller *zaibatsu* were
enterprises which had grown by copying the techniques already
employed by the established *zaibatsu* (Tsuchiya 1977). Most of
these dependent enterprises, however, chose not to diversify their
production or were prevented from diversification. They grew
slowly as single product enterprises, with company promoters
playing a leading role in ensuring successful flotation.

The *zaibatsu* form of group organization had as its main purpose
the maintenance of family control over a diverse range of enterprises. The wealthy families sought 'a device to assure that they
would not be interfered with by outsiders in their efforts to keep
the closed character of the business' (Yasuoka 1977, p. 94). The
practice of pyramidding within the group allowed external funds to
be raised by the subsidiary operating companies, with direct family
holdings being limited to the parent holding company. In this way
the *zaibatsu* family could retain control over a massive operation
on the basis of a relatively small personal shareholding, and the
family could not have retained this control over such a large group
if the various companies had been amalgamated into a unified
enterprise. The groups which were created, based around a family
strategy aimed at maintaining control, were tighter and more
centralized than the French and Belgian holding systems, and can
be seen as extensive industrial and financial combines. Techniques
of control used by the families to co-ordinate their combines were
ties of share-ownership, generally taking the form of majority
control, the use of the group bank to make credit available to
group enterprises, the centralization of commercial relations within the group, and the appointment of directors and executives to
subsidiaries by directors and executives of the holding company.
The *zaibatsu* banks played a central role in their groups, acting as
German-style 'universal' banks. The core business of the group,
generally banking or mining, provided the surplus for investment
in other areas, and the banks were the means through which this
capital could be mobilized alongside the money held in their

deposit accounts. Each combine generally aimed at industrial and financial self-sufficiency, and thus was based around a high level of central management co-ordination at the level of strategy and operations.

Table 36 shows how combine organization was reflected in the control of the top 200 enterprises of 1936. As in the USA at that time, there were a small number of large enterprises subject to majority control – though rather more were wholly-owned. The major difference between the USA and Japan, however, is to be found in the composition of the 'minority control' category. This category in Japan included not only enterprises which were minority-controlled by entrepreneurs and their families, but also those which were tied through intercorporate minority participations into *zaibatsu*. Similarly, many of those enterprises in which there was no single dominant interest were, in fact, subject to a system of intercorporate control (Hadley 1970, pp. 66–7; Lockwood 1968). For this reason, the conventional categories of modes of control fail to come to grips with the complexities of strategic control in Japan. Thus, in 1940, the Iwasaki family held 47.5 per cent of the Mitsubishi holding company, while other companies controlled by this holding company and its subsidiaries held a further 11.9 per cent (Yasuoka 1977, p. 97). An enterprise which conventional procedures would classify as minority-controlled in fact had a majority of its shares held by associated shareholders;

Table 36 *Strategic control in the 200 largest Japanese non-financial enterprises (1936–66)*

| | Number of enterprises | | |
Mode of control	1936	1956	1966
Wholly-owned	12	0	0
Majority control	13	4	4
Minority control	93	64	76
No dominant interest	82	132	120
Totals	200	200	200

Source: Kiyonari and Nakamura (1977), p. 268, table 4.

Note: A 10 per cent cut-off point was used for minority control. The original source contains a misprint in the 1966 data; this has been corrected.

and each of the corporate shareholders involved would show a similar pattern. Because of the practice of intercorporate shareholdings within *zaibatsu*, the precise control status of any one enterprise can be determined only when the control status of all others is known. This indeterminacy at the level of immediate control, however, was counterbalanced by the clarity with which the *zaibatsu* families appear as the ultimate controllers. The intercorporate holdings within the Mitsubishi group, for example, were a means of buttressing the control of the Iwasaki family over the whole group.

The power of the *zaibatsu* was challenged during the 1930s with the rise to power of the army in Japanese politics, but the combines were so necessary for the militaristic policies of the army that they soon regained any lost ground (Allen 1940). The massive demands of production for the Second World War forced a number of the controlling families to incorporate the parent holding company itself so as to seek outside capital. In this way the tight organization of the combines began to loosen, and family control was weakened (Yasuoka 1977, p. 93). This loosening was considerably advanced by the policies followed during the post-war Occupation. The American Occupation authorities attempted to break the economic power of the *zaibatsu* through a policy of 'dissolution': holding companies were made illegal and the controlling families were forced to sell their shares. When, later, large numbers of shares were acquired by group companies, the extent of intercorporate shareholdings was massively increased. The authorities made no real attempt to break up the groups themselves, and so the combines were able to continue on a restructured basis (Hadley 1970; Livingston *et al.* 1973b, part 2). Although internal executives rose to fill the gaps left by the divested families, this resulted not in share dispersal and management control but in the consolidation of intercorporate control (Kiyonari and Nakamura 1977). Instead of the spread of 'institutional' share ownership which was discovered in the Anglo-American economies, post-war Japan experienced the spread of what may be called aligned participations. Within the aligned groups there has not been a growth in control through a *constellation* of interests, but of control by *coalitions of aligned interests*. This situation has been described by Japanese writers as 'corporate capitalism' to distinguish it from 'institutional capitalism'; non-financial corporations join with banks and insurance companies to hold shares in aligned non-financials (Okumura 1983).

Table 37 *Beneficial ownership of Japanese company shares (1950–80)*

| | % of corporate shares held by each category | | | |
Type of holder	1950	1960	1970	1980
Government, public sector	3.2	0.2	0.3	0.2
Financial companies	24.5	34.3	33.5	40.5
Non-financial companies	11.0	17.8	23.1	26.0
Foreign companies	0.0	1.1	3.0	4.0
Persons	61.3	46.6	40.1	29.3
Totals	100	100	100	100

Source: Ohtani (1984), p. 50, table 8; see also Miyazaki (1973), p. 304, table 3; and Okumura (1975), cited in Clark (1979), pp. 101–2.

Table 38 *Strategic control in large Japanese enterprises (1966)*

| | | Type of control | | | |
Mode of control	Family	Cor-porate	Govern-ment	Inter-corporate	Total
Majority control 90% or more	3	5	1	13	22
50–90%	7	4	4	27	42
Minority control 30–50%	12	3	1	22	38
10–30%	42	11	3	77	133
Limited minority control	18	0	0	21	39
No dominant interest	—	—	—	191	191
Totals	82	23	9	351	465

Source: Miyazaki (1973), pp. 312–13, table 6.

Note: Limited minority control has been used to describe Miyazaki's category of minority control with a holding between 3 per cent and 10 per cent. The figures are based on the top 492 companies, of which twenty-seven were mutuals, public enterprises, or other special situations. The data consisted of the ten largest holders in each company.

It can be seen from Table 37 that the proportion of shares owned by persons in companies listed on the Japanese stock exchanges fell over the post-war period much as it did in Britain and the USA, though the proportion remains higher than in either of those societies. Although the proportion owned by financials has increased, the most obvious trend is the marked increase in the proportion owned by non-financials. In the Anglo-American systems this is an important factor only in the case of foreign subsidiaries, while in Japan over one-quarter of all shares in quoted companies are owned by domestic non-financials. During the 1960s these holdings even began to grow at the expense of the share of the financial intermediaries. Turning to the figures on ownership in Tables 36 and 38, it can be seen that most of those enterprises in 1966 that could be classified into the categories of majority and minority control or no dominant interest were, in fact, controlled through intercorporate shareholdings. There were twenty-four cases of majority control and ninety cases of minority control where a single interest was unambiguously in control, but 191 enterprises were subject to varying levels of control by constellations of interests or by coalitions of aligned interests (Kiyonari and Nakamura 1977, p. 267; Caves and Uekusa 1976, p. 10). In some of these enterprises a situation of control through a constellation of interests similar to that found in the largest Anglo-American enterprises can be discovered, albeit with a larger number of holdings by other non-financials. But in many other enterprises, coalitions of aligned interests tied the enterprises into co-ordinated combines. In the case of Hitachi, for example, the ten largest shareholders in 1979 held 23.9 per cent of the shares, the large holders comprising a mixture of competing financial intermediaries. On the other hand, Mitsubishi bank had 30.6 per cent of its shares held by the ten largest holders, of which six (with a total of 19.8 per cent) were part of the Mitsubishi group (Dodwell 1980).

Clearly, the group structure of aligned participations is central to an understanding of the Japanese economy; and while the contemporary situation has some similarities with that which existed before the war, there are a number of fundamental differences.[20] The economy today has a clear hierarchical structure, with three major combines at its head. These three combines are the former *zaibatsu* groups of Mitsui, Mitsubishi, and Sumitomo, and though each embraces a range of bank, insurance, commercial, and manufacturing enterprises they are particularly strong in heavy industry and chemicals. Figures for 1966–8 showed that the combines ranged in size from Sumitomo's fifteen enterprises to Mitsubishi's eighteen, and Mitsui's twenty-seven; and the proportion of shares in each company held within the group ranged from 3 to 66 per cent (Hadley 1970, pp. 216–17; Miyazaki 1973, pp. 320–1). The big city banks were the main sources of funds for post-war recovery and modernization, and the companies which benefited most from recovery were those that were most closely allied to the banks. These were, naturally, the former *zaibatsu* companies, and so the largest groups were able to restructure themselves around the group bank. As in Germany bank funding created a multiplier effect on industrial investment, with the level of internal funding being lower than in Britain or the USA (Clark 1979, p. 69ff.; Adams and Hoshi 1972; Thompson 1977, p. 60; Halliday 1975, p. 273). Each combine is less hierarchical in its internal structure than was the case before the war, though they are centred around financial enterprises and co-ordinated through trading companies. The main basis for unity is provided by the reciprocal share participations which run among the group enterprises. During the post-war period these groups have been increasing their reciprocal holdings, especially since the late 1960s, and so the groups have tended to become tighter in structure (Miyazaki 1973, p. 55; Bieda 1970, p. 210ff.; Caves and Uekusa 1976, ch. 4). They remain relatively decentralized federations of aligned enterprises, and Japanese commentators tend to use the term *kigyoshudan* to distinguish them from the hierarchical and family-dominated *zaibatsu* (Okumura 1983; see also Lockwood 1965a, pp. 495–7; Hadley 1970, p. 299).

Of all the countries considered in this book, Japan shows the strongest evidence for the existence of the rival financial interest groups depicted in the theory of capitalist society and its model of finance capital. Group members engage in preferential trading, joint ventures, and technical integration, and the aligned participations are reinforced by preferential loans supplied by the group bank and by funds from the trust and insurance companies within the group. Ueda (1983) has shown that strong and weak interlocks are much more closely associated in Japan than in the USA, most interlocks being carried by executives and contained within combines. Interlocking directorships are largely confined to the big *kigyoshudan* and are not involved in the creation of an extensive national network. Most directors were executives and in most enterprises the executives constituted a majority on the board, though these executives were sometimes also large shareholders. In 1964, 44 per cent of the 397 largest enterprises had no outside directors, and 33 per cent had only one or two (Caves and Uekusa 1976, p. 11). Thus, most outside directorships were those within combines which were held by group directors, and Steven shows that directors of the big combines in 1980 held 47 per cent of all directorships in quoted companies (Steven 1983, p. 52). These intra-group directorships were an important source of unity for the combines, though corporate strategy is largely worked out in each group's 'President's Club' (*shache kai*). Presidents of the combined enterprises meet regularly to discuss matters of mutual concern, and the club exercises the voting rights of all shares held by group companies.

Three other groups join the big three to make up the 'big six' groups: the Sanwa, Fuyo, and Daiichi Kangyo (DKB) combines. Each of these three is based around a bank and each incorporates the remnants of some of the lesser *zaibatsu*. Fuyo and Sanwa are both centred around banking hubs and have fewer cross-holdings than in the big three; links tend to run from the bank to the other enterprises, rather than among the enterprises themselves (Futatsugi 1969, p. 81). On the other hand, DKB has a financial core which links two semi-autonomous industrial groups – Kawasaki and Furukawa – each of which has a high degree of internal cohesion but are linked mainly through group financials.[21] The newer members of these groups were added in the 1950s and 1960s as the big city banks built up shareholdings among their clients so as to counter the in-roads of foreign capital. Around the *kigyoshudan* and their smaller affiliated combines, circulate a number of large industrial enterprises with varying degrees of attachment to the big groups. Hitachi, Nissan, Toyota, Nippon Steel, Matsushita, Sony, and others tend to have financial links with the big combines and are often members of one or more of the Presidents' Clubs, but they are autonomous decision-making centres which are organized in a similar way to large enterprises in the Anglo-American economies.[22] They are somewhat less centralized, as their subsidiaries are not always wholly-owned, but the parent company is invariably a majority or large minority shareholder and inter-group holdings are less common. Okumura (1983, pp. 9–10) terms this a group linked through vertical alignments rather than through the horizontal alignments of the *kigyoshudan*. While the combines are made up of companies controlled through coalitions of aligned interests, the parents of the autonomous enterprises are controlled by families or by constellations of interests: Nissan, for example, is controlled by a twenty-member constellation with 54 per cent of the shares, and Sony is controlled by the Morita family with 9.6 per cent. The major contrast between the Anglo-American constellations and those in Japan is that the latter include more individuals and industrials and the total pool from which the interests are drawn is smaller.

Below the *kigyoshudan* and the autonomous enterprises are a mass of small- and medium-sized enterprises which are heavily dependent on the activities of the large enterprises and combines, and which often act as subcontractors to them. Japan has a very large proportion of small firms (Caves and Uekusa 1976, p. 3), and in 1982 about two-thirds of all small- and medium-sized enterprises were subcontractors (Okumura 1983, p. 9). Although frequently described as a 'dualistic' economy, involving a division between monopoly capital and a dependent non-monopoly sector (Broad-bridge 1966), the Japanese economy is best seen as hierarchical with a continuous 'gradation' from the big three *kigyoshudan* to the small subcontractor (Clark 1979, p. 64). There is a division between hegemonic and subordinate enterprises, but financials *per se* are not hegemonic. The big six combines are effectively self-controlling through aligned participations, and they stand as hegemonic groups, alongside some other financials, in relation to the smaller combines and the autonomous enterprises. This oligarchic combine hegemony is a system in which the big combines have tight control over the flow of capital and so dominate the structure of activity in major areas of the economy.

Other patterns of capitalist industrialism

The patterns of capitalist development discussed so far do not exhaust the variety of patterns found in the advanced capitalist societies, but they do comprise the clearest exemplars of particular routes. Other patterns are less clear-cut, showing elements of each of the types delineated, but these variants can be illuminated by comparison with the major types. The Netherlands and Switzerland, by contrast with their European neighbours, are both marked by an overseas economic orientation, and in neither country was big business characteristic of the manufacturing sector until late in the nineteenth century. Prior to 1900 about three-quarters of the Dutch labour force was employed in small enterprises, but by 1909 this had fallen to a half. The beginning of the century was, therefore, an early turning point in industrial concentration (De Vries 1978, p. 10). An analysis of interlocks in the top 142 enterprises of 1886 shows the great similarities between the Netherlands and Britain at that time, though the overall density of interlocks was higher in the Dutch network (see Table 39). At the core of the interlock network were the financial and commercial enterprises, the most central enterprises including a large number of banks together with insurers, railways, and shippers. In an analysis of interlocks in 1910, Wibaut (1913) tried to show that Jeidels (1905) analysis of interlocks in Germany could be extended to the Netherlands; but Schijf (1979) shows that there is little evidence that the Dutch banks followed German practices. Wibaut's error was to start from the banks and trace their interlocks, so building bank centrality into his data. Schijf, by taking a larger selection of enterprises, put bank interlocks in context, showing that the interlocks presented in Table 39 involved close interlocks between banks, other financials, and colonial traders, but few interlocks between banks and industry.

Manufacturers such as Philips, Van den Berghs, and Jurgens

Table 39   *Distribution of directorships in the Netherlands (1886–1969)*

	Number of directors				
Number of directorships per person	*Top 142 of 1886*	*Top 107 of 1894*	*Top 98 of 1902*	*Top 93 of 1910*	*Top 147 of 1969*
2	110	79	76	79	190
3	43	25	24	22	103
4	21	22	8	9	70
5	9	6	10	4	35
6	4	5	5	3	26
7		2	2	1	10
8 or more		2	3	2	21
Totals	187	141	128	120	455

Source: 1886–1910 from Schijf (1979), table 1; 1969 from Helmers *et al.* (1975), table 5.3.

Note: Schijf selected the top 142 companies of 1886 and traced the survivors of this selection in each succeeding period. The only truly cross-sectional data, therefore, are those for 1886 and 1969.

arose in independence of the banking system, and even the large Royal Dutch petroleum, which traded throughout the Dutch colonial territories, had few links with the Amsterdam banks. The industrial development of the early twentieth century did, however, stimulate concentration in the banking sector, leading to the emergence of the 'big five' between 1911 and 1930. Later industrial mergers were associated with a further burst of bank mergers in 1964, reducing the number of big banks to just two – AMRO and ABN – though rival co-operative banks emerged during the 1970s (De Vries 1978, pp. 25–6). In the post-war period, therefore, the Dutch economy was centred on a small number of big banks and large industrials such as Unilever, Royal Dutch, Philips, AKZO, and Hoogevens; with the relationship of banks to industry conforming to the Anglo-American pattern. Banks acted as intermediaries in the underwriting and private placement of share issues, but were otherwise involved only in the provision of short-term credit. 'Institutional' shareholders have far greater importance than in Germany, France, or Belgium, with a major role being played by insurance companies, pension funds, and the investment companies of the Robeco group (Readman *et al.* 1973, ch. 6). The pattern of interlocking directorships, however, was significantly different from the Anglo-American pattern. A study for 1969 (see Table 39) found an increase in the proportion of multiple directors with large numbers of directorships, reflecting a relatively dense network of interlocks, and found the commercial banks to be involved in more interlocks than were any other enterprises (Mokken and Stokman 1974, p. 12; Helmers *et al.* 1975). In 1976 the top 250 enterprises had a particularly dense core, held together through the interlocks created by bank executives, but the major multinationals remained as peripheral to the network as they had been earlier in the century (Stokman *et al.* 1985). Unlike the German economy, where the universal banks had close relationships with most large industrials, the Dutch banks were close to a number of domestic industrials but had little connection with the most important industrial enterprises in the Dutch economy. Although ABN and AMRO spheres of influence could be identified, the main structural characteristic of the Dutch economy was a sharp separation between a dense domestic network and a number of large multinationals on its periphery. The hegemony of financial intermediaries in the mobilization of capital did not extend to those multinationals which had access to international sources of finance.

Swiss banking was dominated by relatively small private banks until the 1850s, when three German-style universal banks were formed with foreign backing. Their primary orientation, however, was not towards the development of Swiss domestic industry, but towards the expansion of Swiss overseas markets. Only as they began to acquire a number of the private banks in the twentieth century did they achieve any size or significance in the Swiss economy. Unlike the Netherlands, therefore, the banks in Switzerland have had very close relationships to the Swiss multi-nationals, making the intercorporate network much more like the German model. In 1976 (see Table 32), a large number of the top 250 Swiss enterprises were interlocked into a dense network in which the big three banks – Crédit Suisse, the Union Bank, and the Swiss Bank – held central positions (Rusterholz 1985; Schreiner 1984).

Although French capital was involved in the formation of invest-ment banks in Italy in the 1860s, these banks invested mainly in railways and Italian industrialization was further inhibited by poli-cies pursued by the Italian state. Not until German, Austrian, and Swiss banks formed Italian associates in the 1890s did any signifi-cant industrial development take place. These universal banks were especially important in the newer electrical and chemical industries, but a series of banking crises prevented the establish-ment of the close and continuous relationship of banking and industry which developed in Germany. In the older industries entrepreneurial families remained important, the scale of produc-tion was much smaller, and the rate of growth was even less than in the new industries (Cafagna 1971; Gershenkron 1962, ch. 4). The slow and hesitant 'take-off' led to early state involvement in the economy, with the consequence that insurance companies, pension funds, and the stock exchange have never been important sources of industrial finance. State intervention began on a large scale in the fascist period and was extended after the war, and most long-term industrial finance by the 1970s was provided by state banks and credit agencies. The state holding company, IRI, was set up to rescue three of the failed universal banks in 1929, and acquired their industrial participations along with their banking operations. Since that time IRI has set up a number of associated holding companies in various sectors and two new and separate state holding companies have been set up in electricity and oil. State intervention, therefore, has transformed a chronically disabled system of bank hegemony into a state-controlled holding system. Unlike the French state holdings, those in Italy are not pre-existing private holding companies but were forged from the industrial participations of the universal banks and from subsequent extensions of public ownership. Outside the state holding system, however, a number of wealthy entrepreneurial families such as Agnelli, Pirelli, and Pesenti have established holding companies and combines of their own. Although Table 32 shows the distribution of interlocks in Italy in 1976 to be similar to that found in Belgium and Germany, a more detailed investigation showed that there was a sharp split between the 'state pole' and the 'private pole' of the network (Chiesi 1985). Each part of the network had a dense pattern of interlocks, but the state and private worlds were only loosely connected with one another. Nevertheless, a group of directors based in financial enterprises did bridge the two sectors – the main links running through IRI and the Falck and Pesenti groups (Chiesi 1982, figure 1). Few studies of ownership and control have been carried out in other countries of capitalist Europe. In Spain, Portugal, Denmark, and Finland, the traditional economy of land ownership, agriculture, and commerce prevails. Despite their general level of economic development, neither their industry nor their joint stock organization is as fully developed as in the other countries discussed in this chapter. For this reason it is difficult to draw any general conclusions from the strong survival of family ownership and family enterprise in the Iberian societies and the importance of co-operatives in the Scandinavian societies. Studies of Sweden and Norway, however, do throw further light on the trends identified in this chapter.

Swedish industrial development followed closely on the establishment in 1856 of the Stockholm Enskilda Bank, which was formed as a universal bank (Kindleberger 1984, pp. 131–4). The bank was controlled by a single family, unlike the more dispersed forms of ownership found in the German banks, and this family – the Wallenbergs – used it to achieve a pre-eminent position in the Swedish economy. In the 1960s fifteen families owned the corporations that employed almost a half of those working in private industry, with the Wallenberg family alone employing 20 per cent of private employees. The family controlled seventy enterprises, such as Electrolux, Saab-Scania, L. M. Ericsson, Swedish Match, Alfa-Laval, and SKF. Concentration of shareholdings in Swedish enterprises was so great that the ten largest shareholders had a majority of the shares in all corporations quoted on the Stockholm stock exchange (Commission on Concentration 1968, p. 37; Gustavsen 1976). In Norway there was no such all-pervasive family as the Wallenbergs, but there was a high concentration in share ownership. In 1963 the twenty largest shareholders held a majority of the shares in 85 per cent of all corporations, most of these large shareholders being individuals and families (Higley *et al.* 1976, p. 132; Seierstad 1968, pp. 100–1). Even in Norway, with its highly concentrated system of family ownership, there is evidence for the emergence of a group of finance capitalists who control the large enterprises which 'because of the large amounts of capital, long lead times, and large markets necessary to their operations, are dependent on each other for capital supplies and co-operative arrangements in production and marketing (Higley *et al.* 1976, p. 145). There had begun to emerge a number of larger enterprises where family control was diminishing and more dispersed forms of control were arising. It might be expected that these would develop in the direction of control through a constellation of interests, but that many of the participants in the controlling constellations would be individual and family shareholders.

The evidence reviewed here has been uneven in both quality and quantity, but a remarkably clear picture has emerged. The Anglo-American pattern of a move from personal, entrepreneurial control to control through a constellation of interests and polyarchic financial hegemony is a major pattern in the advanced capitalist economies, but a number of countries, with differing starting points, have pursued varying routes to the present. Variations in banking systems, state involvement, and private wealth have produced oligarchic bank hegemony, the holding system, combines of aligned enterprises, and a host of intermediate cases. All the countries discussed show that a sector of small- and medium-sized firms exist alongside, and dependent upon, a 'big business' sector of large monopolistic enterprises. The previous chapters have concentrated on documenting the variations to be found in the organization of big business. Considerable evidence has been discovered for the survival of family enterprise within big business; even in the USA entrepreneurial capitalists are an important force in the economy. Similarly, internal capitalists, the salaried executives of managerialist theory, have enhanced opportunities for action wherever owner-control is diluted. But perhaps the most striking fact is the emergence of a group of finance capitalists in each economy; a group which grows in importance as constellations of shareholding interests become the major forces in corporate ownership and control. The finance capitalists play an increasingly important role on the boards of the large enterprises, especially the banks, in the advanced capitalist economies as formulators of corporate strategy and co-ordinators of corporate affairs. Little evidence was found to support the Marxist idea that capitalist economies are internally structured into rival 'financial empires' within which finance capitalists are all-powerful. Only in Japan was this structure observed, and there entrepreneurial capitalists and internal capitalists participated in the exercise of strategic control alongside the finance capitalists. With their pre-eminence on the boards of the hegemonic enterprises in all capitalist economies, however, the finance capitalists have increasingly become the dominant partners in the interplay of finance capitalists, internal capitalists, and entrepreneurial capitalists which structures the patterns of corporate development.

Notes

1 In fact, Swiss law recognizes both the 'German' board system and the 'Latin' variant described below.

2 Not all corporations in these countries are organized as public joint stock corporations, but the various limited liability companies and corporate partnerships approximate to this pattern.

3 These banks were formed as joint stock companies by Royal Charter and pre-dated modern Company Law.

4 In fact the number of companies selected varied between 103 and 116. For a related study of an earlier period see Piédalue (1976).

5 For a classification of control in forty-eight large French Canadian enterprises see Niosi (1981), table 3.1.

6 Carroll's own figures for density are calculated for multiple interlocks only. Recalculations for all interlocks show a level of 0.100 in 1946 and 0.134 in 1966. These density levels are much higher than those found in Scotland, where a similar number of enterprises were studied. On the problems of

measuring density see Scott and Griff (1984), ch. 1. Primary interlocks in Canada are discussed in Ornstein (1982).

7   A 20 per cent cut-off was used.

8   These figures are based on recalculations from the original sources because Wheelwright and Miskelly based their definition of 'owner control' on the total of all personal shareholdings, regardless of their size and regardless of what connections may or may not exist among these shareholders. The figures reported in this paragraph are based on calculations comparable with those used in the other studies discussed in this book.

9   There were also family shareholders in the controlling constellations who had smaller holdings or no board representation.

10   In this context 'foreign' includes English enterprises.

11   See the evidence on this in Niosi (1981).

12   Many German companies issue bearer shares rather than registered shares. That is to say, the shares are not registered in the name of a particular shareholder, as in the Anglo-American system, but are regarded as the property of whoever is the current bearer of the certificate. Individually-owned bearer shares are generally deposited with the banks and so enhance the voting power of banks. On legal forms of business enterprise in Germany see E. O. Smith (1983) ch. 7, where it is calculated that two-thirds of the top 100 in 1978 were *Aktiengesellschaften*.

13   For a criticism of Morin (1974b) see Bleton (1976a). This debate was extended in Morin (1976) and Bleton (1976b). Though critical of Morin, Bleton gives considerable support for the notion of technocratic control.

14   Holding companies are units of finance capital and their operations are limited to the financial sphere, but they are not intermediaries in the monetary system in the same sense as banks and insurance companies.

15   The British government holding dates from the formation of the original Suez Canal company, when the Rothschilds arranged the purchase of a holding for Disraeli's Conservative government.

16   The technical problems of defining 'groups' and 'sets' are discussed in Bellon (1977).

17 Empain is Belgian and Schneider is French, the two being linked through holdings and joint ventures.

18 See Daems (1980), p. 210, for a comparison of Belgium and Japan.

19 Despite following German corporate law, Japan adopted the Anglo-American single board system. The Japanese form of the joint stock company is the *kabushiki kaisha*. On the Meiji period see Yasuoka (1977), Nakagawa (1977), and Morikawa (1977).

20 The following description draws on Dodwell (1980), Clark (1979), p. 73ff., Bieda (1970), and Okumura (1983).

21 DKB was formed as a merger in 1971, Furukawa and Kawasaki being former *zaibatsu*. Fuyo is based around the former Yasuda *zaibatsu* and includes newer clients of the Fuji Bank (formerly Yasuda Bank). Sanwa Bank was formed in the 1930s and built up a new group in the 1960s. A further industrial group with an important role in the economy is that of the Industrial Bank of Japan, which specializes in rescue operations and has a number of dependent clients but has no central policy-making forum for the group.

22 Toyota split from Mitsui in the post-war dissolution and became independent, but it has moved closer to that combine in the 1970s. Nissan is the remnant of a *zaibatsu* which originally included the now-independent Hitachi

6 Corporate strategy and operational management

The sectional managerialism which prevails among economists holds that the separation of ownership from control engenders the uninhibited play of managerial self-interest. Corporate strategy, they argue, is centred on the pursuit of those goals which enhance managers' prospects of career advancement through promotion and job transfer (Williamson 1964; Marris 1964). It has been argued in the preceding chapters that there is little evidence to support the conventional view of the divorce between ownership and control. Entrepreneurial capitalists remain an important element in all capitalist economies, but the dominant form of enterprise, most notably in the Anglo-American economies, is not management-controlled but controlled through a constellation of interests. It is, nevertheless, possible that sectional managerialists may have correctly identified important alterations in corporate goals, even though they have been mistaken in their understanding of the causes of these changes. If this is, indeed, the case, it is necessary to show the causal links which actually exist between mode of control, corporate strategy, and managerial motives.

A major problem in the writings of those who have tried to spell out the implications for the economic behaviour of enterprises of these assumed changes in control and motives is that they have continued to regard market forces as the fundamental determinants of corporate action; market forces being understood in the relatively narrow sense of conventional supply and demand analysis. Though they claim that the 'invisible hand' of 'free competition' has been replaced by the 'visible hand' of corporate planning (Chandler 1977), they see the corporate planners as taking account only of conventional economic variables. It must be recognized, however, that the changes in the structure of capitalism which are documented in this book have brought about a situation in which both the nature of the market and the causal impact of market forces have altered in directions unseen by sectional managerialism.

Paradoxically, this was recognized by one of the founders of managerialist theory in a report to the *American National Resources Committee* of the 1930s. Means argued that the relative importance of commercial market relations and 'non-market controls' has altered: 'Where policies with respect to the use of resources are only limited and not dominated by market controls, the nonmarket controls become a significant factor making for more or less effective use of resources' (Means *et al.* 1939, p. 154). The implications of this neglected and forgotten insight are fundamental.[1]

Business leaders may be subject to constraints which impel them to depart from pure market considerations, and such departures may not threaten their survival if their company is part of a larger enterprise or group which will 'protect' it. The clearest cases of this are companies which are wholly-owned or majority-controlled subsidiaries of other companies, where the behaviour of each company is subordinated to the strategy of the parent company. Transfers of goods and services between subsidiaries do not pass through the external market and so can be priced on criteria internal to the enterprise. Purely notional prices enter into the accounts of subsidiaries, and their 'profits' and 'losses' become equally notional as losses in one part of a large enterprise can be offset against profits in another. The *Temporary National Economic Committee* investigators argued that the same was true of family interest groups held together through majority and minority shareholdings:

> While all of these concerns are independent enterprises, with complete freedom to determine their own policies, it seems hardly likely, in view of the extent to which they are owned by the same people, that anyone of them would pursue a course which was prejudicial to the interests of the others [Anderson *et al.* 1941, p. 24].

Similarly, Fitch felt that relatively small shareholdings by banks, if backed-up by interlocking directorships, could be the basis for 'reciprocity' within bank interest groups in which each enterprise is subordinate to the profitability of the bank (1972, p. 126; Fitch and Oppenheimer 1970c, pp. 77, 81). Certain problems of this notion of bank control in the Anglo-American economies have already been given in Chapter 4, and it must be added here that there are limits to the extent to which any bank could depress the profitability of an enterprise with which it seeks a *continuing* relationship;

if a bank forced reciprocal dealings to such an extent that some of its associated enterprises began to make losses, the banks would be forced to intervene with financial support to prevent the enterprise going out of business (O'Connor 1971). Extreme use of non-market controls by banks is likely to prove counter-productive. However, the fact remains that, within the limits of their market situation, enterprises may follow strategies which do not bring them as high a profit as might have been earned, but which are profitable enough to allow them to survive.

The environment within which business enterprises operate is an intercorporate network of capital, commercial, and personal relations which together comprise a mixture of both 'market' forces of supply and demand and 'non-market' forces of power and influence (Scott and Griff 1984, ch. 1). This intercorporate network, the new invisible hand of finance capital, has become a crucial determinant of corporate behaviour. But corporate behaviour cannot be seen solely as a response to environmental conditions; business leaders have a degree of choice as to the course they steer through environmental constraints (Child 1972). For this reason, it is necessary to examine the processes through which corporate strategy is actually formulated and implemented. This has been discussed most recently in the debates over two influential theses: the Chandler thesis and the Braverman thesis.

Chandler (1962; 1977) argued that alterations in corporate strategy have followed from changes in share-ownership and from expansion of markets. Changes in strategy have, in turn, been responsible for managerial restructuring. In the same period that the USA developed from an economy of small entrepreneurial firms to an economy of large 'managerial' enterprises, management structure has proceeded through holding companies and 'functional' organizations to a multidivisional structure. Clearly, questions can be raised about the significance of management control in this thesis, but Chandler's description of managerial structures has stimulated much fruitful discussion (Channon 1973; Hannah 1976a). Braverman (1974) attempted to outline the ways in which the introduction of techniques of scientific management led to the 'deskilling' of craft work and a consequent reduction in the power of workers. Manual work, he argues, has been progressively reduced to the level of unskilled labour, and much non-manual work has undergone a similar 'proletarianization'. 'Scientific management' – the application of principles of job design to industrial work – extended capitalist control over the labour process from the purely 'formal' level which existed through most of the nineteenth century to 'real' active control. In the earliest capitalist enterprises the employer simply brought together skilled workers to produce in his workshop; the workers possessed the requisite skills and knowledge and the capitalist remained purely external to the process of production. The new forms of management which were introduced towards the end of the nineteenth century brought about the 'real subordination' of labour to capital. Advanced machine production no longer required the traditional skills of the worker, and labour became fragmented so that the worker became simply a detail labourer performing one task in a complex division of labour. The planning of production and the supervision of labour were separated from the routinized 'degraded' labour process itself. Deskilling reduced, if not eliminated, the power of the worker within the labour process, and so enhanced the power of the capitalist and his or her managerial representatives. The Braverman thesis has attracted much critical attention (Thompson 1983; Wood 1982), not least because of its underestimation of the power of workers to resist and its unsatisfactory understanding of 'skill'. Nevertheless, some powerful accounts of corporate management have emerged from the fruitful confrontation of the Chandler and Braverman theses. In the following sections these accounts will be related to the analysis of ownership and strategic control presented earlier in this book.

Corporate strategy: functional organization and technical control

Chandler (1962) made the concept of 'strategy' into his central explanatory variable, though the word has subsequently been applied to a wide range of processes at various levels of the corporate hierarchy and has, in consequence, lost much of its original force as an explanatory factor. In the earlier chapters of this book, corporate strategy has been restricted to its original sense of the long-term goals and objectives of the enterprise in relation to investment, corporate organization, and executive recruitment; and the exercise of strategic control has been seen as participation in the processes through which corporate strategy is formulated. Corporate strategy has been distinguished from those lower-level processes of decision-making which concern the operational administration of the enterprise within the constraints set by the corporate strategy. These lower-level processes are, in one sense, equally 'strategic' – involving deliberate manoeuvring for tactical advantage – but confusion arises if they are not distinguished from the concept of long-term corporate strategy. The 'strategic' aspects of operational administration are the outcome of a continuing series of short-term decisions in which middle managers respond in an *ad hoc* and pragmatic way to the pressing demands of their superiors. Because it is an unintended consequence of actions which are constrained by the over-arching corporate strategy, the process tends to be 'blind'; the managers who implement it being only partially aware of the overall 'logic' of the strategy. By contrast, corporate strategy is the outcome of a more conscious and deliberate process of decision-making in which long-term planning and the monitoring of the consequences of decisions are a central part.

Chandler's account[2] of the gradual separation of strategic decision-making from operational management begins with an analysis of the way in which they were fused in the single-unit firm of the nineteenth century. In this type of firm, typically subject to family ownership and control, production took place exclusively in one location. The plant was typically small enough for the owner to supervise production personally, and the fact that production was for local markets meant that the owner-manager could also oversee the sales of the product. Only in such industries as the railways were business operations spread over a large number of locations; and it was the railways which spearheaded the drive to a distinctively *national* scale of operations. The system of management in the railways involved the creation of an extensive managerial hierarchy and the division of management into two branches: 'line' management responsible for the enterprise's main operations (the movement of passengers and freight by train); and 'staff' management responsible for specialist tasks such as accounting and equipment supplies. Towards the turn of the century the scale of industrial production expanded to meet the needs of a national market, partly through internal growth and partly through mergers and amalgamation, and the new large enterprises had to evolve systems of management capable of co-ordinating their multi-unit activities.

A major development was the transformation of the line-staff system of railway administration into a 'functional' system of departmental administration. 'Line' management became simply the production function alongside a number of other specialist functions, each assigned to a head office department. This required a highly centralized form of organization, with the constituent units having virtually no decision-making autonomy. By the First World War, therefore, a significant proportion of large businesses took the form of the centralized, functional enterprise. But not all large, multi-unit enterprises took this form; many were organized as loose federations of firms under a 'holding company' which acted simply as a central selling agency or a market sharing device.[3] In these holding companies, most strategic issues were decided at the level of the constituent firms rather than on the board of the holding company. Even where the parent board sought to determine an overall group strategy, the decentralized system of management did not contain the machinery necessary to formulate and implement a coherent strategy.

The main stimulus to the creation of large enterprises was the desire to internalize transaction costs between firms; the non-market 'reciprocity' of administered transactions resulted in lower prices than did the system of market exchange. But the advantages of a system of internalized transactions could only be fully achieved in those enterprises which had already established a managerial hierarchy capable of co-ordinating and planning the internalized processes. The holding company form of organization arose where merger of enterprises took place without the prior creation of an effective managerial system, and the resulting enterprises were unable to lower costs to reap the advantages of amalgamation. Chandler argued that the large enterprises that adopted a centralized system of management – predominantly in the newer, expanding industries where mass production and mass distribution coincided – were those in which the principal shareholder or bankers which had a controlling interest adopted a different management style from the entrepreneurial majority owner. The controllers became the core of a top management team and recruited salaried managers to run the operations and participate in the formulation of strategy. As shareholdings became more dispersed, he argues, the salaried executives achieved a firmer power base. By the end of the First World War big business in the USA was divided between a majority of 'functional' enterprises, epitomized by DuPont and General Electric, and a minority of 'holding companies', epitomized by General Motors and Standard Oil. In neither type of enterprise, argued Chandler, was there an adequate separation of strategy from operations; the holding company left them fused at the subsidiary level, while the functional enterprise tended to fuse them at head office level. In both cases, therefore, long-term planning was inhibited by the continued involvement of key managers in the details of day-to-day operations.

In Britain, France, and Germany, the holding company form of organization was far more widespread than in the USA. Holding companies in Britain were the characteristic form of business amalgamation in the late nineteenth century and early twentieth century, and they persisted through the inter-war years. They were formed as defensive alliances of personal and entrepreneurial firms, each of the leading families seeking to maximize the amount of control which they could retain over their firms (Hannah 1976b, 1980). Holding company boards became arenas in which the rival families struggled with one another, and there was virtually no attempt to recruit professional managers or to engage in long-term strategic planning. Only in ICI and Unilever was there any marked move away from this form of organization before the Second World War (Hannah 1974; 1976c, ch. 6; Chandler 1977, p. 499). In France, the holding company organization was an integral part of the holding system itself, and, in consequence, management structures were even weaker than in Britain.

Morikawa (1977) studied management in the big *zaibatsu* of Japan and showed that the established family trading house of Mitsui had, by the 1890s, adopted the holding company structure, while the newer entrepreneur-led Mitsubishi had created a more centralized functional organization. After 1917, however, Mitsubishi was reorganized as a holding company – the classic organizational form of the *zaibatsu*. This strengthening of the holding company structure was specifically designed to cope with the problem of perpetuating concentrated control. Not only did it allow the controlling families to retain control of large groups of enterprises, it also enabled them to build up a system of delegated managerial administration. The particularly rapid industrialization of Japan created great opportunities for managerial careers, and the big groups had to find a way of recruiting and retaining the services of salaried managers. The fact that the Japanese holding company had centralized family control at the level of the parent company, and that the latter controlled its subsidiaries through majority and minority holdings rather than owning the whole of their share capital, meant that there were unique opportunities for achieving this goal. Each subsidiary was headed by a person with the title of 'President', giving a status superior to that of subordinate executive in a centralized enterprise, and the top managers in a subsidiary could be permitted to acquire shares in the subsidiary company without this threatening either the parent's control of the subsidiary or the family's control of the group. Managers could be retained through the rewards of status and share-ownership (Morikawa 1977, pp. 59–60; Mishima 1977). Unlike the British holding companies, where the subsidiaries had effective autonomy from the parent, the Japanese holding company was the centre of ultimate control over group operations; and this gave unrivalled opportunities for managerial development in a situation of rapid industrialization. With the demise of the *zaibatsu* the holding company has remained the predominant form of business organization in Japan,[4] with the central board or President's Club of the new *kigyoshudan* becoming a meeting place for subsidiary Presidents to evolve group strategy. The economic success of the *kigyoshudan* organization has meant that the major groups have faced few pressures to modify their management structures. The holding company organization is an integral part of Japanese 'corporate capitalism'.

The early capitalist entrepreneurs, owner-managers of their single-unit firms, were able to carry out virtually all management tasks themselves, only occasionally employing subordinates. When the capitalist's role in production was essentially external, or 'formal', the extent of supervision was minimal; but as the scale of production increased, so the task of management became more complex and began to be separated into a role separate from that of the capitalist. The managerial agents of the early capitalists were of two types: internal contractors and foremen. When an internal contractor was used, the capitalist paid a block fee to a person – the subcontractor – who became the direct employer of other workers, paying them out of his fee and often employing members of his own family. Thus, the capitalist was direct employer of only the subcontractors and so had no need to be actively involved in the managerial supervision of the workforce (Pollard 1965, p. 51ff.; Littler 1982, ch. 6). The system of internal contracting was widespread in Britain until the 1870s and 1880s, when the practice of direct employment by the capitalist became more common. With this transition, the employment of a supervisor, often a former subcontractor, became necessary. This system of management can be designated *close surveillance*:[5] the entrepreneur and foremen specified the task to be carried out and directly observed its performance, and they were able to apply appropriate disciplinary action if this performance was inadequate. The ruthless and assertive 'entrepreneurial ideology', with its emphasis on competitive success and the struggle for survival, was the means through which this exercise of power was legitimated (Bendix 1956, pp. 99ff., 254–67; Perkin 1969, p. 221ff.), but it was in some cases supplemented by paternalistic ideas. This concern for employee welfare was, in both Britain and the USA, a minority response, being limited in Britain mainly to Quaker firms which were adopting practices of close supervision in the 1890s and later. In the USA, the entrepreneurial ideology came under little challenge from paternalist ideas.

In Japan, however, a form of 'corporate paternalism' emerged as the dominant characteristic of the big business sector. Japanese industrialization was very dependent on a form of internal contracting where the subcontractor (*oyakata*) recruited workers into a hierarchically structured work group dependent on him and over which he exercised considerable power. The system centred on low wages, with the *oyakata* adopting an arbitrary and coercive attitude to those he employed. He expected personal loyalty to himself, and rewarded such loyalty with preferential treatment for those with long service. Workers were treated virtually as dependent kin, and the power of the *oyakata* was expressed in a system of extreme patriarchal authority (Okayama 1983). As the *zaibatsu* grew in the period up to the First World War, they attempted to replace the *oyakata* with directly employed workers – but so entrenched was the subcontracting system that many *oyakata* had to be incorporated into positions of formal authority in the managerial hierarchy of the group, and their dependent work groups became the basis of the company unions. Those *oyakata* that were not incorporated in this way became external contractors to the *zaibatsu*, laying the foundations of the 'dualistic' structure of the inter-war Japanese economy. The fusion of *zaibatsu* family ownership and *oyakata* patriarchal exploitation produced what has been described as 'corporate paternalism' (Littler 1982, ch. 10; Yamamura 1978, pp. 254–8; Dore 1973) as the entrepreneurial capitalists who headed the big combines moulded 'traditional' ideas to the requirements of modern management.[6]

In Britain and America the growth in size of enterprises meant that the entrepreneur, now often a majority or minority shareholder, and the foremen could no longer manage through simple personal supervision of the workforce, and more complex systems of management began to evolve. Layers of clerical workers and specialist managers involved in purchasing and sales were established alongside the levels of foremen and supervisors who became the nascent system of 'line' authority. This resulted in a hierarchical variant of close surveillance in which each level of management was able to undertake the close surveillance of its subordinates while, at the same time, being subject to the close surveillance of its superiors. This system of *hierarchical control* involved little departure from earlier patterns of authority, but the increased scale of production, the withdrawal of the entrepreneurial capitalists from absolute control, and the increased market power of large enterprises all contrived to undermine it as a system of management. Edwards has argued that 'Hierarchical control declined because it could not cope with those characteristics . . . that specifically differentiated the new giants' (1979, p. 52). In Britain, with its protected markets and its tenacious family capitalists, this system of hierarchical control persisted as the dominant form of management well into the inter-war period, even where family firms had been amalgamated into federal holding companies (Gospel 1983b, pp. 104–6; 1983a; Littler 1982, ch. 7).

The growth of the centralized, functional enterprise in the United States, however, involved a further restructuring of management functions, a restructuring which today goes under the name of 'Taylorism' but was then regarded as 'scientific management' (Chandler 1977, p. 412; Salaman 1982, p. 48). The amalgamation of large numbers of enterprises in heavy industry into massive national enterprises produced resentment among those engineers who felt that they were losing control over their conditions of work. This resentment found its expression in the writings of professional engineers who claimed that labour management should be placed in the hands of a separate department managed by specialists in the principles of labour management. Since labour was an adjunct to machinery, it was felt, it was appropriate that those who best understood the principles of machine technology – the engineers – should fill these key management posts. Engineers could formulate an engineering solution to the question of labour control by carrying out studies into the standardization of tools and tasks, the restructuring of payment incentive systems, and the avoidance of fatigue. The aim of this 'scientific management' was to design the form of machinery and work flow which would make labour as efficient as possible (Layton 1971; Armstrong 1984; see also Thompson 1983, ch. 5; Littler and Salaman 1984). Taylorism was one particularly clear and influential statement of this view, but scientific management can best be seen as an inchoate series of practices which emerged at different times and in different places without, at this stage, forming a coherent system of thought. In the practices of *technical control*[7] which began to be established in the functional enterprises, formal controls over labour were institutionalized in the physical organization of the labour process (Edwards 1979, p. 110). There was no need for arbitrary and inefficient personal supervision of workers, as the rate and quality of their work were paced by the machines to which their skills had been transferred. The principles of technical control proved very effective and were widely adopted in the USA, but they proved so easy to understand that engineers could claim no special competence to apply them and so the growth of large managerial hierarchies did little to enhance the power of engineers. Management was becoming more 'professionalized', but the knowledge and skills required for business management were not specifically those of the trained engineer.

While forms of technical control had become widespread in the USA, it was not until the 1930s and 1940s that this had any significant impact in Britain. The depression led to massive problems of industrial re-organization and to the involvement of banks and insurance companies in the formation of large-scale horizontal and vertical amalgamations of enterprises. Where this involved the use of industrial consultants in re-organization at the plant level there was often an attempt to introduce forms of technical control. Central to this re-organization of management was the international Bedaux management consultancy firm (Littler 1982, chs. 8 and 9) which drew up schemes of re-organization based on time and fatigue studies, schemes of job analysis, and alterations in payment systems.[8] There was considerable worker resistance to the systematic application of these ideas, and they had far less impact, in any case, in family enterprises and in the holding companies. Not until the post-war period did less systematic, but more effective, systems of technical control become widespread in Britain.[9]

Corporate strategy: divisional organization and bureaucratic control

It has been argued that the failure to separate strategic control from operational administration created grave problems of management in both the functional and the holding company structures. In an expanding economy, such as that of the United States prior to the First World War, these managerial weaknesses were less obvious and could normally be dismissed. But in the conditions of the post-war depression they were highlighted and could no longer be ignored. During the 1920s, therefore, alternative structures of corporate management began to be adopted. The major enterprises began to build a system which combined centralized strategic control with decentralized operational administration. In the case of the centralized, 'functional' enterprises this involved the building of autonomous operating units; in the case of the decentralized 'holding companies' this involved the creation of a large general office and general staff. Proposals for 'divisional' restructuring accorded with the occupational interests of accountants, who began to propose that the auditing techniques which were used to regulate relations among enterprises and between them and the state could also be applied to the internal control of enterprises. The economic difficulties of the early 1920s had exposed the need to identify and control costs more closely, and the creation of a structure of divisional organization involved a shift of business accountancy from its former position as a 'staff' function separate from line authority to a new position at head office. The accounting staff introduced the techniques of central budgeting which permitted head office to exercise control over autonomous operating divisions. By contrast with the turn-of-the-century engineers who pressed their sectional skills as a solution to the problems of business management, the accountants of the interwar years were successfully able to claim a monopoly of certain skills and competences required in the central financial staff of the divisional enterprises (Armstrong 1984). This occupational strategy was available to accountants in the USA and, later, in Britain because the stock exchange system of industrial finance had already given accountants a role in the joint stock company (Johnson 1982). In Germany and Japan, where bank funding was more important, the legal requirements of company reporting differed and the role of professional accountants was far more limited. For this reason, accountants in Germany were not able to tie their own occupational interests to the establishment of divisional organization. Engineers, on the other hand, had achieved some success in establishing systems of technical control, and were able to buttress their position in management by instituting a form of professional training in which they could acquire the limited budgetary techniques required by German enterprises alongside their technical expertise as engineers (Lawrence 1980).

In the divisional form of organization the general office at headquarters was given the task of strategic planning, and accounting and budgetary principles were used to co-ordinate the operational units. The diversification of production within enterprises from a single product to a group of related products or to a collection of unrelated products meant that the operational units came to be structured as 'product divisions', each of which contained its own functional specialists and was responsible directly to the general office (Chandler 1976, pp. 27–8). Through the inter-war years this form of 'multi-divisional' organization rapidly became the typical form of administration in large American enterprises, and this led to the almost complete separation of strategy and operations in the big business sector. Corporate headquarters housed the top executives and their large advisory and financial staffs who were responsible for planning the long-term strategy of the enterprise as a whole and for co-ordinating, monitoring, and evaluating divisional performance. The dispersed operating divisions were responsible for production and distribution of a product line in a specific market, and had complete autonomy within the financial targets and limits set by head office. The concerns of the operational division were materials and labour management, with the senior operational managers co-ordinating materials and labour not in terms of physical quantities but in terms of the financial quantities which appeared in the budgets produced by head office.

Only in the period after the Second World War did the many British holding companies begin to restructure their management along divisional lines – and only then because of the competitive pressures imposed by the expansion of American enterprises in British markets. Table 40 presents the results of a study by Channon (1973) of the top 100 manufacturers of 1970 and their corporate structures in earlier decades. He discovered that just 12 per cent of these enterprises had adopted multi-divisional organization by 1950, and that even in 1960 less than one-third had made

Table 40 *Administrative structure in top 100 British, French, and German non-financial enterprises (1950–70)*

Administrative structure	Britain			France			Germany		
	1950	1960	1970	1950	1960	1970	1950	1960	1970
Holding company	28	40	20	20	18	12	15	14	12
Functional	52	22	8	50	32	14	36	21	20
Functional/holding	—	—	—	24	29	20	43	48	18
Multi-divisional	12	30	68	6	21	54	5	15	50
No information	8	8	4	0	0	0	1	1	0
Totals	100	100	100	100	100	100	100	100	100

Source: Calculated from Channon (1973), tables 3.3 and 3.4, pp. 72 and 74; Dyas and Thanheiser (1976), table 6.5 and figure 12.2, pp. 72 and 184.

this move. Only four of the twelve pioneers were fully British-owned – eight were foreign or bi-national, mainly American subsidiaries.[10] By 1970, largely because of American success and American management consultants, more than two-thirds of the top 100 were multi-divisional enterprises. Table 40 shows clearly the pattern of corporate development in Britain. In the first decade after the war many of the enterprises which had adopted a centralized functional administration moved over to a holding company organization, and in the second decade the large number of holding companies built their divisional structures. That is to say, the holding company form was retained by those enterprises that had adopted it before the war and was employed as a transitional form of decentralized administration by those that had not. In similar studies for France and Germany Dyas and Thanheiser (1976) introduced the category of 'functional/holding' organization to refer to the transitional form adopted in these countries, where the main pattern of corporate development was from functional to functional/holding to multi-divisional. It can be seen from Table 40 that the number of functional/holding enterprises in France in 1970 was high, reflecting the legacy of the French holding system which, as shown in Chapter 5, was tightened into the functional/holding combines of the 1950s and 1960s.

Though used for management control over labour, and increasingly for control over 'deskilled' clerical workers, technical control was not used to control members of the managerial hierarchy themselves. Under hierarchical control, superiors could closely supervise subordinates, but this was no longer possible in functionally specialized systems of management; and the 'technology' used by managers was too rudimentary to make technical control a feasible proposition. Alongside the system of technical control, therefore, emerged systems of *bureaucratic control*, often based on principles of 'formal organization' which management consultants such as Fayol and Urwick formulated to complement Taylorist ideas of job design. The work of operational managers was controlled by a system of authority based on impersonal rules: job titles, salary scales, promotion procedures, and career structures became ways of institutionalizing impersonal controls over the work of management (Edwards 1979, p. 85ff.). Although managers had a great deal of autonomy in their work situation, bureaucratic procedures, which were much strengthened in the development of divisional organization, ensured that operational managers were constrained to act in conformity with the requirements of the corporate strategy (Williamson 1970, ch. 7; see also Cutler *et al.* 1977, p. 277).

Thomas (1981) has shown how the idea of a managerial 'career' is a central element in such control. To the extent that managers share expectations concerning the legitimacy of their occupational advancement through the bureaucratic hierarchy and perceptions of the role of their superiors in securing this advancement for them, this subjectively meaningful concept of 'career' will be an important control over their actions. Both actual and anticipated advancement, through promotion or job transfer, reinforces their commitment to their current employer and their current position. Furthermore, the identity of 'management' as a distinct group within an enterprise is strengthened by the exclusion of other workers from these same prospects of advancement. The career structuring of work is a means of social differentiation within the workforce; but at the same time it fragments the management group itself, encouraging managers to seek individual solutions (promotion and job change) to their shared interests. The work situation autonomy of managers is a consequence of the absence of close surveillance and technical control, and is expressed in the 'high trust' characteristics of managerial work (Fox 1974).[11] Managers are 'high trust' workers, controlling 'low trust' clerical and manual workers but controlled themselves through the very concepts of career and discretion which differentiates them from those they control. Corporate careers depend upon effective contribution to the success of the enterprise, and managers tend to become subjectively committed to this through the 'selective and moulding effects of institutions on the personnel that operates them' (Baran and Sweezy 1966, p. 49).[12] Marxist and non-Marxist writers are agreed on the point that the corporate goals of size, strength, and growth through profits 'become the subjective aims of the business world because they are the objective requirements of the system' (ibid., p. 53; Parsons 1940).

The trends discussed in this chapter are reflected also in the evolution of the multinational enterprise. While overseas investment and overseas trading has a long history, multinational production is a fairly recent phenomenon. The multinational enterprise has been defined by Vernon as 'a cluster of corporations of different nationalities that are joined together through bonds of common ownership, that respond to a common strategy, and that draw on a common pool of human and financial resources' (Vernon 1971b, p. 694; 1971a, pp. 11–15). In an extension of the Chandler thesis, Vernon has claimed that geographical diversification is impelled by the same mechanisms as product diversification. Routinization of activity within a market after initial entry and innovation results in a weakening of the barriers to entry and a fall in profitability. In order to protect its chances of survival and prosperity, therefore, the large enterprise is impelled to seek new markets where competitors cannot match the scale and complexity of the technology required, and where, in consequence, the profits are higher (Vernon 1971a, pp. 26–7; 1977, ch. 5; Kurth 1975; Michalet 1976, p. 106ff.). Geographical expansion is an alternative to product diversification, and in this way enterprises progress from the local to the regional and national level and, eventually to the international level. Thus, the rise of the multinational enterprise is 'a change in degree, not kind, from the world of very large expansive enterprises still contained within national borders' (Heilbronner 1976, p. 73; Papandreou 1973, p. 109; Hymer 1972).

Multinational enterprises were generally organized as variants of the holding company until the 1960s and 1970s. In the case of American enterprises, the American and major overseas subsidiaries were internally structured as divisional organizations, but the international structure itself took the form of a holding company. American overseas subsidiaries, therefore, had a degree of autonomy from their parent companies and were often majority-controlled with share participations and board representation from the financial interests of the overseas country. European multi-nationals had an even looser structure, reflecting the predomi-nance of the holding company form in their national economies. As the European enterprises began to adopt multi-divisional or-ganization, so the European multinationals, from the 1970s, organized their foreign operations in a 'matrix' in which the product-division structure of the group as a whole was cross-cut by separate national subsidiaries which co-ordinated all group activi-ties within their particular country. Only since the middle of the 1970s has there been any significant move towards the creation of international product divisions co-ordinated by the head office (Francko 1976). Many American multinational enterprises, by contrast, adopted a thorough-going multi-divisional structure in the 1960s. Minority and majority shareholdings were increasingly transformed into wholly-owned subsidiaries, and lines of com-munication between overseas divisional executives and parent headquarters were strengthened. Divisional executives of American enterprises in Europe, for example, increasingly filled the board seats of the American subsidiaries, so tying them into a cohesive group which was isolated from or peripheral to the Euro-pean national networks of interlocking directorships (Fennema and Schijf 1985). Table 41 shows some of the consequences of these differences for ownership patterns of multinational subsidi-aries. In 1970 almost three-quarters of American foreign sub-sidiaries were wholly-owned, while this was true for only a half of European subsidiaries and one-third of Japanese subsidiaries. Japanese multinationals operated mainly through minority par-ticipations, reflecting the translation of the combine organization of aligned participations from the national to the international scale.

The emergence of a global strategy and an integrated interna-tional divisional organization has major implications for the flow of funds within the enterprise. Within the multinational enter-prise, non-market administrative controls can be used to by-pass market exchange on an even wider scale than in the purely national enterprise. The global strategy may involve the pursuit of profits for the enterprise as a whole, but not necessarily for each of its overseas subsidiaries. The power of the multinational enter-prise to override market pricing considerations in its own internal transactions means that foreign subsidiaries do not need to behave

Table 41 *Ownership status of foreign subsidiaries in industrial economies (1970)*

Ownership	180 US companies Number %		135 European companies Number %		61 Japanese companies Number %	
Wholly owned	2612	72.5	1788	55.8	6	13.0
Majority-owned	657	18.2	802	25.0	8	17.4
Minority-controlled	302	8.4	404	12.6	30	65.2
Unknown	32	0.9	213	6.6	2	4.4
Totals	3603	100.0	3207	100.0	46	100.0

Source: Calculated from Vernon (1977), p. 34, table 4.

Note: Subsidiaries in the Third World are not included. This distorts the picture for Japan, most of its subsidiaries being in Asia (see Weinstein 1976). Percentage figures for Japan are included for illustrative purposes only.

in the same way as locally-owned enterprises in the overseas markets in which they operate:

Although the multinational system as a whole must make a profit in order to survive, each of the affiliates in the system does not independently have to meet that test. Moreover, the price in any given transaction between a pair of affiliates need not be tested against competing offers in the open market [Vernon 1977, p. 128; Brooke and Remmers 1970, pp. 68–76].

The key to these activities at the international level is the practice of 'transfer pricing' through which the possibilities of discretionary pricing of internal transactions which are available to any multi-company enterprise are considerably enhanced by international variations in currency exchange rates and taxation rules. Transfer pricing permits the parent company to reinforce the net flow of funds from subsidiary to parent which is inherent in the multinational enterprise (Brooke and Remmers 1972, p. 30ff.; 1970, p. 172ff.; Hughes 1973, pp. 172–3; Holland 1976, p. 153; House 1977, p. 5). Transfer pricing, like any internal transaction, should not be seen as necessarily involving an attempt to reduce the profitability of foreign subsidiaries in order to enhance the profitability of the parent company. Indeed, it is often used to *reduce* its profitability.[13] The significance of transfer pricing has, in any case, often been overstated. The move towards multi-divisional organization has involved the creation of decentralized 'profit centres' which have considerable autonomy within the constraints of the headquarters' budgetary targets, and the fact that divisions are required by their parent to show a particular level of profit actually militates against any attempt to secure centralized transfer pricing (Hood and Young 1979, p. 122). The global strategy of the multi-national enterprise is a way of co-ordinating affairs through budgetary targets; it is inherent in the separation of strategy from operations that headquarters executives should not intervene in the pricing policies of the operating divisions.

The various forms of corporate administration can be seen to be related to variations in patterns of ownership and control between countries. Chandler (1962) saw the presumed change from private ownership to management control as the economic basis for the transition from the entrepreneurial firm to the centralized and multi-divisional enterprise. Changes in ownership produce changes in strategy which, in turn, produce changes in administrative structure. It has already been shown, however, that management control was a relatively short-lived phase in the history of companies undergoing a transition from family ownership to control through a constellation of interests, and that there is little evidence that management control ever had any real significance in Britain. It is in this light that Chandler's secondary explanation of the emergence of centralized administration becomes more important. He suggests that the merger activities of the big financiers of the 'Money Trust' were important in creating the large enterprises and promoting the creation of a managerial hierarchy. Although undeveloped, this argument is clearly compatible with that presented in the first part of this book. Centralized administration in the United States was largely the result of control by banking interests and was transformed into divisional administration as this control weakened and gave way to control through a constellation of interests. The separation of City and industry in Britain meant that banks did not achieve the same kind of control over industry as their American counterparts before the First World War – and family ownership persisted as an important element in big business for longer than was the case in the United States. The close relationship of City and industry which came about during the inter-war years was a response to the economic difficulties of leading enterprises in heavy industry and was not associated with any significant administrative restructuring as many of the holding companies survived into the post-war period. The growth of institutional shareholdings and of control through a constellation of interests was an important precondition for the transition from holding company to divisional organization in the 1950s and 1960s, when the inroads of American enterprises highlighted the inadequacies of British management organization. The post-war American penetration of the French economy was a stimulus to managerial restructuring in that country, but this involved the emergence of the hybrid 'functional/holding' organization and the overall predominance of the holding system was reinforced by the creation of the Paribas and Suez 'sets' of associated enterprises. The relative weakness of control through a constellation of interests in France and Japan is associated with the smaller proportion of enterprises with divisional organization and their long traditions of the holding system and aligned participations.

Managers, motives, and market forces

Entrepreneurial capitalists, finance capitalists, and internal capitalists 'are those who participate in the formulation of corporate strategy, and each is subject to a different set of constraints on their actions. Entrepreneurial capitalists are constrained by their personal interests in maintaining and enhancing their wealth; finance capitalists are constrained by their position as nominees of the controlling constellations; and internal capitalists are constrained by the structuring of their work through a managerial career hierarchy. But each of these sets of constraints is, to a certain extent, shared by all participants in strategic control. All those who hold an executive position, whether entrepreneurial shareholders or 'mere' salaried managers, are subject to the same organizational constraints on their actions, just as all those with even a nominal shareholding in the enterprise for which they work are interested in enhancing its value. Most important, the dominance of control through a constellation of interests and the rise of financial hegemony has ensured that all participants in strategic control must respond to the interests of the financial intermediaries. Corporate strategy is the outcome of the alliances and conflicts among the capitalists who make up the 'dominant coalition' (Child 1972) of each enterprise; but the actions of this coalition are shaped by the network of intercorporate relations in which the enterprise is embedded and, beyond this, by the actions of the state and other political agencies and by both organized and unorganized workers (Child 1969a, p. 14; Wood 1980, p. 59). Different groups within the dominant coalition may seek to realize conflicting corporate strategies, reflecting their conflicting interests, and so the dominant coalition will be beset by internal conflicts as well as by conflicts with outside interests which seek to influence it. Corporate strategy, therefore, is the result of a continual, though sometimes latent, struggle for control.

The focus of this struggle is the board of directors, and the composition of the board is an important indicator of the membership of the dominant coalition. Table 42 shows that those who sat on the boards of thirty-five large American non-financial enterprises in 1935 comprised three groups: executives made up just under a half, and financiers and large shareholders made up just under one-fifth each. Allowing for the fact that a number of the executives would also have been shareholders, some substantial, these data give a clear picture of the major forces involved in the struggle for control.[14] Of particular importance is the fact that financiers were the group most likely to hold two or more directorships and that the thirty-five boards had an average of 2.5 bankers

Table 42   *Board composition in thirty-five large US non-financial enterprises (1935)*

	Number of directors					
	Executives	Commercial bankers	Investment bankers	Large share-holders	Others	Total
25 large industrials	191	29	27	69	56	372
5 large utilities	22	14	4	11	25	76
5 large railways	13	8	7	19	31	78
Totals	226	51	38	99	112	526

Source: Gordon (1945), pp. 122–3.

Table 43 *Primary interests of directors of top 100 US industrial enterprises (1972)*

Primary interest	Number	%
Executive in top 100	633	44.0
Retired employee of top 100	80	5.6
Other	725	50.4
Totals	1438	100.0

Source: Herman (1981), table 2.5, p. 39.
Note: Herman does not give a useful breakdown of 'other' interests for present purposes.

Table 44 *Primary interests of multiple directors of top 250 British enterprises (1976)*

Primary interest	Number	%
Top 50 financials	97	34.4
Top 200 non-financials	112	39.7
Retired from top 50 financials	7	2.5
Retired from top 200 non-financials	17	6.0
Other financial	14	5.0
Other industrial	13	4.6
Other	22	7.8
Totals	282	100.0

Source: Scott and Griff (1985), table 12.5
Note: The enterprises analysed are those described in Tables 15, 18, 19, 22, and 23.

among their directors. Many of the 'other' directors were retired executives and bankers, a finding which still held true in 1972. Table 43 shows that the executives formed an almost identical proportion of the top 100 directorate as their counterparts had been in the large enterprises of 1935, though it may be assumed that fewer would have had substantial shareholdings in their company. Herman's breakdown of the 'other' category in Table 43 refers only to the number of directorships held and to the characteristics of companies, but he does add that a related study for

1972 discovered that there were three main groups in this category; bank and financial executives, executives of smaller non-financials, and lawyers (Herman 1981, p. 43). Barratt Brown (see Table 13) reported that the directorate of the top 120 British enterprises of 1966 was made up of about one-third entrepreneurial capitalists, one-third internal capitalists, and just under a half finance capitalists. Table 44 shows the primary interests of multiple directors ten years later. Multiple directors made up 10.5 per cent of the total directorate of the top 250 and the figures underestimate the proportions of internal and entrepreneurial capitalists in the total directorate, but some important findings emerge. Two-thirds of the multiple directors were executives in one of the top 250 enterprises, and a further 11 per cent had their primary business interest – as shareholder, member of the dominant family, or holder of an important internal role – in one of these enterprises. Financial executives contributed disproportionately to this group: financial enterprises contributed an average of 1.9 of their 'insiders' to other boards, while non-financials contributed an average of 0.6 insiders. A substantial number of the multiple directors had retired from an executive position in the top 250 or had their primary interest, as shareholder or executive, in smaller enterprises. The study concluded that finance capitalists frequently held executive posts, generally the position of chief executive or managing director,[15] and that they continued as active participants in corporate control after their retirement from executive positions (Scott and Griff 1985, p. 230). Stokman and Wasseur (1985, table 2.7) report that the proportion of executives in the directorate of the top 250 enterprises in various European countries varied from less than one in five in France and Belgium, to one in four in Italy to one in three in Austria, Germany, the Netherlands, and Switzerland. This finding is clearly related to variations in board systems and corporate structure. Those countries with a 'German' two-board system showed a high proportion of executives, while those countries which developed through the holding system had a low proportion of executives.

An important area of debate in studies of the business enterprise has been the impact of mode of control and the composition of the dominant coalition on economic performance. It has often been claimed that the increase in the number of salaried executives and of those subject to the constraints of bureaucratic control has altered the prevailing pattern of motives among business leaders and so has had an influence on the behaviour of large enterprises. Dahrendorf (1959, p. 46) has argued that 'Never has the imputation of a profit motive been further from the real motives of men than it is for the modern bureaucratic manager', and Shonfield (1965, p. 377) states that 'the manager, who is not the owner, is neither driven into automatic responses by the forces of the market place nor guided by the exclusive desire to make the maximum profit on behalf of his shareholders'. Changes in patterns of control are held to create the conditions under which management may exercise a certain amount of discretion and so may move away from an exclusive concern with profit. Monsen and Downs (1965), for example, argue that, while the shareholders of a company look for a steady dividend income and capital gains, managers seek to maximize their lifetime incomes.

In opposition to this position it has been argued that the motives and interests of business leaders are irrelevant in understanding corporate behaviour. Those who advocate a 'natural selection' model of the enterprise (Alchian 1950; Becker 1962) have argued that the uncertainty inherent in the market is such that no rules of decision-making can guarantee survival. Actions can be successful only if market conditions permit, and business leaders have imperfect knowledge of these conditions. Enterprises may employ any of a number of procedures and criteria in the calculations they make in pursuing their strategies, and rational procedures may turn out to be no more successful than any others. Instead, they argue that the market is to be conceptualized as a device which selects enterprises for survival according to their success in realizing profits. In order to survive an enterprise must earn sufficient profits to meet its current commitments, and in order to prosper it must do better than its competitors; but there is no way in which business leaders can evolve a corporate strategy which will ensure them either survival or prosperity. In the long run, surviving enterprises will be found to be those which have actually succeeded in maximizing their profits; but this is a consequence of market conditions and not of the perspicacity of business leaders. The 'long run', however, like the 'last instance', never arrives. Market conditions are constantly altering, and so the enterprises operating at any given time may not be maximizers (Winter 1967). An adequate understanding of corporate action must be based on the decision procedures actually employed by enterprises in the formulation and implementation of their strategies.

A particularly influential approach to this question draws on the work of Simon (1945), who argued that corporate decisions are the outcome of choices made within the constraints of the perceived environment of the enterprise. Business leaders are faced with imperfect knowledge of their environment and so evolve a more or less adequate definition of the situation on the basis of their perceptions of the consequences of past actions (Simon 1945, p. 67). The logic of the situation in which they find themselves suggests a range of alternative possible actions from which they have to choose a specific course of action to follow (Marris 1964, p. 47; Karpik 1972). Traditional economic theory assumed that enterprises would choose that course of action which would maximize their profits, but Simon argues that the uncertainty of outcomes which is inherent in imperfect knowledge means that no action can guarantee maximization. Business leaders can never be sure that they have chosen the optimal course of action; all they can do is seek out decision criteria that ensure them 'satisfactory' outcomes. The 'satisficing' behaviour of the large enterprise involves the search for those courses of action which will generate sufficient profits for them not to go out of business. From this standpoint it is possible to begin to examine the question of the links between control and performance, and there is surprising agreement between Marxist and non-Marxist writers on the general approach to be adopted. According to Baran and Sweezy, large enterprises are involved in a 'systematic temporal search for highest practicable profits' (1966, p. 37). In a given market situation, they argue, this level of profit is generally the greatest increase which will not ruin later opportunities. Short-term profit maximization would involve 'a reckless and wholly irrational pursuit of immediately realizable profit, regardless of any longer-term consideration' (Miliband 1968, p. 54), and Mandel has argued that the modern enterprise eschews such 'reckless' hedonism:

In conditions of monopolistic competition short-term maximization is a completely senseless goal. Company strategy aims at long-term profit maximization, in which factors such as domination of the market, share of the market, brand familiarity, future ability to meet demand, safeguarding of opportunities for innovation, i.e., for growth, become more important than the selling price which can be obtained immediately or the profit margin which this represents [Mandel 1972, p. 232; see also Blackburn 1965, p. 172; Baran and Sweezy 1966, p.51; Aaronovitch and Sawyer 1976, p. 42ff.; Westergaard and Resler 1975, p. 165].

This Marxist position finds its echoes in the writings of some leading managerialists:

The compelling constraint ... is that the firm's health, indeed its survival depend on the relation within it of revenues and costs. .... Pursuit of profit does not mean that management spends much of its time contemplating profit as such but that its time is spent on decisions regarding the planning, providing, pricing, and selling of products, which govern revenue, and the organizing, equipping, and carrying on of production, together with the purchase of labour, supplies, and other requirements, which govern costs. ... This is the essence of profit-seeking and of capitalist behaviour in employing resources [Peterson 1965, p. 9; Baumol 1962; Marris 1964, pp. 59, 107ff.].

The large enterprise, therefore, is a long-term profit seeker rather than a short-term profit maximizer, and attempts to evolve decision criteria that give it the most rational chance of achieving a relation of revenue to costs which is likely to give it the best chance of survival and prosperity in the market. The imperatives of the market are such that enterprises that are not profitable will not survive, and the dominant coalitions are constrained by these market forces in the formulation of corporate strategy. Business leaders must strive to pursue policies which will allow them to be profitable enough to earn a rate of profit which does not fall too far below the average. Enterprises that depart from these principles of long-term profitability will face problems of bankruptcy or decline. Far from undermining the pursuit of long-term profitability, the creation of hierarchies of professional managers subject to bureaucratic control can actually be seen as reinforcing it. Professional managers have the technical knowledge and information processing capacity to interpret market constraints more effectively than was the traditional capitalist entrepreneur. All the various techniques of modern business management and corporate planning serve to reduce the market uncertainty facing the large enterprise and enable it to more effectively pursue long-term profitability (Blackburn 1965, pp. 168–70; Baran and Sweezy 1966, pp. 40, 58; Mandel 1972, p. 233; Pahl and Winkler 1974, p. 118).

Clearly managerial motives cannot be ignored in the analysis of corporate behaviour, but their significance may be very different from that conventionally assumed. Although managers are constrained to pursue long-term profitability, a number of studies have produced evidence that their subjective commitment to this is not unambiguous. Nichols (1969) and Francis (1980b) both found evidence that managers expressed a belief in long-term financial goals, most frequently maximizing the growth of total profits and maximizing the rate of return on capital; but there was a tendency for these goals to be allied with the notions of 'social responsibility' and 'community service' which appear in non-sectionalist managerialist theory. These notions are reconciled through a belief in an underlying harmony of interests in the business enterprise. Fidler (1981, ch. 5) found that chief executives in large British enterprises espoused a 'balancing of interests ethos', seeing their occupational role as involving an attempt to balance the varying short-term interests of shareholders, workers, and customers with the long-term interest in profitability which they were all assumed to have in common. This system of beliefs, argues Fidler, is fundamental to what Fox (1973) has called the 'unitary' viewpoint of British management. Managers believe that, because of the underlying harmony of interests, there should be a unified hierarchy of authority, with managers having 'the right to manage' unchallenged by trades unions or other forms of worker resistance (Storey 1980, pp. 41-2; 1983, ch. 6). This unitary view is grounded in conceptions of the rights of property ownership – managers seeing themselves as the trustees of the mass of shareholders – and the requirements of economic efficiency, and it involves the belief that managers have to secure compliance from workers who lack the detailed information which would enable them to perceive the underlying harmony of interests. Industrial conflict is seen as due to poor communication between managers and workers, the action of union 'militants', or outside interference, and it is seen as soluble through good management. At the same time, most senior executives have little contact with employees other than other managers and their own secretaries (Winkler 1974). Industrial relations, that is to say, is regarded as an operational matter rather than as something that should figure directly in the corporate strategy. Personnel managers in the operating divisions must secure pay settlements which enable their division to meet the budgetary targets set by headquarters.[16]

The beliefs of managers must be seen as aspects of the legitimation of control. Although the operation of market forces leads managers to specify levels of effort and production which they attempt to secure through technical and bureaucratic control, they must also secure a degree of *consent* to the employment relationship.[17] Ideas of 'humanization', 'participation', and 'enrichment', no less than the espousal of 'social responsibility' are social meanings upon which managers draw to justify the acceptance of a system in which they perceive themselves and their subordinates as having little choice. The role of such vocabularies of motive (Mills 1940) is to legitimate both the corporate structure and the position of managers within it.

The strategy formulated by the dominant coalition is constrained by the operation of market forces, with the subjective motivation of managers having its major impact in the legitimation of the search for long-term profitability. Business leaders, nevertheless, have a degree of choice in the ways in which they meet this requirement – and, of course, they have absolute choice as to whether they observe the requirements at all; though failure to do so is likely to result in the collapse of their enterprise. The way in which this choice is exercised depends on the non-market controls to which an enterprise is subject, and it is here that a number of studies have sought to find a link between control and performance.

The members of the controlling group in an enterprise may have the power to make an enterprise act at a particular point in the range of possibilities open to it in its market situation. Executives may strive to benefit themselves through salaries, fees, share options, and pensions, dominant shareholders may attempt to increase the dividend payment on their shares or the capital value of their holdings, and bankers may attempt to increase the indebtedness of the enterprise and hence the interest which it must pay. The opportunities available to each of these groups is dependent on the mode of control of the enterprise, and it might be expected that control and measures of economic performance would be statistically associated. Although the size and rate of 'profit' earned by an enterprise are dependent on its accounting practices and may not, therefore, provide strictly comparable yardsticks, many investigations have attempted to relate strategic control to measures of profits. In some cases this has been allied with measures of performance such as capital appreciation and the dividend payout ratio. It has been claimed, for example, that enterprises with family or other personal majority owners will pursue a strategy of long-term growth and capital appreciation as a way of maintaining the value of the capital invested, while enterprises controlled by financial intermediaries will have to make high dividend payouts to meet the pension and insurance commitments of their major shareholders (Wilson Report 1977, p. 22; Pahl 1977a, p. 15). This leads to the conclusion that the transformation in ownership patterns from personal majority control to control through a constellation of interests results in more money coming out of the enterprise in the form of income and so limits the funds available for expansion.

Attempts to investigate such hypotheses empirically have generally proved inconclusive. Investigations carried out in the United States in the 1960s discovered a slight tendency for 'owner-controlled' enterprises to have a higher profitability and a better return on capital than those with no dominant ownership interest; though the main factors found to be associated with profitability were the size of the enterprise and obstacles to market competition (Kamerschen 1968; Monsen *et al.* 1968; Larner 1970; Palmer 1973). Later studies, too, have found little influence of control on profits.[18] An investigation of eighty-nine large British enterprises over the period 1957–67 also found that owner-controlled enterprises had higher profit and growth rates than those with no dominant ownership interest, but it was discovered that this reflected an inverse association between size and profitability; owner-controlled enterprises tended to be smaller, and smaller enterprises tended to be more profitable (Radice 1971, pp. 558–61; see also Steer and Cable 1978). Savage (1979), in a study of the long-term growth of French enterprises, found a complex pattern. His data suggest that enterprises in which the chief executive was not a major shareholder had a better growth record than those run by family heirs, and Savage interprets this in terms of corporate development profiles. Owner-controlled enterprises had a high growth rate under their founder and then stagnated under the heirs; enterprises with no dominant shareholder followed a more sustained growth pattern (Savage 1979, pp. 10–11).[19]

Managerial compensation has been investigated by some who have studied the influence of mode of control. McEachern (1975) has argued that managerial salaries and other rewards will vary with the existence of a dominant shareholder and the representation of this shareholder on the board. Dominant shareholders, he argued, would structure managerial incentives in such a way as to constrain managers to act in their interests. In a study of forty-eight industrials for 1969–72 he discovered that enterprises with a dominant shareholder had systems of management compensation which geared managers to profits and to the market value of shares, and he shows that this resulted in these enterprises showing a higher rate of return on capital (McEachern 1975, pp. 112–13). In a larger study of 218 industrials for 1975–6 Allen (1981) argued that the power of the chief executive was the important intervening variable between mode of control and managerial compensation, and he demonstrated that the level of compensation was inversely associated with mode of control. Allen argues that a chief executive's power is highest if he or she is the dominant shareholder; it is lowest if the chief executive has a negligible shareholding and is faced on the board by susbstantial shareholders. Even after allowing for size and performance, chief executives who were low in power were also low in compensation. But this relationship was not unilinear, as the most powerful chief executives were found to have the lowest rates of compensation. Allen suggests that this was a deliberate tactic of such executives to divert any criticisms that they were using their power for their own benefit, and he claims that they were, in any case, able to offset their low salary with their high dividend income.

Research on the relationship between control and performance has generally failed to produce unambiguous generalizations about sharp differences in corporate behaviour between 'owner-controlled' and other enterprises. Although this has led Herman (1981, p. 112) to conclude that mode of control has no impact on performance, Zeitlin and Norich (1979) confirmed the general impression of inconclusiveness when they examined the relationship between ownership and profitability in the top 300 American industrials of 1964. These writers compared the results from an investigation based on the definitions and methods of Palmer (1973) and one based on the definitions of Burch (1972), finding that neither method yielded any significant result.[20] Lawriwsky (1984) however, recognizes that certain unambiguous, though hardly startling, results do emerge from the various studies. 'Owner-controlled' enterprises are more profitable than those with no dominant ownership interest, but this has not generally been a statistically significant result.[21] There is similar weak evidence that 'owner-controlled' enterprises have faster growth rates, a lower dividend payout ratio, and more risky patterns of investment. In part the weakness of these results derives from the fact that any effect of control on performance is likely to be small. Profit seeking involves a surplus of revenue over costs and, since the surplus is always small in relation to revenue and costs, behaviour aimed at marginally altering the size of the surplus is unlikely to produce any significant variations between broad classes of enterprise (Peterson 1965; Lieberson and O'Connor 1972). In fact, it can be argued that these weak results are also a consequence of poor theorization and inadequate methods. Improvements in these respects might be expected to yield less ambiguous results.

Two sets of problems have beset previous studies. At the methodological level, the definitions of 'control' employed have generally been inadequate. Typically a contrast is drawn between 'owner control' and 'management control', with the division between the two being based on arbitrary and variable percentage shareholdings. Even the more sophisticated classifications, such as those of Larner (1970) and Palmer (1973) have tended to ignore the difference between control by personal owners and control by corporate owners, and have ignored the importance of share-ownership by financial intermediaries (Reeder 1975). Thus, McEachern (1975) defined a dominant shareholder as any holder of 4 per cent or more of the shares; a definition which includes not only cases of majority and minority control, by both corporations and persons, but also many cases of control through a constellation of interests. Similarly, Allen (1981) defined a substantial shareholder as one with 5 per cent or more – and his ignoring of control through a constellation of interests is particularly unsatisfactory in the light of his finding that the relationship between compensation and power still held if the shareholding level was reduced to 1 per cent. The second set of problems are theoretical and concern an inadequate understanding of the mechanisms through which mode of control may have a causal effect on corporate performance. Lawriwsky (1984) argues that the causal complexity is such that there should be no straightforward correlation between mode of control and performance. Economic performance is affected by internal organization, and by the product and capital market situation of an enterprise, and its mode of control comprises the non-market context within which these other mechanisms operate. An adequate understanding of the interdependence of these mechanisms has to take account of the interest which corporate controllers, whether families, managers, or financial intermediaries, have in maintaining their control. Although managerialism, following classical economics, assumed that enterprises controlled by personal owners will seek high profits, Lawriwsky argues that owners may perceive the need for a trade-off between higher profits and retaining control; a strategy of growth aimed at securing the highest profits involves the risk that expansion will dilute the controlling shareholding to the point at which it becomes too small to ensure continued control (Lawriwsky 1984, pp. 27–30; Reder 1947; see also Pitelis and Sugden 1983). The influence of personal ownership on economic performance will, therefore, vary from case to case. Similarly, an enterprise with no dominant shareholding interest is constrained in its strategy by an interest in avoiding a takeover bid, and may choose a strategy of growth in order to forestall such bids – but it may depart from growth if the dominant coalition feel that the chance of a possible takeover is slim. The performance of the enterprise varies with the state of these non-market controls.[22] Although the influence of control on performance is variable, it varies within certain limits. Each mode of control comprises a different mixture of the mechanisms governing managerial incentives and constraints, and so will be associated with a *range* of performance values. To illustrate this argument, Lawriwsky investigated large Australian enterprises, classifying them into three categories: private ownership control, company control, and dispersed ownership. Enterprises subject to majority or minority control by private individuals showed a growth rate which was strongly and negatively associated with the size of the controlling holding: the larger the size of the shareholding, the lower the growth rate. These same enterprises also showed a lower profitability and a higher retention rate, and Lawriwsky interprets these findings as demonstrating a striving to maintain control (1984, p. 116). In enterprises where the controlling block was held by another enterprise there was no specific relationship to performance, and Lawriwsky argues that this was because the performance of subsidiaries and associates depends upon the circumstances of the parent (ibid., p. 126). Finally, enterprises with dispersed ownership – control through a constellation of interests – showed a number of patterns, varying according to the presence of family influence or institutional dominance. In enterprises where a family participated in the controlling constellation and was represented on the board there was higher profitability and higher retention, though such enterprises were invariably smaller. In enterprises where financial intermediaries collectively held a high proportion of the shares there were higher growth rates as their controllers sought to avoid takeover (ibid., pp. 133–5).

Lawriwsky's study, therefore, came up with strong and un-ambiguous findings and, while it is possible to question some of his interpretations, he has certainly established his case. Mode of control, understood as a set of non-market controls, does have an impact on corporate performance, but its causal impact is mediated through other factors, is exercised alongside other mechanisms, and must be understood as setting limits for eco-nomic performance rather than determining a specific corporate strategy. It may be concluded that research based on the concepts employed in the earlier part of this book would yield reliable – though as yet unpredictable – results.

The results of such an analysis might be expected to show that the effect of mode of control on performance is mediated through the composition of the dominant coalition. The mode of control of an enterprise is a determinant of the limits and opportunities available to the participants in business leadership in their struggle for control over corporate strategy. It is to be expected, therefore, that economic performance will also be associated with the balance of power and interests in the dominant coalition and the resources of capital and intelligence which its members are able to mobilize on behalf of the enterprise. The availability of these resources is determined by the structure of the capital, commer-cial, and personal relations in which the enterprise is entwined; by the network of intercorporate relations which constitute the enter-prise's environment of action. 'Mode of control' as conventionally defined grasps one aspect of this network; it grasps that aspect of the capital relations which is dependent on the ownership of share capital, the possession of the associated voting rights, and the opportunities which these present for making further capital avail-able. The network of personal relations between enterprises is, primarily, a set of connections created by the presence of people on the boards of directors of two or more large enterprises, and has been studied through investigations of interlocking director-ships.[23] There has been far less research on the impact of inter-locks on economic performance, but the results have generally been conclusive. Burt (1980) for the United States and Ziegler (1982) for Austria and Germany have shown that interlocking within product markets occurs as an attempt to reduce uncertainty and enhance profit seeking, though there was little evidence that such strategies of horizontal co-optation were successful. On the other hand, both Pennings (1980) and Carrington (1981) have shown that profitability is positively associated with bank interlocks in both the United States and Canada. Meeusen and Cuyvers (1985) confirmed this in their study of interlocks in the top 250 Belgian and Dutch enterprises of 1976. They discovered that the profitability of non-financials was significantly associated with the number of bank interlocks which they had, but that this relationship did not hold for interlocks with the Belgian holding companies. Enterprises interlocked with the holding companies performed less well than others, suggesting that the holding companies did indeed use non-market controls to enhance their own profitability and depress the performance of their associates. The argument which Fitch (1972) put forward about bank interlocking and bank power held not for the banks but for the Belgian holding companies.

The invisible hand of finance capital – the intercorporate network of capital, commercial, and personal relations – structures the interplay of finance capitalists, entrepreneurial capitalists, and internal capitalists and constitutes a nexus of market and non-market controls which structure patterns of corporate administration and performance. The organization of the management hierarchy, with its systems of careers and compensation, the forms of control over the labour process, and financial parameters such as rates of growth and profitability are all conditioned by the nature of the corporate strategies formulated by the dominant coalitions which have control of the large business enterprises. The composition of the dominant coalitions, and hence the balance of power and interests which determine corporate strategy, are a reflection of the changes which have altered the intercorporate networks of the major capitalist economies, of which the transformation of ownership and control is one major element. The varying patterns of capitalist development which have been identified in the capitalist world are the major sources of variation in patterns of corporate structure and operational management.

Notes

1   An extract from the report was reprinted in the first edition of Bendix and Lipset's textbook *Class, Status and Power* (Bendix and Lipset 1953), but was deleted from the second, and more widely-cited edition (Bendix and Lipset 1967).

2 This summary is drawn from Chandler (1962; 1976; 1977).

3 The concept of 'holding company' used by Chandler refers neither to the Franco-Belgian holding system described in Chapter 5 nor to the mere 'parent' company, though it is related to both. As will be apparent from the discussion, it refers to a specific form of federal management. For a definition and justification of this usage see Simons (1927).

4 Holding companies *per se* were made illegal, but the same organizational structure exists where an operating company is effective parent or there is a central Presidents' Club.

5 Edwards (1979, ch. 2) terms it 'simple control'.

6 As Dore (1973) remarks, there was no straightforward survival of traditional 'feudal' ideas. Paternalism as a form of workforce control was a conscious creation from various cultural elements and was legitimated by its appearance as 'traditional'. On the general 'creation of tradition' in Japan in the Meiji period see R. J. Smith (1983).

7 Woodward (1965) calls this 'mechanical control'.

8 For a brilliant and rigorous sociological analysis of such ideas see Baldamus (1961).

9 On scientific management and technical control in Germany see Kocka (1978), p. 574ff., and Homburg (1983).

10 These four were Smiths Industries, Spillers, British-American Tobacco, and ICI. Unilever was treated as part foreign.

11 Friedmann (1977) describes this as 'responsible autonomy'. Trends in management thought are discussed in Child (1969b). For a study of ambivalence in career commitment of British managers see Pahl and Pahl (1971).

12 For more general statements of this thesis see Bourdieu (1974) and Gerth and Mills (1954), p. 165ff.

13 On the use of international base companies and tax havens such as Switzerland, Liechtenstein, Panama, the Bahamas, and the Netherlands Antilles, see Brooke and Remmers (1970), p. 206ff. and Raw *et al.* (1971). Detailed accounts of particular multinational enterprises can be found in Sampson (1973; 1975) and Cronjé *et al.* (1976).

14 Evidence on directors' shareholdings can be found in Chapter 8.

15 The American equivalent is 'President'.

16 This argument draws on various contributions to discussions

made by Howard Gospel, Bryn Jones, and others at the British Sociological Association Annual Conference at Bradford in April 1984, though no individual should be held responsible for my claims. A number of contributors to these discussions suggested that the salience of industrial relations at the operational level was related to the economic cycle. The economic recession of the 1970s and 1980s weakened worker bargaining power and made it possible to resolve pay deals through the fear of unemployment. For this reason personnel management became less important as a specialist skill and personnel managers lost power at the operational level to engineers and other line managers.

17 Littler and Salaman (1984) call this the 'dual nature' of the capital–labour relation. See also Littler (1982).

18 See Stano (1976) and Kania and McKean (1976). The latter are criticized in McEachern (1978) and reply in Kania and McKean (1978).

19 Additional studies are Jacquemin and Gellinck (1980) on France and Thonet and Poensgen (1979) on Germany.

20 They did discover a significant relationship between 'rate of exploitation' (measured by census of production figures showing 'man-hour' equivalents of value added, wages, etc.) and rate of return on capital.

21 It could be argued that tests of significance are not the appropriate measure where the study involves no sampling and the assumption of normally distributed measures is unlikely.

22 Some economists term this the 'market for corporate control'. See the debate on these points between Holl (1977; 1980) and Lawriwsky (1980).

23 Personal relations between enterprises are also created by bonds of kinship, friendship, and political association between directors.

7 Concentration, internationalization, and intervention

The development of industrial capitalism has involved a massive expansion in the scale of economic activity. Through internal growth and through amalgamation large business enterprises have concentrated ever larger portions of national output and employment in their hands. For the theory of industrial society this is an inevitable consequence of the technical 'logic of industrialism', and the growing power of the large enterprises is rendered benign by the countervailing power of worker and consumer groups (Galbraith 1952; Kerr *et al.* 1960). For the theory of capitalist society, on the other hand, the monopolization of production through cartels, trusts, and other business associations only serves to reinforce the power held by those at the head of the large enterprises. The theory of capitalist society also relates national monopolization to a process of internationalization: as capitalist interests seek to overcome declining domestic profitability by investing overseas, so competition is displaced from the national to the international level. The struggle between rival imperialist powers replaces the struggle between competing national enterprises. In this struggle private businesses become more closely allied with nation states, as centralized state power intervenes to buttress the concentrated economic power of the monopolies (Lenin 1917a; Ryndina and Chernikov 1974, p. 198). This vision of an increasingly centralized state dominated by private capital is rejected by the theory of industrial society in favour of an image of 'pluralistic democracy': all power generates countervailing power, and the state becomes simply an arena for the interplay of power relations. Government policy is the outcome of negotiations and comprises among a plurality of more or less equal pressure groups.

The ideas debated in these theories have generated considerable dispute in recent discussions. The international operations of business enterprises have raised the question of whether an enterprise operating in many countries and pursuing a global strategy is able to disregard both its own national base and the frontiers of the national economies in which it operates. Such a situation would have important implications for national patterns of economic development, as economies would reflect the movement of international capital rather than the policies of national governments. If, on the other hand, nation states have the power to counter the actions of multinational enterprises, then the national economy might be subject to increased levels of state intervention and the international economy would reflect the rivalries of sovereign states. In order to try and resolve these questions it is first necessary to outline the extent to which economic power has become concentrated.

Concentration in the national economy

The main focus for studies of economic concentration, as for studies of ownership and control, has been the national economy. This is the level of economic activity at which 'certain crucial parameters and conditions' of the operation of capitalist relations of production are determined (Cutler *et al.* 1978, p. 244). These conditions include the framework of property and company law, taxation, regulation of the supply of money and credit, and regulation of the supply of labour through rules of nationality, immigration, population, and hours and conditions of work. The central determinant of these conditions is the state, and so national economies tend to coincide with effective state territorial power. Within such territories there occur varying degrees of differentiation of industry into sectors and markets, disparate levels of dependence on foreign trade, diverse relations between banking and industry, and so on. It is the mix of such variations within a particular territory which constitutes the specificity of such national economies as Britain, Germany, and Japan. Enterprise behaviour is constrained not by the 'capitalist mode of production', conceived as some general and ahistoric structure, but by the structures of specific national economies.

Both managerialists and Marxists have seen the degree of concentration in a national economy – the transfer of a large proportion of economic activity to a small number of enterprises – as an important condition of corporate behaviour. Early theorists of 'imperfect' and 'monopolistic' competition (Robinson 1933; Chamberlin 1933) attempted to formulate alternative market models to that of atomistic, 'perfect' competition, but not until the rise of managerialist theory did any viable alternative to neo-classical economics emerge. The model of market oligopoly was premised upon the enhanced market power possessed by large enterprises, and this power was assumed to result from the separation of ownership from control. Although the assumptions of managerialist theory have been questioned in this book, it has been argued that sectional managerialism has correctly recognized some of the ways in which the market behaviour of large enterprises has been modified. The enterprise is a long-term profit seeker operating under market constraints, but its scope for choice within these constraints is much greater than was the case for the classical entrepreneurial firm. Under conditions of market concentration the enterprise becomes a 'price maker' rather than simply a 'price taker'. The uncertainty and 'anarchy' of the market mechanism can be reduced through the enhanced information upon which large enterprises can draw and through tacit or overt co-operation between enterprises. Price-setting can, therefore, be made a more rational feature of corporate behaviour. Marxist writers such as Baran and Sweezy have suggested that the growth of intercorporate alliances permits enterprises to co-operate on a monopoly pricing policy and then to compete vigorously in non-price areas, such as advertising, so as to determine the distribution of the monopoly profits among themselves (Baran and Sweezy 1966, p. 68; see also Baran 1957, p. 196ff.; Holland 1975, p. 56; Giddens 1973, pp. 143, 161).

The level of concentration within markets and within overall national economies varies considerably from one country to another, and so, in consequence, does the power of large enterprises. There is, however, little agreement as to how it should be measured and, therefore, little consensus on the precise facts of concentration. Concentration results from the formation of a small number of large enterprises in each market or sector, and also from the formation of capital, commercial, and personal relations among large enterprises.[1] Although economists have often recognized the importance of 'rings', 'trusts', and 'cartels' in linking independent enterprises, they have rarely studied these alongside interlocking directorships as components of economic concentration. It should be clear, however, that a national economy in which large enterprises are connected through a dense network of intercorporate relations has a higher level of concentration than a similar economy with a less dense network. These two aspects of concentration – through the formation of a small number of units and through the formation of a dense network – are interdependent, yet they need not move in the same direction. Under some circumstances both may be increasing and reinforcing one another, but at other times they may show different trends. In the discussion that follows, both aspects of concentration will be analysed.

Monopolization through the concentration of economic activity in a small number of large enterprises increased steadily in Britain from the 1870s until the Second World War, with a particularly rapid increase taking place in the merger boom of 1919–20. The amalgamation of family enterprises into large units prior to the First World War was associated with the creation of defensive cartels and trusts aimed at controlling sales and output, but this resulted in a considerable concentration of economic activity (Pollard 1962). Table 45 shows that the 100 largest manufacturers of 1909 accounted for 15 per cent of total output and that by 1930 this share had risen to 26 per cent. Over this same period, as shown in Chapter 4, the density and intensity of interlocking directorships among the top manufacturers was also increasing: by the 1930s a large proportion of national output was accounted for by large enterprises which were themselves closely connected through a network of capital, commercial, and personal relations. Hannah (1976c) claims that the modern corporate economy had been established in the heartlands of the British economy by 1914, and a contemporary observer remarked that

While . . . a greater part of our industrial system still continues to be competitive, the area of the power of capitalist combination is growing and the effective protection furnished by competition to the consumer is diminishing [Hobson 1906, p. 215].

Table 45 *Share of the top 100 British manufacturers in net output (1909–68)*

	1909	1919	1930	1939	1948	1958	1968
% of output	15	17	26	23	21	33	42

Source: Hannah (1976c), table A.2, p. 216.

Economic concentration had created a big business sector in which competition was overlain with a network of combinations and alliances, and this sector was sharply divided from the small- and medium-sized businesses which still operated under conditions of atomistic competition. The enterprises of the big business sector prior to the First World War came disproportionately from textiles and brewing, though non-manufacturers operating on a national scale included the railways and banking. By the Second World War 'big business' was a more diverse, and more powerful, sector of activity, and it was increasingly determining the conditions under which smaller enterprises had to operate. From the late 1930s until the late 1940s the level of concentration fell back slightly, but through the 1950s and 1960s it once again increased as American inroads stimulated defensive mergers and takeovers. By 1968 the top 100 manufacturers accounted for 42 per cent of output and 65 per cent of corporate assets (Meeks and Whittington 1975; 1976; Prais 1976; Jewkes 1977). This burst of merger and takeover activity was not, however, associated with any increase in the density of interlocking directorships; on the contrary, the level of interlocking declined consistently over the post-war period.

The large enterprises created before the Second World War were formed mainly as holding companies exercising only a loose control over their autonomous subsidiaries, while the merger boom of the 1960s was associated with the adoption of divisional organization. But neither form of big business has been associated with any substantial reorganization of plant-level production. The top 100 manufacturers of 1904 had an average of six plants each, those of 1958 had an average of twenty-seven plants, and those of 1972 had an average of seventy-two plants. Although concentration of economic activity in a small number of enterprises was greater than in any other country in the world by 1972, the proportion of the labour force employed in large plants had remained constant since the inter-war years. Most British workers in private employment worked in large *enterprises*, but they did not necessarily work in large *plants* (Utton 1982, p. 22).

Merger activity in the United States led to increased concentration during the period 1890–1904, producing a level of concentration higher than that found in Britain in this period. This was reinforced by the large number of interlocking directorships created by the 'Money Trust' of investment bankers which had been responsible for many of the largest amalgamations. The level

Table 46 *Share of the top 100 US non-financial enterprises in net assets (1909–75)*

	1909	1929	1933	1975
% of assets	33	49	57	35

Source: Herman (1981), table 6.2, p. 191.

of concentration continued to increase until the early 1930s, by which time the levels of concentration in Britain and the USA were broadly comparable,[2] but the inter-war years saw a fall in the level of interlocking as the power of the investment bankers declined. In the latter part of the inter-war years the share of the top 100 in total assets declined also, and not until the post-war period did concentration begin to level-off. Table 46 shows that the figure for 1975 was below that achieved fifty years before. Figures on the proportion of total value produced by the top 200 manufacturers suggest that the fall in the level of concentration may have been less than Herman's data suggest, with the figure for the mid 1960s being somewhat higher than that for 1929 (Means 1964, p. 15; Chandler 1969, p.278). Nevertheless, the American economy did not experience the massive increase in concentration found in Britain during the 1960s. Directly comparable data show that the top 100 manufacturers in the United States accounted for 33 per cent of output, while those in Britain accounted for 42 per cent in 1968 (Jewkes 1977, p. 15).

It can be seen from Table 47 that concentration in the United States was associated with a considerable diversification of manufacturing activity. The number of large manufacturers operating in only one or two industries declined considerably from 1909 to 1935 and again during the 1950s. Conversely the number operating in ten or more industries increased slowly until 1929, after which time it increased substantially. By 1960 most large American enterprises operated in five or more industries. Chandler has argued that this reflects the growth strategies of large enterprises. A small number of key industries that were science-based and where size and vertical integration gave advantages were the first to become highly concentrated. And from these industries – such as electrical and transport engineering, primary metals, oil, and chemicals –

Table 47   *Diversification in the top 100 US non-financial enterprises (1909–60)*

Number of industries operated in	Number of enterprises					
	1909	*1919*	*1929*	*1935*	*1948*	*1960*
10 or more	3	4	7	16	24	33
3–9	29	43	43	50	43	45
2	20	8	9	4	4	8
1	29	33	23	12	12	4
Missing information ⎫ Non-manufacturers ⎭	19	12	18	18	17	10
Totals	100	100	100	100	100	100

Source: Calculated from Chandler (1969), table 2, pp. 290–8.

Note: The original lists related to the top 100 non-financials, but Chandler gives information only on those involved in manufacturing industry.

the giants enterprises diversified into other industries at the same time as they adopted the divisional form of organization. Because large enterprises had subsidiaries in many markets, overall concentration of aggregate economic activity was associated with increased concentration at the level of particular markets (Chandler 1969, p. 257).

It has been suggested, however, that company mergers in the post-war period have not resulted in increased plant size: acquired plants tend to be run as parallel operations rather than being integrated into a restructured production process (Thompson 1978, p. 12). Nevertheless, average plant size in the United States is considerably higher than in many European countries. The proportion of the labour force employed in establishments of more than 1000 people varied from high levels of 28 to 30 per cent in the USA, West Germany and Holland, to low levels of 13 to 17 per cent in Italy, France, and Japan (Morvan 1972, p. 221). Of all European countries, only Germany shows any significant association between economic concentration and technical reorganization (George and Ward 1975, pp. 44; Daems and Van der Wee 1974).

The concentration of economic activity in a small number of large enterprises is far less marked in Japan than in Britain, the top

Table 48 *Control over top Japanese enterprises by the big six combines (1979)*

Combine	Number of enterprises controlled Top 200 non-financials	Top 50 financials	Totals
Mitsubishi	19	5	24
Mitsui	15	4	19
Sumitomo	14	4	18
DKB	16	2	18
Fuyo	13	5	18
Sanwa	14	6	20
Totals	91	26	117

Source: Calculated from Dodwell (1980).

Note: Only strong group affiliations are included, and one joint venture of Mitsui and Sumitomo was not counted.

Table 49 *Share of the big six combines in Japanese industry, banking, and insurance (1974)*

Combine	% of industrial turnover	% of bank lending	% of insurance premium income
Mitsubishi	13.2	8.5	8.3
Mitsui	10.0	6.0	6.0
Sumitomo	10.1	7.9	11.0
DKB	9.1	6.0	7.8
Fuyo	8.5	7.0	—
Sanwa	8.5	6.4	20.8
Totals	59.4	41.8	53.9

Source: Stokes (n.d.), pp. 76, 77. The original source was Dodwell (1975).

Note: No insurance figures were given for Fuyo, and so it must be presumed to be unimportant in this sector.

100 manufacturers of 1967–8 accounting for 29.2 per cent of total sales (Caves and Uekusa 1976, p.18). This comparison does not, however, take account of the great significance of the capital, commercial, and personal relations which tie these enterprises

together. The pattern of aligned participations which produced the combine structure of the Japanese economy brought about a level of overall concentration higher than that in Britain. The big six *kigyoshudan* in 1981 accounted for 5 per cent of business employment and held 26 per cent of business assets (Okumura 1983, p. 14). Table 48 shows that this high concentration resulted from the control exercised by the largest enterprises. Almost a half of the top 250 Japanese enterprises were under the control of the big six groups, and many more were subject to their influence. Table 49 shows that these groups were thereby able to control over a half of industrial turnover and insurance income, and that they were responsible for over 40 per cent of all bank lending. Diversification in Japan has led to a massive fusion of capital in manufacturing, mining, banking, and insurance, and so has created giant units of finance capital which control the major parts of the Japanese economy. Table 50 shows that this is no recent phenomenon, but it also shows that concentration is particularly marked in heavy industry and in chemicals. The proportion of capital controlled by the big four *zaibatsu*[3] and their descendants increased substantially between 1937 and 1966. The massive increase which took place during the 1940s was abruptly ended by the post-war *zaibatsu* dissolution, but the level of concentration soon began to increase once more.

Table 50   *Share of the big four combines in Japanese capital (1937–66)*

Industrial sector	% of capital by big four combines in					
	1937	*1941*	*1946*	*1955*	*1960*	*1966*
Heavy and chemical industries	12.1	16.5	33.3	18.4	23.8	25.4
Other primary and secondary industries	11.6	13.7	17.8	15.4	13.5	19.2
Finance, distribution and communications	9.2	8.2	17.3	6.7	8.9	12.0

Source: Miyazaki (1973), table 10, pp. 326–9.

The internationalization of capital

Variations in the level of concentration at the level of the national economy generate a pattern of concentration at the international level. The largest national enterprises, operating on an international scale, constitute the central agents in the world economic system, and their actions constrain the possibilities open within any one national economy. In 1972 there were ninety manufacturing enterprises in the western world with 40,000 or more employees.[4] Britain and the United States dominated this group, with thirty and nineteen enterprises respectively, and France and Germany (with twelve enterprises each) occupied the middle ranks (Prais 1976, pp. 221–3). The predominance of Britain, France and Germany among European enterprises was confirmed in a study of 1981. British enterprises made up 44 per cent of the top 100 European enterprises in this year, Germany accounted for 22 per cent, and France for 12 per cent. Among other countries, only Switzerland and Sweden had five or more enterprises in the top 100 (*Financial Times* 1982; see also George and Ward 1975, p. 55; Jacquemin and de Jong 1977, p. 98). In world banking the dominance of Britain and the United States was less marked: although the United States provided the two largest banks in the world, the twenty largest banks of 1981 included six from Japan and four from France. Britain and the United States supplied three each and Germany provided two[5] (*Financial Times* 1982).

Table 51 *Strategic control in the world's 487 largest non-financial enterprises (1978)*

Mode of control	Type of controller						
	Family	Corporate	Bank	State	Foreign	None	Totals
Majority control	25	9	1	38	26	—	99
Minority control	72	33	124	9	16	—	254
No dominant interest	—	—	—	—	—	134	134
Totals	97	42	125	47	42	134	487

Source: Grou (1983), p. 45.

Note: Because some bi-national and other enterprises appeared on two or more of the lists consulted by Grou, the total number of independent enterprises was reduced from 500 to 487. The cut-off point for minority control was 5 per cent.

The patterns of ownership and control in the world's largest enterprises naturally reflect the predominance of American enterprises. In a selection of the 487 largest enterprises in the world there were 237 from the United States, and the figures in Table 51 show that this significantly influenced the degree of dispersed ownership found in the world's biggest businesses. Control through a constellation of interests prevailed in those with no dominant interest and in many of those in which the minority holding was less than 10 per cent. Grou (1983) shows that the percentage of shares held, though not the number of enterprises controlled, by financial intermediaries increased substantially between 1965 and 1978, largely at the expense of family enterprise. The proportion of large enterprises subject to family control declined from 39 to 20 per cent, and both state and foreign ownership contributed to this decline: between 1965 and 1978 state control increased from 4 to 10 per cent, and foreign control increased from 3 to 9 per cent. Thus, the enterprises that dominated the world economy comprised four groups: a dominant group of multinationals controlled through constellations of interests and owning subsidiaries in a number of countries; a large group of family enterprises; a significant number of British, French, and German state-controlled enterprises; and a group of French, Belgian, and Japanese enterprises controlled through aligned participations. These enterprises have achieved powerful positions within their own national economies, and their power has been strengthened by the growth of international intercorporate relations among them. Commercial relations of international trade, capital relations of foreign ownership, and personal relations of interlocking directorships have tied the world's largest enterprises into a web of international connections.

The modern world system has not always been dominated by large enterprises; this is a consequence of the concentration of economic activity within each national economy. Some of the earliest forms of European capitalist enterprise – such as the British East Africa Company and the Hudson's Bay Company – were indeed giant international traders, but international investment was relatively limited until the early nineteenth century. The City of London had an important role in funding international trade and in government finance, but became involved in foreign investment only from the 1830s. By 1855 the volume of British overseas investment was £230m, but declining domestic investment

opportunities after the 1870s led to a massive export of capital
and resulted in this figure rising to £4000m by 1914 (Cottrell 1975;
Cairncross 1953; Kennedy 1976). The main destinations for this
investment were the railways, mines, and ranches of the United
States, Canada, Australia, and Argentina. Before the First World
War the bulk of overseas investment was 'portfolio investment' –
ownership of foreign shares and bonds by British residents and
British investment companies. American overseas investment,
however, was 'direct' investment in overseas manufacturing by
American manufacturers. Direct American investment grew considerably after the First World War and spread into Canada, many
parts of Europe, and South America (see Table 52). From the
1930s direct investment replaced portfolio investment as the major
form of international capital relations, its growth corresponding to
the transformations of strategy and structures described in Chapter 6. It can be seen from Table 52 that a marked change occurred
in the direction of American foreign investment during the 1960s.
A fairly constant one-third of all American investment has gone to
Canada, but there has been a substantial shift from Latin America
to Europe. Multinational enterprises do not go where resources
are cheapest, regardless of national boundaries. They invest in or
near their main markets, and so the most favoured sites for
American investment are other advanced industrial economies
(Magdoff 1970; Williams *et al.* 1983, pp. 30–1). By the early 1970s,
US investment in Canada took $21,075m from a total of $67,702m.
Within Europe, Britain received $7158m and West Germany
$4252m. Furthermore, the rate of increase of US investment in
Europe was twice that in Canada (Vernon 1971a, p. 19; Hughes
1973, p. 161). Figures for British foreign investment in the 1960s
show that the total was equivalent to just under 10 per cent of net
domestic investment and that the total foreign assets of British
companies (£6000m) was divided equally between the developed
and the 'underdeveloped' nations, although investment in Europe
was growing more rapidly. Increasingly, foreign direct investment
has become an interchange of capital relations among the advanced capitalist economies, and it has been estimated that about
a half of all their capital exports are to one another (Barratt
Brown 1974; Dunning 1970, pp. 49–50; Hood and Young 1979,
pp. 10–11).

Nowhere is this trend clearer than in Japan. The self-imposed
economic isolation of Japan was broken by the post-war American

Table 52   *US direct foreign investment (1929–68)*

Area	% of total investment stake in			
	1929	*1949*	*1959*	*1968*
Europe	19	14	16	30
Canada	25	31	33	33
Latin America	33	39	35	17
Other	23	15	16	20
Totals	100	100	100	100

Source: Adapted from Barratt Brown (1974), pp. 208–9, table 20.

occupation, though there was very little inward or outward foreign investment until the 1960s. While British overseas investment represented 20 per cent of GNP in 1969, the corresponding figure for Japan was only 1.6 per cent (Halliday and McCormack 1973, p. 33). Most Japanese investment at this time was in South East Asia and the Middle East, the involvement in Asia being encouraged by the United States' withdrawal from this area because of its entanglement in the Vietnam War. The main countries which have received Japanese investment have been Indonesia, Hong Kong, Taiwan, and, above all, South Korea, though Britain's entry into the EEC forced Australia to move into closer contact with Japan. From the 1970s Japan has increased its investments in Europe, at the same time as European and American enterprises began to invest in Japan. In 1970, eighty-three of the top 200 American industrials had Japanese operations; and they were especially important in the electrical, oil, and chemical industries, where IBM and Standard Oil were major forces in Japanese markets (Halliday and McCormack 1973, pp. 5–6). Even though American investment has benefited from Japan's role as an American military base in the Far East, it has not had a great influence on the economy. A major obstacle to foreign investment is the combine structure, as mutual shareholdings can be used by groups to prevent the growth of foreign ownership. There has, as a result, been no example of the successful takeover of a Japanese enterprise by foreign interests; virtually all foreign investment consists of newly established subsidiaries or minority holdings in joint ventures with Japanese interests (Okumura 1983).

The expansion of American investment in Europe began after the Second World War, and American multinationals quickly overshadowed many of the older British, German, Swiss, and Dutch multinationals which had spread their interests in Europe. This 'American challenge' to European industry (Servan-Schreiber 1967) led many European enterprises to modify their practices and to respond to the challenge. By 1970, virtually all of the eighty-five largest European manufacturers had overseas operations; three-quarters of them operated in six or more countries. Much of this expansion took place within Europe itself and a number of unstable bi-national liaisons were set up.[6] Nevertheless, American enterprises remain a potent force in key industries such as oil, chemicals, telecommunications, and electronics. This investment is highly concentrated by industry and by company; in the 1970s 85 per cent of total US investment in Europe was in four industries (vehicles, chemicals, mechanical engineering, and electrical and electronic engineering), and 40 per cent of US investment in Britain, Germany and France was made by General Motors, Ford and Exxon (Hughes 1973, pp. 162–4; Turner 1970; Hodges 1974, p. 53). American companies in Europe accounted for only 6 per cent of manufacturing sales, although the figure was highest in Britain, at 10 per cent, and lowest in Italy, at 3 per cent (Vernon 1971a, p. 21). The real significance of this dominance lies in the importance of American ownership in specific industries which are oligopolistic and have an advanced technology:

the more narrowly one chooses to define an 'industry', the more commonly one encounters extreme rates of US participation. In Italy, during the 1960s, US enterprises were reported as controlling 100 per cent of the ball-bearing industry and most of the heavy electric industry; in Great Britain, more than 75 per cent of the carbon black industry, more than 40 per cent of the computer industry; in France, more than 90 per cent of the carbon black output, more than 40 per cent of the telegraph and telephone equipment and more than 35 per cent of the tractor and agricultural machinery output [Vernon 1971a, p. 24; Steuer *et al.* 1973, p. 91].

This growth in overseas investment has produced an international network of capital and personal relations. In 1976 the top 250 American enterprises held majority control in 116 of the 2000 largest European enterprises, while these same European enterprises had only two such controlling holdings in the United States.[7] The countries with the largest numbers of foreign subsidiaries among their top 250 enterprises were Belgium with seventy-two (thirty-two of them American), Germany with twenty-seven, and Britain and Austria with twenty-five each. The most active parents of these subsidiaries came from the United States, Britain, France, and the Netherlands. A study of the largest enterprises in thirteen countries in 1970 found that they were linked into an extensive international network of interlocking directorships. Japanese enterprises were isolated from this network, having no international interlocks, but American and European enterprises had numerous connections. Britain and the United States were especially well-connected internationally, as were Canada and the Netherlands. This pattern of interlocks reflected American investment in Canada and the wide international orientation of Britain and the Netherlands. The Continental EEC economies were not closely integrated as a group, and the German economy, in particular, tended to have few international interlocks. Those German enterprises which were internationally connected, had intense links with a small number of Dutch enterprises. Banks such as the Deutsche Bank of Germany and J P Morgan of the United States were especially important in the international network, reflecting their centrality in national economies. Fennema and Schijf (1985) suggest that there is some evidence for a division between Anglo-American and Continental European groups of directors. Continental European directors tended mainly to link neighbouring national economies – Belgium/France, Germany/Netherlands, and, to a lesser extent, Germany/Switzerland and Italy/Switzerland. All of these had weaker links to Britain and the United States, which were allied internationally mainly through their links to Canada. The international interlock network, therefore, was extensive but fragmented along national lines, its main significance being to create channels of communication and consultation between national enterprises.

The structure of the international network of intercorporate commercial, capital, and personal relations is both a consequence of processes internal to national economies and a constraint upon those processes. The centre of the world economic system comprises the advanced industrial economies of North America, Western Europe, and Japan, and the internationalization of capitalist production has tied these economies very closely together (Rowthorn 1971). The interlinking of national economies through the global operations of the multinational enterprise means that crucial areas of economic activity are removed from national arenas of decision-making. The powers of nation states and indigenous capitalist interests are increasingly countered by the powers of foreign interests; and the power of those who manage branch plants and subsidiaries is limited by the power of the international corporate leadership. Any one advanced economy is likely to experience two tendencies – a decline in its national autonomy alongside the enhanced power of its domestic multinationals over other economies – but this only serves to increase the 'anarchy' of the world economic system, and so creates greater unpredictability for national decision-makers.

The main point at issue in relation to the 'nationality' of the multinational company is not national sentiment but the fact that centralized decision-making is associated with the repatriation of profits to the base country, and the fact that this repatriation inhibits or distorts capital accumulation in the 'host' economy (Amin 1973, pp. 211, 236; Hymer 1972). 'Nationality' determines the flow of funds and so determines the world pattern of capital accumulation. The growth of the 'centre' of the world economy occurs at the expense of the 'periphery'. Yet important differences arise within the centre itself. The challenge presented to European business by the growth of American multinationals after the Second World War was manifest in the pattern of accumulation between Europe and the United States, and the recent expansion of European and Japanese multinationals has again altered this pattern. In areas such as Europe, where there is a complex interweaving of international capital movements, the development of each national economy is significantly influenced by the operation of foreign multinationals. The European pattern of accumulation emerges as the unintended consequence of the intersecting global strategies of the multinationals.

The size of the multinational enterprises gives them an enhanced ability to determine in which national economies they will operate. In consequence they, unwittingly, produce and reproduce the structure of the world economic system. Their effects on particular national economies may further undermine the limited capacity of the state to control the economy:

The capacity of any government to command a particular firm to undertake a specified task in support of public policy, such as settling in a backward region or holding down a key price, has been reduced; large firms now have a capacity that they never had before for choice between competing nations [Vernon 1977, p.63].

The 'fundamental dilemma' of the modern state, according to
Vernon, is to reconcile national control over economic events,
with the recognition that accumulation is determined by external
forces beyond its control (Vernon 1976, p. 256; Hughes 1973,
pp. 166, 169; Holland 1976, pp. 56, 152–3).

The consequences of foreign direct investment for the 'host'
economy have generally been seen in terms of the process of
'disarticulation' or structural distortion of the national economy.
'Disarticulation' means that the economy 'is made up of sectors, of
firms, which are juxtaposed and not highly integrated among
themselves, but which are, each on its own, strongly integrated in
entities whose centres of gravity lie in the centres of the capitalist
world' (Amin 1971, p. 289). There are 'empty boxes' in the inter-
industrial tables, such that 'the density of the flow of external
exchanges of these atoms, being much greater, and that of the flow
of internal exchanges very much less' than in the countries of the
capitalist core (Amin 1973, p. 237). Within the centre as much as
the periphery, the activities of multinational enterprises, produce
symptoms of disarticulation; the external linkages of those industries that are dominated by foreign capital become more important
than their linkages with other national industries. Thus, Murray
(1971, p. 96) has argued that such tendencies bring about a 'growing territorial non-coincidence between extending capital and its
domestic state'. He claims that

There is . . . a tendency for the process of internationalization to increase
the potential economic instability in the world economy at the same time
as decreasing the power of national governments to control economic
activity even within their own borders [Murray 1971, pp. 102–3; Picciotto
and Radice 1973, p. 63; Mandel 1972, p. 316; 1970].

At the same time, multinational enterprises do have national
bases and necessarily retain important links with their national
states. An American *multinational* is an *American* multinational
because it is embedded in the American system of corporate and
commercial law, its profits are subject to the American taxation
system, and its activities are a determinant of American economic
growth and balance of payments (Warren 1971, p. 139). It is in this
sense that the internationalization of production in Europe has
correctly been seen as an 'American' and, later, a 'Japanese'
challenge. This problem has, however, been most forcefully discussed in Canada, where the inroads of British and American

multinationals have stimulated much concern over the transfer of control from Canadian hands.

From its earliest years, Canada has been the target of British overseas investment. Although total foreign ownership of Canadian business declined from 38 per cent before the Second World War to 32 per cent in 1954, this same period saw a rise in American ownership from 19 to 25 per cent. Foreign investment became concentrated in the manufacturing sector, and by 1959 more than a half of all manufacturing assets were foreign-owned. American investment, therefore, has become an increasingly significant feature of the Canadian economy, being strongest in the automobile, chemical, oil and electrical industries (Drache 1970, pp. 24–5; Porter 1965, p. 267; Safarian 1966, p. 14; Aitken 1959a, pp. 7–8; Blyth and Carty 1956). Increasing interdependence of capital relations was matched by closer commercial relations: by the mid 1950s the United States bought 60 per cent of Canadian exports and provided 75 per cent of Canadian imports. Similar trends are observable in Australia: over a half of all foreign investment in 1964 came from Britain, and a further third came from the United States (Encel 1970, p. 337; Brash 1970). Wheelwright and Miskelly have estimated that 36 per cent of the share capital of the top 200 Australian companies in the 1960s was owned abroad. The British portion of this, which was still channelled through the City of London, was concentrated in petroleum, chemicals, non-ferrous metals, iron and steel, food processing, textiles and electrical engineering. American capital was concentrated in petrol, chemicals, metals and food but was equally strong in motor vehicles and agricultural equipment (Wheelwright and Miskelly 1967, cited in Encel 1970, p. 338; Lawriwsky 1982).

On the basis of evidence such as this, it has been argued that the Canadian economy occupies a 'satellite' position in the world economy because much of the strategic decision-making power lies outside the country. As a consequence, the development of the Canadian economy reflects 'the imperatives of more advanced areas' (Aitken 1959a, p. 3), and Canadian patterns of capital accumulation are subordinate to those of Britain and the United States (Porter 1965, p. 269; Gonick 1970; Aitken 1959b). Executives in foreign subsidiaries are uninvolved in strategic control as their responsibilities are limited to operational matters (Levitt 1970, p. 77). Foreign investment in Canada has produced, reproduced, and consolidated Canada's position in the world economy, creating a set of constraints on the ability of indigenous decision-makers to influence this satellite status. But it has been suggested in Chapter 5 that this is only a part of the picture. Although many Canadian firms are mere 'branch plant' operations of American and British multinationals, a substantial role is played by the controllers of indigenous Canadian enterprises. An important base from which these people are able to influence the operations of foreign subisidiaries has been the banking and insurance system (Carroll 1982). The maintenance of an autonomous financial system has been an important factor in, partially, offsetting the disarticulation of the economy. Evidence from Scotland (Scott and Griff 1984, ch. 3) supports this argument. Although English and foreign investment has considerably reduced Scotland's economic autonomy, the maintenance of a banking and investment system in Edinburgh has served as a focus for Scottish capitalist interests in preventing the loss of all decision-making powers.[8] The 'challenge' of foreign investment to an economy is especially great if it can be aimed at reducing the power of indigenous banks and other credit-giving financial intermediaries.

Private capital and state intervention

Nation states play a crucial part in maintaining the integrity of national economies and in enhancing the international power of their multinational enterprises, and it is for this reason that Marxist theory has posited the emergence of 'state monopoly capitalism'. For some Marxists this close alliance of state and private capital is a response to declining profitability. Whether a result of an underlying tendency for the rate of profit to fall[9] or a simple consequence of *de facto* profitability problems, state action in support of private capital has been seen as a consequence of a lack of profitability.[10] The state can intervene in order to discriminate against one sector and in favour of another through taxation, subsidies, and general expenditure, and so can help to bring about the restructuring of capital which private capital itself is incapable of producing (Urry 1977, pp. 12–13). A number of Marxists, however, have pointed out that state intervention is contradictory in its consequences. Although intervention occurs in response to problems of private profitability, expenditure which improves the position of private capital in the long term may have short-term effects which are the exact opposite. In order to finance its expenditure, the state must borrow or raise taxation; it must take funds away from the private sector. Private capital may be unwilling or unable to provide the facilities upon which its long-term survival depends, but it must, willingly or unwillingly, pay for the collective provision of these facilities. A rise in state expenditure involves a deduction from current private investment funds. For this reason, the productivity of capital must be sufficient to meet both the immediate needs of capital and the needs of the state. When state expenditure is growing, productivity must also increase, or there will be a contraction in the rate of capital accumulation. While past state expenditure may be increasing the productivity of capital, a portion of this increased productivity is required to finance present and future expenditure. It is in this way that an increase in state expenditure creates the need for further state expenditure. O'Connor concludes that 'The socialization of costs and the private appropriation of profits creates a fiscal crisis, or "structural gap", between state expenditures and state revenues' (O'Connor 1973, pp. 9, 40; Yaffe 1973, p. 225; Fine and Harris 1976, pp. 102–5; Rowthorn 1976, pp. 66–7). State intervention, therefore, has been seen as a necessary prop for private capital which, nevertheless, poses problems for private profitability and public expenditure.

The economic role of the state has altered in both a quantitative and a qualitative sense. Quantitatively the scale of state expenditure has increased massively. Although spending by the British state reached an all-time high level of 75 per cent of GNP during the Second World War, the level of peace-time expenditure increased steadily from the 1920s to reach a figure of over 50 per cent of GNP by the 1960s (Gough 1975, p. 61). With the exception of Japan, and, to a lesser extent, the United States, this trend occurred in all the advanced capitalist economies. Britain, France, West Germany, and Italy showed remarkably similar high levels of state expenditure in the 1970s, with American public expenditure being somewhat less than in the European countries. State expenditure in Japan, expressed as a percentage of GNP, was only half as great as in Europe (Gough 1975, p. 59). The bulk of this public expenditure has been directed towards the collective provision of posts and telecommunications, police and military activities, education, welfare, transport, and housing (Pahl 1977b; Pickvance 1976), and has thus been an expression of the move from facilitative to supportive state mediation of economic relations. 'Facilitative' mediation is grounded in a belief in the self-regulating nature of atomistic competition, and its ideology of *laissez-faire* saw the role of the state limited to the provision of those conditions that would facilitate the market regulation of economic activity. Thus the state concentrated on questions of law and order, currency, and taxation. The economic dislocations which arose as economic activity became more concentrated led to the state becoming more 'supportive' of private capital by undertaking to provide those education and welfare facilities which private capital was unable to provide (Winkler 1976; 1977; Cawson and Saunders 1983). Supportive and facilitative state expenditure could be used as an instrument of demand management as western governments became more concerned to maintain aggregate public and private expenditure at a level of demand sufficient to ensure full employment.

Alongside this mainly quantitative evolution was a qualitative transformation in state activity. Weak and unprofitable sectors of the economy became targets for public ownership or subsidy as the state intervened in the interplay of private interests in an attempt to solve these problems. The unprecedented depression of the inter-war years saw the initiation of a series of state-sponsored economic reforms aimed at the restructuring of private capital (Yaffe 1973, pp. 216–17; Fine and Harris 1976, p. 107; Westergaard 1977; Booth 1982). From the early 1960s this 'interventionist' mode of action has involved the extension of indicative planning. France and Japan made the first moves in this direction, with Germany and the United States being the last of the advanced capitalist economies to adopt planning of a long-term kind. By promoting mergers and joint ventures, by extending state ownership, by restructuring whole industries, and by tax and incomes policies, governments have attempted to ensure that private capital meets the goals of public policy (Shonfield 1965; Warren 1972; Causer 1978; Halliday 1975, pp. 53–60; Lockwood 1965a, p. 501ff.).[11]

Figure 1 shows the main dimensions in terms of which the economic role of the state can be analysed. Public enterprise is 'minimal', where it is predominantly organized through ministries and official agencies, and state ownership is limited to those assets required by these departments. By contrast, it is 'strategic' where public corporations and state shareholdings reach into the banking system and key industries and so give public authorities power and

Figure 1 The economic role of the state

Form of mediation	Nature of public enterprise	
	Minimal	*Strategic*
Facilitative	1	2
Interventionist	3	4

Note: Box 2 would seem to be a null category.

influence over the commanding heights of the economy. Although economies may be located at any point in the space defined by the intersection of these two dimensions, four major clusters can be identified.[12] The dominant feature of capitalist development since the middle of the nineteenth century has been for economies to move from positions in box 1 to positions in box 3. The British economy, for example, shows a particularly marked move from the 'top-left' *laissez-faire* system in box 1 to a contemporary position towards the centre-right of box 3. Before the First World War there were very few autonomous public enterprises in Britain, most large operations being organized as direct units of departments of state; but by the 1960s the state owned the Bank of England, had nationalized the coal, electricity, and gas industries, and major parts of the steel, shipbuilding and transport industries, and had controlling interests in numerous other enterprises. The Australian and Canadian economies moved to similar levels of state intervention but retained minimal public sectors, as did the less-interventionist United States and Japan. West Germany, the Netherlands, and Belgium had all come to occupy a central position in box 3, reflecting moderate levels of state intervention and enterprise. Of the major capitalist economies, only Italy, France, and Austria had moved into box 4. All three economies have long histories of strategic public enterprise and state intervention, though the French public sector has only achieved the scale of that in Austria since the nationalizations of 1981.

The growth of public enterprise and state intervention is a response to economic dislocations but produces political dislocations within the state itself. In Habermas's words, economic 'crisis tendencies' do not disappear but are 'displaced' into the internal structure of the state. The fiscal problems of the budgetary gap are compounded by problems of administrative efficiency (Habermas 1973, pp. 39–40, 47).[13] While it may be possible for a state to accommodate to its budgetary problems and attempt to co-ordinate private production in a planned way, there are definite obstacles to the achievement of this. In a capitalist economy, no planning authority has sufficient control over production because of the inadequate knowledge possessed by the planners. The goals set out in a plan rest upon projections from past tendencies which may not hold under altered circumstances, and the information which the state receives is, in any case, obtained from capitalist enterprises which may seek to use their links with particular state agencies and departments as instruments of competition with their rivals. The competition between enterprises is, in part, displaced into conflict and inadequate co-ordination between the various parts of the state apparatus (Habermas 1973, p. 62; Mandel 1972, pp. 233, 235–6; Miliband 1977, p. 96).

All states that have adopted a more interventionist role have had to evolve mechanisms of information gathering which enable them to achieve the goals which they seek but which become also mechanisms through which capitalist interests seek to pursue their strategies. Although trying to pursue what it seeks as being re-quired by its own fiscal policy and by the need to maintain produc-tion, a state must also respond to the views of the business world. The state must, therefore, attempt to distil a general point of view from the myriad particular views pressed upon it through its in-formation gathering activities. Some Marxists have gone so far as to argue that state policy becomes 'a specific form of expressing the general interests of capital' (Altvater 1972, p. 99; Israel 1974; Hirsch 1977), but this cannot be assumed to be the case. There is no guarantee that the state will be able to recognize, let alone express, the general interests of capitalist enterprises. The impor-tant fact to which these writers point, however, is that interven-tionist states must establish structures of representation and policy formation which enable them to determine the goals and pro-cedures which figure in their economic planning.

The structures which have evolved to cope with these problems are shown in Figure 2, where the two dimensions of interest representation and policy formation are used to define a typol-ogy.[14] The categories of 'pluralist' and 'corporatist' representation are distinguished by the degree to which interest organizations are compulsory, hierarchical, and monopolistic. Thus, corporatist

Figure 2 Economic interests and the state

	Patterns of policy formation	
Form of interest representation	*Pressure politics*	*Concertation*
Pluralist	1	2
Corporatist	3	4

Source: Modified from Schmitter (1982); see also Schmitter (1981) and Lehmbruch (1982).

representation is at its strongest when such organizations are formed into statutory 'chambers' or 'estates', while pluralist representation operates through a variety of competing and voluntary bodies (Schmitter 1974; 1977). 'Pressure politics' designates a system where pluralistic or corporatist organizations influence the policy process from the outside through consultation and lobbying. On the other hand, 'concertation' describes that situation where organizations are incorporated directly into the governmental policy process as negotiators and can be made responsible for policy implementation. In the latter situation organizations and their members are co-opted into official committees and agencies and may also be formally represented in political parties through the cumulation of offices. Concertation has typically been described as involving a 'social partnership' or 'social contract' in which centralized or 'tripartite' negotiations take place within a framework of consensus.

Boxes 1 and 4 in Figure 2 describe the polar types in this typology, with the United States and Austria being the exemplars. Business interests in the United States are only loosely organized into representative bodies and their members typically attempt to influence government by lobbying political parties, supporting candidates with donations, sitting on advisory bodies, and other methods of pressure group politics (Wilson 1982). In Austria, on the other hand, corporatist representation was a deliberate constitutional development of the 1930s and was expanded by the Conservative–Socialist coalition which held power from the Second World War until 1966. Public enterprise, too, began in the 1930s with the takeover of the failed Credit-Anstalt and other banks. Further nationalization took place after the Second World War, when numerous enterprises were in danger of confiscation by the Allies as 'German' property. The state sector is now dominant in the economy and directorships are filled in such a way as to maintain a party balance. The corporate interests of Austria are formed into a strong 'corporatist' system (Ziegler *et al.* 1985). Only slightly weaker in character is Japan, where an alliance of business and government is strengthened by the paternalistic incorporation of labour (Lehmbruch 1982, p. 25). Between the two poles, almost at the mid-point of the typology, is Italy, where corporatist structures and public enterprise were employed in the 1920s as a response to the dependence of the economy on foreign capital and to its uneven development. The fascists appropriated this strategy as a deliberate and conscious policy, and the instruments of intervention were refined after the war by the governing Christian Democrats. This apparently strong development of corporatism was undermined, however, by the loose federal structure of the Italian state, which ensured limited and unstable concertation and sharply competing interest groups (Donolo 1980, p. 165). Different sections of Italian capital used different branches of the state for their own purposes, and state action was ineffective and poorly co-ordinated. Formal mechanisms were supplemented, especially at the local level, by 'arrangement and illicit practices', and the trades unions and the Communist Party were outside this structure (ibid., p. 168; Regini 1982). Mid-way between Italy and Austria, in the centre of box 4, can be found the Netherlands and Sweden, where formal corporatist institutions are well-established and are combined with a degree of concertation in planning (De Vries 1978, p. 73). In Sweden this has been associated with attempts to establish shareholding funds controlled by employees. Under the so-called Meidner Plan, incomes policy is supposed to ensure that profits above a collectively negotiated level are paid into a shareholding fund. This plan was first put forward in 1975 and began to be established in 1984, though recent work has suggested that its viability is being undermined by the fragmentation of labour markets which limits the possibilities for solidaristic support for incomes restraint (von Otter 1980; Korpi 1978; Lash 1984).

Although business interests in France have developed along corporatist lines, they have tended to operate through the mechanisms of pressure politics. France has a long history of intervention by a centralized state, and in the post-war period this centred around planning and nationalization geared towards industrial reconstruction to meet the American challenge. Under De Gaulle state policy revolved around a government/civil service axis, which reduced the role of parliament and parties as the political system came to be dominated by appointed officials. The appointed executive attempted to act in economic matters in what it saw as a 'technical' rather than a 'sectional' party way, and this was reinforced and legitimated by an education in the École Normale d'Administration which encouraged the view that the civil service was the voice of business. The closed circle of political decision-makers stepped into business positions late in their careers,[15] but it was only during the 1970s that this began to be a two-way interchange between business and politics. Thus, business organizations only belatedly came into close contact with the economic machinery of the state, but their incorporation was not associated with any attempt to use the state to concert private interests (Birnbaum 1980). Only with the electoral victory of the Socialists in 1981 and the subsequent extension of the nationalized sector has there been any marked shift of the French political economy towards box 4.

Germany and Britain have moved, in different ways, to a position between boxes 3 and 4 which has variously been described as 'bargained corporatism' (Crouch 1977) and 'corporate bias' (Middlemas 1979). A strong state emerged in Germany in the 1870s and protected the German economy through tariff barriers and the encouragement of cartels. From a very early period the state endeavoured to link business with national goals and a degree of planning, this role being expanded in the 1920s and during the Second World War (Feldman 1981). The Nazi regime and wartime conditions extended this into a form of 'statist corporatism' (Schmitter 1974), but most enterprises in Western Germany were returned to private ownership after the war. The system which has evolved in the Federal Republic involves considerable state intervention but no apparatus of economic planning. Because the banks had produced a highly concentrated economy, the state has been able to intervene in key areas without the need for extensions of the state machinery itself. The state has both supported and legitimated the actions of the banks in reconstructing the economy in which they hold central positions in the mobilization of capital (Hirsch 1980, p. 121). Since the 1960s, however, there have been moves to strengthen the executive powers of the state and to build a planning apparatus (Offe 1981; Streeck 1982).[16]

Britain's system of 'corporate bias' has been traced back to the end of the First World War, when a number of the practices developed by the coalition government under wartime conditions were retained into the post-war period (Middlemas 1979). The transition from the facilitative to the interventionist state began in this period, but for most of the inter-war years such 'intervention' in industry as took place was a result of private rather than public intitiative. In the slump conditions of the early 1920s a number of bankers, industrialists, and politicians turned to the idea of 'rationalization' as a remedy for Britain's archaic industrial structure, believing that conscious and deliberate intervention had to replace the 'invisible hand' of the market (Hannah 1979c, ch. 3). Governments of the late 1920s supported this move towards rationalization but refused to become actively involved as agents of public intervention, seeing the banks, who had their capital tied up in overdrafts to the ailing industrial giants, as the most appropriate agents of change; the banks, in their turn, connived in this limitation of state power. 'The City', therefore, dominated strategies of industrial reconstruction in the inter-war years, and the Bank of England played the role of co-ordinator and spokesman for City interests (Booth 1982). Industrial strategy has reflected the City view of economic affairs, a view based around the primacy of certain economic goals: maintenance of Britain's international trading position and the consequent need for policies aimed at maintaining the international role of sterling through restrictions on public expenditure and growth in the money supply.[17] The financial and commercial enterprises of the City have not formed themselves into formal organizations of interest representation and, because of their centrality to government economic policy, have inhibited trends towards corporatist intermediation. The representation of City interests has been informal and personalistic, reinforced by the kinship and friendship links which tie members of the City into the established social orders (Moran 1983, pp. 52–5; Longstreth 1979b; see also Scott and Griff 1984, ch. 4; Lupton and Wilson 1959). The Bank of England has, until recently, been the sole formal channel between the City and the state, and its system of personal and informal links to both the Treasury and other financial interests was perfected under the governorship of Montagu Norman in the inter-war years. The autonomous 'self-regulation' of the Stock Exchange and other City markets was a reflection of the formal separation of state and City on which economic policy was based.

State intervention and public enterprise were expanded under the post-war Labour government, but this was not associated with any substantial increase in corporatist interest representation or concertation in economic planning. The growth of state activity was supported and underwritten by the continued dominance of the City viewpoint, and its main institutional support was what has been called the 'post-war settlement'. This settlement comprised a consensus over the broad aims of economic management and social reform in which governments of either party could depend upon the support of both business and working-class organizations (Jessop 1980). The economic practices of the state in this period, described under the rubric 'Keynesianism', constituted the supportive role of the state which marked the late stage of development from facilitative to interventionist mediation. These practices, drawn from elements of Keynes's economic theory, were aimed at securing a level of output that would ensure full employment without involving any serious departure from 'normal' market mechanisms. Alterations in levels of government spending were supposed to counteract the booms and slumps of private economic activity and so ensure a constant level of aggregate expenditure. The success of Keynesianism depended upon the maintenance of those conditions which supported the post-war settlement. The officials of the Treasury and the Bank of England had the task of designing and implementing a policy which would receive the support of City interests, other business leaders, and the mass of the population. The support of the business community could be ensured because of their common social background as members of the 'establishment', the dominant status group within the upper class, and the support of the rest of the population was achieved partly by the attitudes of deference, respect, and acceptance which had survived from the past and partly by the ability of the managed economy to meet their rising demands.

Keynesianism was undermined in the late 1950s by the decay of traditional authority and the consequent willingness of workers to use the power of organized labour to the full to achieve greater wage increases (Skidelsky 1979). The decay of traditional authority was itself an aspect of the decay of the establishment which was occurring through the 1950s; Keynesianism had, for a time, traded successfully on the support of a declining social formation. The consensus and overlap of personnel between City and government, and the informality of personal relations between them, could no longer be relied upon as business and trades union organizations outside the establishment grew in importance. The concentration of economic activity in the post-war period created major strains for the system of interest representation. From the early 1960s, governments in Britain began to build a machinery for economic planning which was intended to yield the economic benefits which pure Keynesianism had become unable to produce. Tripartite consultation among government, business, and unions became an important means of formulating the goals of economic policy, and so state intervention became less dependent on informal mechanisms of interest representation. New agencies of industrial reconstruction were formed (Young and Lowe 1974; Hague and Wilkinson 1983) as ways of intervening in the economic process. Government began to encroach on areas formerly left to City self-regulation, the Bank of England came to be regarded more and more as a nationalized enterprise,[18] and the Confederation of British Industry, formed in 1965, became an increasingly powerful forum of business opinion (Grant and Marsh 1977; Blank 1973).[19] As the state began to adopt more formal means of consultation with the CBI and the unions, a distinctively 'City' viewpoint became a much weaker influence on government policy.

The City was itself under pressure as family ownership of the merchant banks was weakened by the increased scale of banking activities and by the adoption of divisional organization. As in the manufacturing sector, this restructuring of City enterprises occurred as a response to the inroads of American enterprises in the British financial system and the growth of rival financial centres in the United States and Europe (Channon 1977; Moran 1983, p. 58). City enterprises began to transform old trade associations into effective lobbying organizations, formed themselves into new organizations such as the various institutional shareholders committees, and became members of the CBI. Though it retains a role as a central business forum, the Bank of England has increasingly been by-passed by these collectivities and can no longer be seen as spokesman for the City. While financial intermediaries have achieved enhanced economic power, 'the City' as a bloc of opinion has become of declining significance: 'In place of the old cohesive City is left a series of separate sectors displaying varying levels of organised cohesion and effectiveness' (Moran 1983, p. 67). The CBI, dominated by the big private and public enterprises in both finance and industry, has become the effective representative body of finance capital, though its fragmentation and lack of co-ordination prevents it from acting as a corporatist 'peak organization' within a system of concertation.

The post-war period in all countries has seen regular shifts in the location of particular economies in the typology shown in Figure 2, largely as a result of changes in governing parties and, hence, in the direction of economic policy. In Britain, for example, the election of 1979 reinforced a move away from concertation and a weakening of corporatist organizations, though this has not yet resulted in the wholesale dismantling of the 'corporate bias' (Strinati 1982). Despite such changes, however, and despite alterations in the level of public enterprise, there is no sign of any reversal of the trend depicted in Figure 1. The nation state is central to the maintenance of a national economy in the face of tendencies towards its disarticulation, and to ensure this the nation state has had to both support private capital and intervene in its reconstruction. The 'displacement' into the state of the economic dislocations produced by concentration and internationalization might be expected to make state policies contradictory and shifting, but an enhanced role for the state cannot be avoided. The move from facilitative to interventionist mediation appears to be an irreversible feature of the development of modern capitalism.

Notes

1 In Scott and Griff (1984) these two processes are termed unit and network concentration. They should be distinguished from the Marxist distinction between concentration and centralization.
2 Note that Tables 45 and 46 adopt different measures of concentration. The trends in the two countries can be compared, but the actual figures are not directly comparable.
3 Mitsubishi, Mitsui, Sumitomo, and Yasuda.
4 This study (Prais 1976) excluded steel-makers and made no reference to Japanese enterprises.
5 The remaining two were from Canada and Brazil.
6 The older bi-nationals such as Unilever and Royal Dutch/Shell survived, but liaisons such as Dunlop/Pirelli, AGFA/Gevaert, and Fokker/VFW had all broken up by 1981.

7 The discussion which follows draws heavily on Fennema (1981) and Fennema and Schijf (1985). The latter draws on data from various national economies collected for the research shown in Tables 15, 24, and 32. See also Grou (1983), p. 51.

8 The argument that Scotland has become a branch plant economy can be found in Firn (1975). Similar evidence for Wales is provided in Tomkins and Lovering (1973).

9 Marx saw this tendency as a consequence of the rising organic composition of capital, though he recognized that its effects could be offset by counteracting factors such as joint stock principles of accounting (Marx 1894, pp. 325, 428). Szymanski (1973) has argued that monopoly conditions not only counteract the tendency but introduce a wholly new set of laws. Some developers of Marx's thought have gone so far as to reject the very idea of tendential laws (Hussain 1977; Cutler *et al.* 1977). A persuasive case for the centrality of generative processes and their tendential laws can be found in Harré and Madden (1975).

10 Evidence on profit rates has been debated in Glyn and Sutcliffe (1972), Castells (1976), and Boddy and Crotty (1974).

11 Marxist views can be found in Habermas (1973, pp. 33–4) and Miliband (1968), while a related, but distinctly non-Marxist, view can be found in Berle (1955, p. 23).

12 The categories of 'minimal' and 'strategic' imply a polar category of 'maximal', where all economic assets are state-owned. This category is clearly of limited relevance for the analysis of capitalist economies. Similarly, the polar category to 'facilitative' and 'interventionist' mediation is 'directive' mediation. The combination of directive mediation and maximal public enterprise might be taken to define the Soviet-type of economy.

13 Habermas terms this the 'rationality crisis' and relates it to broader socio-cultural problems of legitimation. On the latter see Habermas (1976), part 4. Habermas's general approach to sociology is discussed in Scott (1978).

14 The typology is limited in its application to economies in which interests are collectively organized and the state pursues an interventionist role.

15 It is for this reason that Morin (1974) refers to control through a constellation of interests as 'technocratic' control.

16 The situation in Switzerland is described in Kriesi (1982).

17 It should be clear from the argument of Chapter 4 that the City is not a separate and distinct fraction of capital. The City is a sector of the economic activity, well-integrated with others, whose hegemonic enterprises were able to ensure that the commercial practices of City enterprises were a major influence on business opinion.

18 The Bank had, in fact, been nationalized in 1946.

19 For a general analysis of business power see Finer (1955) and (1956).

8 The corporation and the class structure

The transformation of property relations which is expressed in the modern corporate form has been widely assumed to involve the disappearance of the class of capitalist property owners whose wealth and power arose from the conditions of nineteenth-century capitalism. Though eschewing the language of class, Berle felt that 'the transformation of property from an active role to passive wealth has so operated that the wealthy stratum no longer has power' (Berle 1963, p. 53). This judgement from the initiator of the debate on the modern corporation is in accord with the views of those advocates of the theory of industrial society who have attempted to explore the contours of the modern stratification system. Bell, for example, has argued that the decline of the 'finance capitalism' created by the turn-of-the-century investment bankers has led to a consolidation of the power of the salaried professional managers. Family inheritance and control over capital become less important, while technical skills increase in importance. The result of these trends is the 'break-up' of the old ruling class of family proprietors, as the mere possession of wealth no longer gives access to economic power (Bell 1957, pp. 40–1; 1958, p. 50ff.). Parsons has argued that the capitalist propertied class has been replaced by a managerial stratum which is 'broad and diffuse ... with several loosely integrated components', and which is based not on property ownership but on 'occupational status and occupational earnings' (Parsons 1954a, p. 431).

The most influential proponent of this idea – and the person who coined the phrase 'managerial revolution' to describe it – is not a mainstream advocate of the theory of industrial society but a former Marxist. Burnham accepts the validity of the orthodox Marxist theory of capitalist society as an account of the distribution of economic power prior to the 1930s. He held, however, that the dominance of the financial oligarchy was a feature of the transition from the family capitalism of the nineteenth century to a new managerial society. The managers, who carry out the 'technical direction and coordination of the process of production' (Burnham 1941, p. 70) are technically indispensable to the new industrial system and so are destined to replace the finance capitalists as a new ruling class. The finance capitalists, who had merged individual enterprises and rationalized the organization of production, had created the base from which the internal managers, who 'are in no way dependent upon the maintenance of capitalist property and economic relations' (ibid., p. 80), could rise to power in their place. Burnham saw the bureaucratization of government and industry leading to a situation where those who filled the administrative posts of society would realize their common interests and seek to make a political revolution. The form of state that they would create, he believed, was that which had already emerged under fascism, and this argument was extended by contemporaries of Burnham who held that the organization of large business enterprises into trade associations and other corporate bodies was a sign of the emergence of the totalitarian 'corporatist' state (Brady 1943; Neumann 1942).[1]

The basis of Burnham's claim for the 'technical indispensability' of professional managers is the work of Veblen, whose argument predates that of Berle and Means (1932). Veblen claimed that corporate organization involved the 'alienation of control' by owners (Veblen 1924). Shareholders become absentee owners, and the investment bankers who participate in strategic control also tend to adopt an 'absentee' orientation in so far as they are concerned with financial matters rather than with the people and physical goods involved in the work of production. While shareholders and financiers have a 'pecuniary' orientation, engineers and skilled workers adopt an 'industrial' orientation which is held in check by their subordination to proprietary and banking interests (Veblen 1919; see also Banks 1959). For Veblen, the creative powers of industrial craftsmanship could be released by liberating them from financial bondage, and Burnham's contribution was to focus on the key role which he believed managers would play in this.

The theses of the managerial revolution and the dissolution of the capitalist class have a long lineage, and writers of all shades of opinion have subscribed to this general picture. Following his critical review of the debate over ownership and control, Zeitlin ventured the tentative conclusion that 'News of the demise of the capitalist classes . . . is, I suspect, somewhat premature' (Zeitlin 1974, p. 46). The purpose of this chapter is to support Zeitlin's suspicion and to document the ways in which capitalist property ownership remains central to the formation of an upper class.

Relations of possession and the upper class

Discussion of class structure at the upper levels has been radically transformed in the last twenty years by the work of Poulantzas (1968) and of Althusser and Balibar (1970), which extended Marxist theory in a novel and stimulating direction. Poulantzas's own book on class structure (1974) attempted to demarcate the boundaries of the 'bourgeoisie' and to discern the basis of class differentiation among the propertyless. Although his emphasis on the distinction between productive and unproductive labour has aroused considerable, and well-earned, criticism, all contributors to the debate on class boundaries owe a great debt to his work.[2] The form of theorization initiated by Poulantzas – an attempt to locate class boundaries within an analysis of the structure of capitalist relations of production, and to show how political and ideological factors interact with these determinants – has been extended in two competing directions. According to Carchedi (1975; 1983), class positions are defined by the *functions* performed by their occupants: the function of capital and the function of labour define the two basic class positions of capitalist and worker, with the 'new middle class' being those whose position in the relations of production involves the performance of aspects of both functions. Wright (1978; 1979; 1980), on the other hand, differentiates classes in terms of the *structure* of the relations of production: the structural contrast between positions involving economic ownership and strategic control and those involving a lack of both ownership and control defines the bourgeoisie and the working class, while the 'new middle class' comprises the occupants of contradictory structural locations between these two poles.

It is argued here that the differences between Carchedi and Wright are of minor importance to those who stand outside the framework of Marxist politics and that both writers provide useful concepts. Their concepts do not, however, tell the whole story of stratification, and they must be combined with concepts from other theoretical traditions.[3] Central to this synthesis is an under-

standing of the implications for class structure of the transformation of property which has been described in this book.

For Wright the bourgeoisie is constituted through the structural
dominance ensured by control over the investment and accumulation of money capital, a dominance which gives such controllers
command over the labour and productive assets which are put to
work in the process of production. The structure of capitalist
possession defines a group of participants in strategic control –
major shareholders and top corporate executives and directors –
who head a managerial hierarchy of supervision and discipline
through which their control over corporate operations is ensured
(Wright 1979, pp. 3–4; 1980, pp. 328–9; see also Wright *et al.*
1982). Wright recognizes that most such 'capitalists' are salaried
employees of an enterprise rather than entrepreneurs, but he does
not accept the claim of Cutler *et al.* (1977) that this prevents them
from being regarded as true capitalists. Capitalist locations are not
necessarily defined by individual, personal possession; such locations result also from membership of a collectivity which exercises
all the powers of possession and, thereby, determines the conditions under which its individual members may be hired and fired.
The position of collective power which constitutes them as capitalists gives the participants in strategic control a part to play in what
Carchedi has called the 'global function of capital', a process
through which strategic and operational matters are decided and
implemented. In a situation of impersonal possession, member
ship of a board of directors constitutes occupancy of a capitalist
location:

Top executives and directors of corporations may be fired, but they are
fired by collectivities of other directors and top executives, collectivities in
which they are participating members. The social mechanisms by which
they lose their jobs are thus qualitatively different from the mechanisms
by which workers lose their jobs. They may not personally possess the
means of production *as individuals*, but they are members of collectivities
that do possess those means of production [Wright 1980, p. 338].

Considerable confusion has arisen because of the disagreement
between Marxist and 'Weberian' writers over the correct usage of
the word 'class'. Although Carchedi and Wright equate capitalist
locations within the relations of production with class positions,
this usage will not be followed here. In the present book, classes
are regarded as collectivities which stand in definite relations to

one another in the hierarchical distribution of advantages and disadvantages. This definitional fiat has no justification other than its compatibility with most non-Marxist usages, but, whatever linguistic preferences may ultimately prevail, the choice of terminology does not prejudge the question of the deeper foundations of hierarchical structures in the relations of production. These relations define economic locations which comprise positions in the structure of strategic and operational control and the associated patterns of recruitment and remuneration through which such positions are filled. These two aspects of an economic location – 'work situation' and 'market situation' in Lockwood's (1958) terminology[4] – are determinants of class situation, understood as the opportunities which a household has for enhancing the life chances of its members on the basis of the economic locations of its members.[5] Alongside the impact of market and work situation on class situation is the role of property *per se.* Where capitalist locations depend in whole or in part on personal possession – through the survival of personal ownership and of majority and minority holdings – property enters directly into the work situation of the capitalist; but the mere fact of property ownership enhances the life chances of a household independently of its relevance for strategic control. Ownership of company shares, even on a small scale, can be a source of income and capital gain to those who own them, and these benefits are in no way dependent upon personal participation in strategic control.

This argument points to the validity of Weber's (1921) claim that property and the commercial use of property are the fundamental aspects of class situation, though it must be recognized that the commercial use of property encompasses both market and work situation.[6] It is thus possible to accept Weber's further concept of 'social class'. Although he recognizes the formation of rentier classes rooted in mere property ownership and entrepreneurial classes rooted in the commercial use of property, Weber argues that the interplay of these mechanisms generates clusters of class situations within which inter- and intra-generational mobility is easy and typical (Weber 1921, pp. 302–7). It is such clusters of class situations which constitute the major social classes of society. Social classes are the result of complex structuring processes and do not, therefore, have sharply defined boundaries. While the core members of a social class may be easily distinguished from those of other classes, those on the fringes of a class will have many characteristics in common with those on the fringes of adjacent classes. As Cole has argued, social classes

are not sharply definable groups whose precise numbers can be determined by gathering in enough information about every individual. They are rather aggregates of persons round a number of central nucleii, in such a way that it can be said with confidence of those nearer each centre that they are members of a particular class, but that those further from a centre can be assigned to the class it represents only with increasing uncertainty [Cole 1955, p. 1; Sweezy 1951].

The core of the upper class in modern industrial capitalism consists of those households whose life chances are dependent upon occupancy of capitalist economic locations. Wright and Carchedi were correct to assign the occupants of such locations to households at the top of the stratification system. By virtue of their property ownership and their participation in the exercise of strategic control, entrepreneurial capitalists, finance capitalists, and internal capitalists collectively dominate the system of impersonal possession and so comprise the 'central nucleus' of the upper class.

The upper class stretches beyond this core to encompass those households with similar life chances but which are not dependent on the participation of their members in capitalist locations. Such households derive their life chances from the inheritance of sufficient wealth to remove the necessity of highly paid work from their members. This is not to say that their members do *not* work – though a life of leisure may be pursued by some – it is merely that the major part of their life chances derives from the income which their property generates. Members of rich households therefore have the freedom to engage in a variety of occupations without the need to ensure that their occupational income is sufficient to meet the totality of their outgoings. At the same time, members of such households *do* have the opportunity of seeking entry to capitalist locations. A social class, it has been argued, consists of class situations among which mobility is easy and frequent; and the unity of the upper class consists in the opportunities which its fringe members[7] have of entering core locations, and vice versa. The upper class as a whole is dependent on the success of the business system which produces its wealth. It is a 'propertied class' in so far as its members are the wealthiest of households, but the dependence of its members on the uses to which this property is put in business enterprises makes the designation 'business class' more appropriate (Scott 1982b, ch. 6).

The finance capitalists, recruited in part from entrepreneurial capitalists and internal capitalists, are those occupants of capitalist locations who epitomize the system of impersonal possession, though internal capitalists have expanded in numbers with the growth of large-scale enterprise. Entrepreneurial capitalists, however, retain an element of personal possession and so show certain distinctive 'work situation' characteristics. For this reason, Abercromby and Urry (1983) were misled into seeing them as the only true capitalists. Personal ownership of the means of production, they argue, is the defining characteristic of capitalist economic locations, and so a distinctly capitalist class becomes more and more restricted to those small enterprises in which such personal ownership is possible. It should be clear from the preceding argument that the 'depersonalization' of property does not lead to the disappearance of capitalist locations in large enterprises, and that entrepreneurial capitalists play an important part in the structure of impersonal possession. While the upper, business class is based on the large, diversified enterprise and the system of impersonal possession, with a substantial but reduced part played by the entrepreneurial capitalists whose shareholdings in these enterprises gives them an element of personal possession, the 'petite bourgeoisie' is that class whose members are the owners or principal shareholders in the small- and medium-sized enterprises whose activities are increasingly dependent on the operations of big business (Scase 1982). The petite bourgeoisie is a class distinct from the upper class, though the growth in scale of an enterprise may be the basis of the social mobility of its owner into the upper class.

The internal capitalists are structurally distinct from the subordinate managers and administrators who Wright has characterized as occupying 'contradictory' economic locations. Managers are workers who are excluded from strategic control over money capital but participate in the operational control of production and labour. Their economic location is contradictory because 'they share class interests with two different classes but have interests identical to neither' (Wright 1980, p. 331). In Carchedi's terms they participate in the performance of some aspects of the global function of capital, while at the same time engaging in the work of the collective labourer (Carchedi 1975).[8] Recent sociological work has pointed to their subordinate role in the service of capital and has described these personnel as a 'service class'.[9] Their economic locations involve a high degree of trust and autonomy in the exercise of delegated authority and are structured into bureaucratic hierarchies in which recruitment and promotion is organized through career expectations (Abercromby and Urry 1983, p. 118ff.; Goldthorpe 1982, p. 168). The core of the service class comprises those households whose life chances are rooted in the progress of one or more of their members through a career in service locations. They have no substantial wealth other than modest domestic property, and thus are dependent solely on their occupational salaries and 'fringe benefits'. The service class is rooted firmly 'in the middle' of the class hierarchy, though it stretches a considerable distance from households dependent on the earnings of a junior manager to households whose members have reached peak career positions and may be on the verge of the upper class.[10] A high proportion of service class households will have members in core locations, the fringes of the class being less extensive than those of the business class. The fringes of the class include self-employed and partnered professionals and 'consultants' who perform similar tasks to those employed in bureaucratic hierarchies, but whose market and work situations have similarities with those of the petite bourgeoisie.[11]

The discussion so far has concentrated on the social class hierarchy and its basis in the class situations of households, but it is important to recognize the analytically distinct contribution to life chances made by the processes described by Weber (1921) as the status situations of households. While class situation describes the determination of life chances through the material consequences of property ownership and economic location, status situation describes the determination of life chances through cultural mechanisms. More specifically, status situation is determined by the 'social estimation of honour' (Weber 1921, p. 932). Social honour, argues Weber, is estimated on the evidence offered of a person's life style: a particular life style is expected of those occupying a particular status, and so the outward trappings of life style tend to become the observable attributes in terms of which household members are 'placed' by others in the status hierarchy. The style of life followed by households of a similar status normally involves the restriction of social contacts through social *closure*. Contacts are restricted to the circle of status equals, the resulting status groups being expressed in conventional, and sometimes legal, regulations concerning informal interaction, intermarriage, and the monopolization of resources.[12] Parkin has argued that the form of closure typically exercised by relatively privileged groups of high status involves a strategy of 'exclusion': agents mobilize power and enter into distributional struggles by denying others access to resources and opportunities (1979, pp. 44–5).

Class and status are analytically distinct, though they inter-penetrate in concrete situations to form complex patterns of strati-fication. In some circumstances status will correspond to and legitimate class differences, but in others it will run counter to them and obscure class relations with a tissue of status considera-tions. Weber illustrates this in the case of property ownership, which he argues has distinct class and status implications. Those with property may claim a superior status, though it is rarely the case that property *per se* guarantees such honour: in a reference to the status disadvantages of the *nouveau riche*, Weber argues that the status evaluation of property 'normally stands in sharp opposi-tion to the pretensions of sheer property' (1921, p. 932); 'old' wealth is superior to 'mere' wealth. Nevertheless, he recognizes that 'property classes', households in which property ownership is a significant component of their class situation, often form them-selves into status groups (ibid., p. 307). The kind of cohesion and solidarity achieved by a fully developed status group is equivalent to that of the 'social class', and so a social class might be expected to constitute itself as a status group or as a hierarchy of status groups.

Adapting the argument of Parkin (1979), it can be argued that upper-class households in a capitalist society might be expected to form themselves into a status group through practices of 'bour-geois' closure based on the criterion of property ownership. The property which has given them their income and their access to capitalist locations is justified on the basis of the legitimate rights of property owners to control the use of that property. The status of service class households – inferior to that of the upper class, but superior to that of the working class – is expressed in the principles of 'credentialism': the possession of educational certificates is both a means of access to service locations and a justification of high status. The transformation of property ownership which has been documented in this book has created problems of recruitment and legitimation for occupants of capitalist locations. If personal possession is of declining significance in the determination of corporate strategy, then internal capitalists and finance capitalists must ensure their recruitment through alternative mechanisms; the credentialism of the service class has provided them with a vocabulary of motive for legitimating those mechanisms and has made plausible the image of a 'middle class' stretching from junior clerks to chief executives. Thus, the higher levels of the stratification system involve a confrontation between the rival status principles of property and credentialism. Upper-class households have typically allied the rights of property with the rights of inheritance, seeing the rights of the property owner as including the right to pass on property to a family heir. Because of the centrality of kinship in the structuring of upper classes and upper status groups, the marriage strategy of upper-class families is one of the most important mechanisms of class reproduction. The choice of a marriage partner is a strategy, intended or unintended, for ensuring the maintenance and accumulation of privilege. Marriage patterns reinforce the mechanisms of schooling, friendship, visiting, and commensality and the more organized unity created by clubs and associations. These mechanisms ensure a similarity of background and attitudes and form a social class whose members possess not merely equivalent life chances, but also a similarity of life style (Domhoff 1967, pp. 3–4; 1971, pp. 21–6, 77, 84; Tawney 1931, p. 53). Kinship and property entwine to form the upper class into a cohesive social class which stands at the head of the status hierarchy. The remainder of this chapter will explore the concrete forms which this has taken in the major capitalist societies.

The managerial re-organization of the propertied class

Impersonal possession, it has been argued, is the basis for the existence of an upper class which derives its life chances from the ownership and use of property, but which does not consist exclusively of property-owning entrepreneurs. The propertied class of early industrial capitalism was formed of families which held the whole or the majority of the shares in a family enterprise. Under the system of 'family appropriation' (Grou 1983, p. 107) which lasted in most capitalist societies until the First World War or, in some cases, into the inter-war years, there was a close correspondence between family wealth and family enterprise. The transformation of property and the emergence of impersonal possession have removed the direct and immediate linkage between property owners and strategic control. Propertied households are less likely to have the bulk of their property tied-up in the majority ownership of a particular enterprise, though they may still provide board members in large enterprises. Conversely, board members, who may rarely own a significant minority stake in the enterprises which they direct, still tend to be major property owners by virtue of small shareholdings in a large number of enterprises. There is considerable evidence that propertied families have diversified their wealth and so brought about an internal transformation of the propertied class. Domhoff has argued that 'Family A does not own Company X while Family B owns Company Y, as it may have been in the past; instead, Family A and Family B both have large stockholdings in Companies X and Y, as does Family C, which used to be the sole owner of Company Z' (Domhoff 1967, p. 40; Bertaux 1977, p. 78). Diversification of family investments and impersonal possession together constitute a 'depersonalization' of property (Birnbaum 1969, p. 12) which has led to what Mills (1956, p. 147) termed the 'managerial reorganization of the propertied class':

The growth and interconnections of corporations ... have meant the rise of a more sophisticated executive elite which now possesses a certain autonomy from any specific property interest. Its power is the power of property, but that property is not always or even usually of one coherent and narrow type. It is, in operating fact, class-wide property [ibid., p. 122; Domhoff 1967, p. 40].

This restructuring of strategic control does not alter the basic features of the system, as the participants in control constitute 'the most active and influential part of the propertied class' (Baran and Sweezy 1966; Sweezy 1951). The most forceful statement of the thesis of the managerial re-organization of the propertied class is that of Zeitlin, who argues that internal, entrepreneurial, and finance capitalists participate as members of the upper class in the control of class-wide property:

Although the largest banks and corporations might conceivably develop a relative autonomy from *particular* proprietory interests, they would be limited by the *general* proprietory interests of the principal owners of capital. To the extent that the largest banks and corporations constitute a new form of class property ... the 'inner group' ... of interlocking officers and directors, and particularly the finance capitalists, become the leading organizers of this class-wide property [Zeitlin 1976, p. 901].

The business class in all major capitalist societies stands at the head of a highly inegalitarian distribution of income and wealth. Kolko has shown that the top 10 per cent of income recipients in the USA received a more or less constant share of 30 per cent of all income before tax throughout the first half of this century (Kolko 1962, pp. 15, 24, 37; Kuznets 1953). The top 1 per cent also received a high proportion of income, though their share fell from 14 per cent to 10 per cent during the 1930s and 1940s. By the late 1950s the share of the top 1 per cent of families stood at 8 per cent (Domhoff 1967, p. 41; Birnbaum 1971; Bottomore 1965, p. 44; Miller 1966, p. 113). Although the increase in the concentration of income which took place prior to 1919 was partially reversed during the Depression and the Second World War, it has remained constant ever since. The picture in Britain is remarkably similar. While the share of the top 10 per cent of income recipients in before-tax income seems to have remained in the region of one-third, the proportion received by the top 1 per cent fell in the post-war period from 11 per cent to between 6 and 8 per cent (Nicholson 1967, p. 42; Lydall 1959; Solgow 1968; Blackburn 1967).[13] The reduction in the share of the top 1 per cent occurred primarily between 1949 and 1957, the proportion remaining constant since then.[14] The main cause of this reduction was the fact that from 1949 to 1957 earned incomes rose faster than income from other sources, while after 1957 the most rapidly growing sources of income were rent, dividends and interest (Nicholson 1967, p. 49). The trend in after-tax income has been slightly less marked, the share of the top 1 per cent being 6 per cent in the 1940s and 5 per cent in the 1950s and 1960s. Even the conservative estimates of Polanyi and Wood suggest that in 1970 the share of the top 1 per cent in after-tax income was 5 per cent (Polanyi and Wood 1974, p. 64). Noble (1975, pp. 178, 199) shows that, while the share of the top 1 per cent before tax fell from 9 to 7 per cent, their share after tax fell from 5 to 4 per cent. Allowing for minor variations in techniques, units and data, the basic pattern is clear. In Britain and in the United States as well as in France and Germany (Atkinson 1973a; Babeau and Strauss-Kahn 1977, p. 41ff.), one-tenth of the population receives about one-third of total income, and has done for most of the century. 1 per cent of the population, about half a million families in the United States, receive between 5 and 8 per cent of total income and have received this proportion since the 1950s, having declined from an earlier position of greater concentration.

With respect to wealth distribution, a major study of the United States by Lampman (1959; 1962) shows that the share of the top 1 per cent in personal wealth fell over the period 1922–49 and then rose again through the 1950s to stand at between 25 and 30 per cent. It has since been suggested that this proportion continued to rise through the 1960s (Smith and Calvert 1965; Domhoff 1967; Lundberg 1969). Lampman argues that much of the reduction in concentration in the period between the wars can be explained in terms of the redistribution of wealth within families and so does not represent a significant change in the social distribution of wealth. Nearly half of the wealth held by the top 1 per cent in 1953 was held by the top 0.11 per cent of the population, about 113,300 people, and there is no evidence to suggest that the situation is different today. Britain appears to show a higher degree of wealth concentration than does the United States. The share of the top 1 per cent fell from 69 per cent in 1911 to 56 per cent in 1936, 45 per cent in 1946, 42 per cent in the 1950s and 1960s, and to about 30 per cent in the 1970s (Lydall and Tipping 1961, p. 253; Noble 1975, p. 175; Atkinson 1972, p. 21; Revell 1965; Blackburn 1967; Atkinson 1975, p. 134). The proportion of wealth held by the top 5 per cent declined from 86 to 55 per cent over the same period, and Atkinson shows that, while the share of the top 1 per cent has declined by a half, the proportion of wealth held by the next 4 per cent remained constant or actually increased over the period. Atkinson draws the conclusion that this reflects redistribution within families in order to avoid estate duty (Atkinson 1972, pp. 22–3; Polanyi and Wood 1974, p. 17). As in the USA, almost half of the wealth held by the top 1 per cent is held by the top 0.1 per cent, about 55,000–60,000 people today (Atkinson 1975, p. 134).

The data in Table 53, based on probate figures, suggest that the number of millionaires in Britain has declined since 1900. The decline is particularly marked in view of the changing value of money over that period. A millionaire of 1976 had equivalent purchasing power to a person with £65,000 in 1900, so clearly the absolute figures give a false impression.[15] The increase in the number of quarter millionaires between 1900 and 1938 was at approximately the level that would be expected simply on the basis of changes in purchasing power, though the number of full millionaires shows a real decline on this same basis. Although the increase in the number of full millionaires between 1900 and 1976

Table 53 *Large estates in Britain (1900–77)*

Size of estate	Number of estates		
(£)	1900–1	1938–9	1976–7
250,000–500,000	51	98	n.a.
500,000–1,000,000	17	30	(11)
More than 1,000,000	9	4	21
Totals	77	132	(32)

Sources: Rubinstein (1981), tables 2.2 and 2.3, pp. 31–2; *Daily Mail Year Book*, 1977.

Note: n.a. = not available. Net values of estates do not include value of land. For 1976–7 the band for medium–large estates was 700,000–1,000,000.

was large, it was substantially lower than would be expected on the basis of constant purchasing power. This could indicate simply that wealthy people distribute the bulk of their wealth to members of their families prior to their own death in order to minimize their liability to estate duty, though Rubinstein suggests that it indicates a real decline in wealth concentration over much of the period. Only since the 1950s, he argues, was there any move back towards higher concentration as entrepreneurial capitalists made fortunes in property, consumer goods, and in some financial services (Rubinstein 1981, p. 61). Despite these 'new' fortunes at the top of the scale, however, there is considerable evidence that inheritance continues to play a major part in wealth distribution. Harbury and Hitchens (1979) have convincingly demonstrated the importance of inheritance in wealthy families and argued that even the new 'self-made' wealthy entrepreneurs have often depended on a small inheritance as the 'seed' for their later fortunes (see also Revell 1960; Harbury 1962; Harbury and McMahon 1974). Daumard (1980) has argued that a similar situation applies in France, where wealth concentration became less extreme during the post-war period, and Zamagni (1980) has suggested that in Italy, where the number of large fortunes is consistently lower than in Britain or France, a similar trend can be observed.

Townsend (1979) has powerfully argued that the material inequalities of households should be assessed with a combined measure of income and wealth. 'Income Net Worth', calculated by converting net assets into an annuity value and adding this to net disposable income, represents the notional annual income of a household, and Townsend argues that the inheritance of wealth, particularly if this occurs on marriage or early in life, is a major contributor to the income net worth of households. Upper-class membership involves a high income net worth, though the balance between income and assets in this total may vary from one household to another.[16] Townsend's data suggest that a household could only show upward mobility into this class if one of its members achieved extremely rapid career promotion to the level of income which would provide a large enough surplus to allow substantial investment. A small seed of inherited wealth, even in the form of a small business, would provide a far more reliable basis for the accumulation of assets by a household.

Large income recipients tend also to be large wealth-holders, with the greatest contribution to real disposable income being made by that part of their wealth that consists of company shares. The study of the *Temporary National Economic Committee* discovered that 7 per cent of the American population in 1937 held the whole of the 60 per cent of company shares held by personal shareholders. This same group was among the largest income recipients, and the higher their income the greater was the contribution from dividends. For individuals with an annual income greater than $100,000, dividend income accounted for 60 per cent (Goldsmith and Parmelee 1940, pp. 10–13). This latter group were also more likely to hold diversified portfolios in an average of twenty-five companies. While the number of shareholders declined somewhat during the Depression and the Second World War, it began to increase again during the 1950s. Lundberg (1969, p. 28) discovered that 1.4 million families held 65 per cent of all investment assets in 1962, with fewer than a quarter of a million families holding almost a third of investment assets.

Atkinson has shown that the wealthiest groups in Britain have the highest rate of shareholding, the top 5 per cent of wealth holders in 1961 holding 96 per cent of all personally owned shares (Atkinson 1972, p. 30; 1975, p. 135; Westergaard and Resler 1975, p. 107ff.). Shareholdings make an important contribution to income: the top 10 per cent of those in receipt of investment income in 1960 received 99 per cent of all income from this source (Blackburn 1967), and the top 1 per cent of income recipients in 1970 received 7 per cent of all income but 17 per cent of investment income (Noble 1975, p. 180). Noble argues that 'About 500,000 people, one per cent of the population, own just over a third of all private wealth in contemporary Britain and receive just over a half of all the personal income derived from possession of wealth.' Within this stratum the very rich 50,000, 0.1 per cent of the population, are the most important group (ibid., p. 182; Westergaard and Resler 1975, p. 119).

It has been argued that the core of the business class consists of those who are actively involved in determining corporate strategy in large enterprises. There is, indeed, considerable evidence that the large personal shareholders whose households are at the top of the hierarchies of income and wealth are drawn disproportionately from corporate directors and executives. Directors and executives of the top 200 American enterprises in 1939 held 5.5 per cent of their shares, the bulk of these being held by the directors. Typically the corporate management held less than 1 per cent of the shares of their own enterprises, though a quarter of all enterprises showed management holdings of 5 per cent or more (Goldsmith and Parmelee 1940, pp. 56–60, 64–5; Gordon 1936; 1938). Kolko estimated that directors owned an average of 9.9 per cent of the shares in the top industrials of 1957, though the figures presented in Table 54 suggest that the average size of the shareholding block held by directors declined between 1939 and 1975. In Britain, this is the case too, though many of the enterprises in which directors held less than 1 per cent in 1976 were wholly-owned subsidiaries or had a majority of their shares held by another enterprise.

The personal shareholdings of managers remain considerable, management comprising 'the largest single group in the stock-holding class' (Kolko 1962, p. 57; Domhoff 1967, p. 58). Even where managers have a low percentage holding, their stake is nevertheless of great monetary value. Larner calculated that the median value of shares held by executives in ninety-four large American enterprises in 1965 was $658,359, generating a median dividend income of $23,605 (Larner 1970, pp. 36–7, 66). A share-holding of 0.017 per cent held by the General Motors chairman in 1967 had a market value of nearly $4 m (Miliband 1968, p. 52; Villarejo 1961b, p. 53; see also Burcke 1976). Nichols (1969, p. 75) showed that while there was a decline in the average holding of British directors in their own companies over the period 1936 to 1951, the actual wealth represented by these holdings remained extremely high. This was confirmed by Stanworth (1974, p. 255)

Table 54   *Directors' shareholdings in Britain and the United States (1939–76)*

% of shares held by directors	Number of enterprises				
	United States			Britain	
	1939	*1960*	*1975*	*1951*	*1976*
Less than 1%	23	68	132	79	136
1–2%	42	45	15	87	26
2–5%		43	25		
5–10%	17	39	8	25	5
More than 10%	33	37	20	42	33
Totals	115	232	200	233	200

Sources: US data from Gordon (1945), p. 27; Villarejo (1961a), p. 51, table X; Herman (1981), p. 87, table 3.9. British data from Florence (1961), pp. 90–1, table IVc; Scott and Griff (1984), p. 103, table 4.1.

Note: Data relate to non-financial enterprises, though the US data for 1939 are limited to industrials. The British data for 1951 relate to a selection of ninety-eight large non-financials and samples of smaller enterprises.

who showed that 37.6 per cent of directors in the top seventy-five British companies of 1971 held shares in their own company worth £10,000 or more: 13.5 per cent held shares with a market value in excess of £100,000. Management shareholdings are encouraged by stock option schemes and bonuses, and income from shares can be six times as great as a manager's salary (Useem 1980, p. 48). Because a manager's total after-tax income is highly dependent on dividends, and hence on profits, their career orientation is by no means incompatible with their shareholder interests. These findings are not confined to Britain and the United States. Many wealthy *zaibatsu* families in Japan were forced by the American occupation authorities to sell their shareholdings after the Second World War as part of the policy of *zaibatsu* dissolution. Nevertheless, a high level of concentration in share ownership persists, and corporate managers are among the leading shareholders. Individuals hold 29 per cent of all shares in Japan, with the largest personal shareholdings being those of executives in their own enterprises (Steven 1983, p. 15; Komiya 1961).

The managerial re-organization of the propertied class which has taken place alongside the emergence of impersonal possession creates a situation in which those who own company shares comprise a 'pool' from which directors and executives are drawn. Corporate 'management' and large personal shareholders are one and the same, though a large shareholding in a particular company is no longer necessary or sufficient for a top corporate career (Florence 1961, pp. 93, 137; 1953, p. 200; Klein *et al.* 1956). Company directors comprise a very small proportion of the population who monopolize the personal ownership of shares and derive a substantial part of their income from this source. The heart of the upper class is the 'corporate rich', and the balance between 'earned' and 'unearned' income in their remuneration will reflect such factors as relative taxation advantages (Westergaard and Resler 1975, p. 162; Baran and Sweezy 1966, p. 47).

The transformation of the propertied class in the United States has been described by Berkowitz (1975) as a transition from a segmental structure of separate 'family compacts' to a nationally integrated upper class. Family compacts are sets of loosely interconnected families engaged in similar business activities. Typically, partnerships between families are established in order to extend the capital base of an undertaking and this results in intermarriage. Thus, kinship relations and capital mobilization reinforce one another. When capital requirements reach beyond the means of the partners, legal incorporation of the firm allows capital to be mobilized from non-family sources. Solidified family dynsasties in which the 'family' and the 'firm' are structurally separated are the outcome of this process, and the upper class exists as an extensive kinship network within which various 'cliques' can be identified around particular firms. Zeitlin has characterized these dynastic families as 'kinecon groups':

The corporation is the legal unit of ownership of large-scale productive property. The set of interrelated kin who control the corporation through their combined ownership interests and strategic representation in management constitute the kinecon group [Zeitlin *et al.* 1975, p. 110].

The merger of family compacts to form extended kinecon groups has been found to be a general feature of capitalist development. In Britain many such dynasties emerged (Scott and Griff 1984, ch. 4; Allen 1982), and in Japan the *zuibatsu* familics had similar characteristics (Yasuoka 1977, pp. 84–5). Berkowitz argues that dynastic kinecon groups become interlinked on a national scale when external credit replaces kinship in the supply of capital. The 'Money Trust' which arose in the United States represented one such form of merger based around the centrality of bank credit in industrial finance. The result of such a merger is the dissociation of family fortunes from the profitability of specific, family enterprises. Conversely, capital mobilization by enterprises no longer depends on the wealth of its directors (Berkowitz 1975, p. 208). By the 1930s the diversification of family wealth in the United States was well advanced, and the corporate rich had become the owners of extensive investment portfolios (Goldsmith and Parmelee 1940, p. 115ff.). The upper class had become a nationally-organized social class whose members 'are parts of interlocking social circles which perceive each other as equals, belong to the same clubs, interact frequently, and freely inter-marry' (Domhoff 1974, p. 86; Mills 1956, pp. 47, 62; Sweezy 1951). This process of managerial re-organization is well-advanced in the Anglo-American economies and in Japan, though evidence from France (Bleton 1966, pp. 134, 144; Landes 1951) and from Sweden (Commission on Concentration 1968, pp. 37, 48; Therborn 1976) suggests that economies in which family enterprise is strongest show the persistence of dynastic kinecon groups.

The reproduction of class domination

The closure which an upper class can achieve results from the strategies which their members pursue in order to defend and enhance their superior life chances. Such strategies are generally pursued for individual, household, and family purposes but have, as their unintended consequence, the reproduction of their class. These processes of class reproduction can be analysed in terms of the two dimensions of 'recruitment' and 'integration' (Giddens 1973, p. 120).

Control over *recruitment* involves the ability of class members to restrict entry to the class, and in particular to its core locations, through the exclusion of outsiders. If a class is successful in this, the advantages enjoyed by its members can be retained for the benefit of their descendents and so the intergenerational conti-nuity of the class can be assured. Advocates of the theory of industrial society have argued that the capitalist class has been unable to secure control over recruitment because of the increased importance of technical skills among professional managers. It is impossible to find the necessary number of technical personnel, it is argued, from within the ranks of the propertied families and so outsiders must be recruited to key positions. In consequence, industrial societies are 'open' societies characterized by high rates of upward social mobility (Kerr *et al.* 1960, pp. 151–2). In the business sphere, entrepreneurial capitalists, both founders and their heirs, are displaced by salaried 'bureaucrats'.

Evidence from the United States shows rather mixed support for this contention. 58 per cent of executives in 1928 were recruited from families with a business background, only 13 per cent being upwardly mobile professional managers (Taussig and Joslyn 1932). Nevertheless, a college education was found to be important for both the mobile and the heirs; and a follow-up study for 1952 found that education had grown in importance for all executives. Three-quarters of top corporate executives in 1952 had been to college, though one-fifth had been to one of the top four universities (Yale, Harvard, Princeton, Cornell). Paradoxically from the standpoint of the theory of industrial society, those from the top universities were the heirs and the sons of executives; the upwardly mobile managers had come through the second rank colleges and universities, especially the larger state and city universities (Warner 1959, p. 112, based on Warner and Abegglen 1955). These results suggest that members of the upper class ensured that their children acquired the necessary training for success in a business career, and that they have also ensured that their children received their credentials from the most prestigious educational institutions. This is confirmed by Allen (1978b, p. 517), who found that an increase in the proportion of college graduates among multiple directors between 1935 and 1970 was associated with a continuing high level of recruitment from the top private colleges. At the same time, executives have had to acquire higher levels of qualification in specific business skills through post-graduate training. A study of chief executives in 1976 discovered that more than a half had been to graduate school, mainly studying for the Master of Business Administration (MBA) or a law degree (Burcke 1976).[17]

Private schooling and attendance at one of the ancient universities has for long been an important factor in entry to the boardrooms of Britain's major enterprises (Perkin 1978; Heath 1981, pp. 88–96). More than a half of the directors in large British enterprises during the 1950s came from families with a business background, 44 per cent having fathers who had been directors, and 58 per cent of the directorate had been educated at private schools. Among those with a higher qualification, those trained in law or accountancy tended to be multiple directors while those with a technical training were found among the executive directors of engineering and chemical enterprises (Copeman 1955, pp. 89, 92–5, 105, 120; Clements 1958, p. 173ff.). Banking has shown a far more restricted pattern of recruitment than has industry: the proportion of former public school boys[18] who sat on the boards of the big clearing banks actually increased from 68.2 to 79.9 per cent over the period 1939 to 1970. During the same period, the proportion recruited from Oxford and Cambridge increased from 45.3 to 60.4 per cent. Although recruitment from all other universities did indeed increase over this period, it remained at an extremely low level: in 1970 just 8.2 per cent of clearing bank directors came from universities other than Oxford or Cambridge (Boyd 1973, pp. 84, 92; Stanworth and Giddens 1974a, p. 89). Clearing bank directors who had not come from a business background were especially likely to have used the private school/Oxbridge route to the boardroom (ibid., pp. 96, 102, 110; see also Thomas 1978, p. 309). Useem discovered that the greater the number of directorships a person held, the more likely was that person to have attended one of the major public schools (1984, p. 68).[19] Nichols (1969, pp. 81–3, 93) found some evidence to suggest that professional management training was becoming more widespread among middle managers, a finding confirmed by Whitley *et al.* (1981). The growth of student numbers on the MBA courses at the London and Manchester business schools in the period 1976–8 was mainly accounted for by those from a small business or middle management background. Over a half of the students had attended a major public school (Whitley *et al.* 1981, p. 94) and the authors conclude that private education was used as a means of access to higher education and, thereby, to the business schools. Directors of the largest enterprises, they argue, were rarely recruited through the business schools; instead, attendance at the public schools and Oxbridge provided the social assets of contacts and connections which can be used to ease entry to the top boardrooms.

For France there is some evidence that levels of both family continuity and technical education are higher than in Britain or the United States. Almost three-quarters of chief executives in a sample of French enterprises in 1976 had attended one of the

Grandes Écoles, the science schools such as the *École Polytechnique, École Centrale,* and *École des Mines* being especially popular, and many chief executives were drawn from a business background (Savage 1979, pp. 119–21; Hall *et al.* 1969; Granick 1962). About two-thirds of the chief executives were heirs in family businesses, the proportion being somewhat lower in the very largest enterprises. Nevertheless, the proportion of the top 100 chief executives from business families increased from 39 to 46 per cent between 1952 and 1972 (Bourdieu and de St Martin 1978, p. 46, cited in Savage 1979, p. 132). Attendance at a technical school was especially important for the chief executives in large enterprises who had few family connections with business. Professionals and civil servants could enhance the business prospects of their sons by sending them to the private schools which could ensure them entry to the *Grandes Écoles*, where they could acquire the technical credentials required for a career in the biggest enterprises. Similarly, those who chose to enter the lower rungs of a managerial career through the acquisition of a business school diploma found that their chances of successful entry to INSEAD were much greater if they had attended a private school (Whitley *et al.* 1981, p. 96; Marceau 1977, p. 133). The most senior business leaders, nevertheless, combined business background with educational credentials. Chairmen of enterprises subject to financial control or controlled through a constellation of interests were especially likely to come from an exclusive social background and to possess technical diplomas, and many had *pantouflé* from administrative careers in the state. By contrast, family heirs had a much lower level of education (Monjardet 1972, p. 139ff.).

Evidence on business recruitment in other European countries is rather sparse. Belgium, as might be expected, shows a similar pattern to France with respect to both family inheritance and technical qualifications. In Germany, top executives have been less highly educated than in France, though the level is considerably higher than that in Britain (Hall *et al.* 1969). In both Spain and Italy business is smaller in scale and family enterprise has been correspondingly stronger, suggesting a lesser reliance on educational credentials (Gallino 1971, pp. 101–3; Giner 1971, p. 151).[20] Top executives in Japan have been highly educated but, as in France, have often been drawn from families with business connections. One-third of top executives in 1960 were the sons of entrepreneurial capitalists, just over 10 per cent were the sons of executives in large enterprises (most being sons of bankers), and a further 17 per cent were sons of land owners (Mannari 1974, pp. 18, 20–1). Most of the entrepreneurs' sons were, in fact, heirs in the family business, but almost one-fifth of the executives' sons worked for the same enterprise as their father had done. Table 55, while using data which may not be perfectly comparable, nevertheless suggests that the 'openness' of Japanese boardrooms is more than that found in the United States and Britain, if 'openness' is measured by the degree of self-recruitment shown by business leaders. If recruitment from land and industry are combined, however, Japanese boardrooms appear even more closed than those in Britain.[21] While direct inheritance of positions is lower in Japan, the level of recruitment from among the wealthy is higher. As in France, the wealthy had to ensure their entry to top business positions through the acquisition of a higher education. Specialist schools and universities provided 91 per cent of Japanese executives, one-third coming from Tokyo University and one-tenth each from Kyoto and Hitotsubashi. Just under a half of these executives had degrees in economics, while one-quarter were engineers and one-quarter had studied law or government (Mannari 1974, p. 65).

The *integration* of a social class depends on the quality and quantity of interactions among its members. Whereas studies of

Table 55 *Social background of business leaders in Britain, the United States, and Japan (1952 and 1960)*

Occupation of father	Percentage of directors		
	Britain (1952)	USA (1952)	Japan (1960)
Professional and administrative	26	16	21.5
Executive, director, or owner of large business	32	31	22.0
Small businessman	19	18	21.5
Landlord or farmer	5	9	24.0
Other	18	26	11.0
Totals	100	100	100

Source: Mannari (1974), p. 61, table 1.5. The British data derive from Copeman (1955) and the US data from Warner and Abegglen (1955).

recruitment have examined the composition of the upper class over time in order to assess its degree of openness to outsiders, studies of integration have attempted to grasp the cohesion and unity of the class at a particular time. The intercorporate network of capital, commercial, and personal relations is a major contributor to upper-class integration, but other factors reinforce its effects and help to tie the core of the class to the surrounding membership. Studies of class cohesion in Britain have shown that the central mechanisms of integration have been the informality and frequency of communication and the similarity of attitudes and opinions which result from a common social background: the exclusivity in recruitment has been a major contributor to social integration. Researchers from the Manchester Business School (Lupton and Wilson 1959; Whitley 1973; 1974) discovered that the directors of the major City financial intermediaries had close kinship links with one another and interacted freely and easily in clubs and on the grousemoors as well as in boardrooms and on committees (see also Stanworth and Giddens 1974a, p. 99ff.; Rex 1974b; Thomas 1979; Lisle-Williams 1984). A common background and pattern of socialization, reinforced through intermarriage, residential propinquity, and other forms of interpersonal interaction, generated a community of feeling among the core members of the British upper class (Scott 1982b, pp. 159–60). Useem (1984) found that membership of exclusive clubs and the holding of a title were both associated with the number of directorships held: 8.9 per cent of those with one directorship in 196 large enterprises of 1976 were members of one of the exclusive London clubs, while 31.8 per cent of those with three or more directorships were members of these same clubs; 3.6 per cent of those with one directorship had a title (a knighthood, baronetcy, or peerage), while 17.5 per cent of those with three or more directorships were titled (Useem 1984, pp. 65, 69).[22] There is some evidence that social exclusivity has been greatest in the City and least in such areas as retailing, where the number of titled directors in 1974 was about half that found in the City (A. B. Thomas 1978).

Similar mechanisms of integration have been identified in the United States. Baltzell (1958, p. 7) has argued that the wealthy American families are integrated into a national upper class through friendship, intermarriage, and lifestyle, schooling being an especially important aspect of upper-class lifestyle. Useem (1984, p. 68) reports that about one in six multiple directors in the top 212 American enterprises of 1976 had attended exclusive boarding schools and that one in five were listed in the *Social Register*. American researchers have emphasized the contribution to class cohesion which has been made by interlocking directorships: the web of interlocks generates a 'unification of outlook and policy' (Mills 1956, p. 123) and reinforces the informality of kinship and friendship by creating 'well-oiled communication channels through which business deals of a wide variety can be furthered' (Sonquist *et al.* 1975, p. 199; see also Koenig *et al.* 1979; Koenig and Gogel 1981). Clement has presented a similar picture of the Canadian upper class, pointing to the 'elite forums' which provide exclusive locales for upper-class interaction (1975a, p. 255ff.), though he recognizes the divisions of orientation and ethnicity which cross-cut the class. The division between the internationally-oriented capitalists and those with purely domestic interests, he argues, is an important source of segmentation (Clement 1975b; Marchak 1979), though it has been shown in Chapter 5 that the two sectors have close economic links. A more important division in Canada, and one with implications for the degree of upper-class cohesion is that between Anglophones and Francophones. While the dominant status group within the upper class is based in Toronto and Montreal and operates nation-wide, the French Canadian businesses of Quebec operate on a somewhat smaller scale and recruit from their own community (Niosi 1981).

Useem (1984) has emphasized the part played in integration by those he terms, following Lundberg (1937) and Zeitlin (1974), the 'inner circle' of the upper class.[23] The members of the inner circle are the multiple directors, those who occupy key positions in the intercorporate network and whose connections generate a high degree of cohesion within the core of the class (Useem 1984, pp. 61–2). On a number of measures of social exclusiveness the inner circle were found to be more exclusive than were those with a directorship in just one major enterprise: in both Britain and the United States they were more likely to have attended a private school, more likely to be members of big city clubs, and more likely to have a title or to be mentioned in the *Social Register* (Useem 1984, pp. 65, 68, 69; Soref 1976, p. 360). Most important, Useem argues that their position in the intercorporate network gives them access to a wide spread of business information and that this leads them to adopt a standpoint in business affairs which 'discourages the specific and fosters the general' (1984, p. 55).

That is to say, over and above their participation in the strategic control of particular enterprises, members of the inner circle have a role in 'consensus building' in the sphere of business opinion and act as the 'leading edge' of the upper class in matters of general business policy (see also Lundberg 1969, p. 302ff.). Through membership of commissions and advisory bodies they are able to bring this viewpoint to the heart of the political system.

In Britain the inner circle has formed part of the 'establishment', a dominant status group within the upper class. The British establishment emerged in the last third of the nineteenth century as the newly powerful industrialists began to fuse with the already powerful financial and landed classes. The business class was forged in a cultural context in which the values of the landed class could be taken over and adapted to legitimate the new forms of corporate power which were based around property and inheritance in all spheres of the economy. The core ideas of the landed class became the defining status symbols of the establishment, the gentlemen of property who monopolized the major political positions and the key posts in the military, the church, and the law (Scott 1982b, p. 104ff.). The inner circle of business leaders have been drawn from this establishment, and they and their sons have been able to transfer from business to politics and the professions with ease. Since the Second World War the establishment has crumbled as a political force, though it survived in an attenuated form as a status group. The inner circle of finance capitalists have had to come to terms with the interventionist and corporatist state practices which have superseded the informality of establishment politics (Scott 1982b, p. 179ff.; Finer 1956; Guttsman 1963; 1974; Johnson 1973; Miliband 1969).

Pluralist writers in the United States have claimed that business leaders form a loose coalition of sub-groupings with divergent interests and that they exercise little influence over matters other than economic affairs (Rose 1967, pp. 102–3; Presthus 1973). Against this position it has been argued that the United States, like Britain, has a business establishment. In a critical review of this idea, Burch (1983) nevertheless concluded that a business establishment, less extensive than that of Britain, emerged in the 1940s and became a major force in policy-making through its participation in advisory bodies such as the Business Round Table, the Business Council, the Council on Foreign Relations, and the Trilateral Commission, and through donations to presidential and party campaigns (Burch 1983; Useem 1984, pp. 73, 87; Domhoff 1975; Freitag 1975; Mintz 1975).[24] Clearly, the notion of an establishment in the United States is employed to describe not a dominant status group but the inner circle of business leaders who themselves monopolize key political positions. Yanaga (1968) has argued that a similar phenomenon is observable in Japan, where the business leaders influence state policy through their membership in various overlapping *batsu*. These 'cliques' or 'circles' reflect the high concentration of business influence, the business cliques (*zaikai*) centred on the employers' association and chamber of commerce, have ensured that the Liberal Democratic Party has been, in effect, the political arm of organized business. In the *zaikai*, argues Yanaga, business interests are discussed and negotiated in order to form a unified general viewpoint which can be conveyed to the government and other bodies as the consensus of the business community. As in Britain and the United States, the inner circle of Japanese business leaders constitutes the political leading edge of the upper class.

It has been argued that members of capitalist upper classes can influence the recruitment and integration of their class through more or less deliberate strategies of social closure. With the declining salience of the direct inheritance of corporate power, alternative mechanisms of recruitment have had to be adopted. The managerial re-organization of the propertied class means that the traditional claims of property and inheritance have had to be supplemented with 'credentialist' claims to relevant education and technical expertise. Bourdieu and his colleagues have argued that this constitutes a transition from the 'personal' mode of class domination appropriate to the atomistic market economy to the 'structural' mode of domination which corresponds to highly concentrated economies. When selection and promotion of business leaders depend on educational credentials, upper-class dominance comes to depend on its success in monopolizing the benefits of the educational system: the class can ensure that its members are well-placed at the start of the contest for corporate positions and so can offset the declining possibilities for direct inheritance. If the established families can monopolize access to the educational system, they can ensure that those most qualified for controlling positions in the corporate system are none other than their own scions. Whereas the personal mode of domination involved the 'direct transmission of social positions between the holder and the inheritor designated by the holder himself', the structural mode of domination operates in an indirect way at the level of the class as a whole: transmission of positions within the dominant class 'rests on the *statistical* aggregation of the isolated actions of individuals or collective agents who are subject to the same laws, those of the educational market' (Bourdieu *et al.* 1973, p. 83).[25]

Thus, wealth gives the means for purchasing a privileged education and thus enables wealthy families to 'convert' their economic assets into the cultural assets of educational certificates and accomplishments. These cultural assets become the means through which access to well-paid jobs in capitalist locations can be achieved, and thus they can be 'reconverted' into further economic assets. Through such 'strategies of reconversion', wealthy families may reproduce and enhance their life chances without having to transmit controlling blocks of corporate shares to the next generation (Bourdieu 1971, p. 73; Bourdieu and Passeron 1970). The majority of those who achieve high levels of education will not enter positions of strategic control, but will take jobs in middle management or in the professions. The success of members of upper-class households in achieving capitalist locations continues to depend, to a substantial extent, on the social assets provided by a person's social background – kinship and connections are necessary for entry to the 'right' school and college and can ensure entry to capitalist locations. Despite the fact that it may be necessary to recruit a small number of outsiders to such positions, 'the controlled mobility of a limited category of individuals, carefully selected and modified by and for individual ascent, is not incompatible with the permanence of structures' (Bourdieu 1971, p. 71). The stability of class relations and their reproduction over time can be ensured so long as the new occupants of capitalist locations are endowed with the attitudes and competences already possessed by the established occupants of these positions. Recruitment through restrictions on entry and integration through similarity of social background and experience are interdependent aspects of the social closure achieved by upper classes.

An upper class of propertied families owing their superior life chances to the income and wealth which their property generates can still be found at the head of the stratification systems of modern industrial capitalism. Far from having their privileges usurped by upwardly mobile career managers, they remain a potent economic and political force. The emergence of impersonal possession has resulted merely in a managerial re-organization of the propertied class. Wealthy families have diversified their income-earning assets and many now participate in strategic control on the basis of mechanisms other than direct inheritance of a place in the family firm. Through strategies of social closure, upper-class households ensure their control over the recruitment and integration of their class and the perpetuation of their privileges.

Notes

1 See the criticisms of these positions made in Bendix (1945) and Mills (1942).

2 Poulantzas was not the first to employ the concept of unproductive labour to define the location of the 'middle class'. A particularly influential work to follow a similar line was Nicolaus (1967). An attempt to extend Nicolaus's work can be found in Urry (1973).

3 Similar conclusions have been arrived at in the thorough and stimulating discussion of Abercromby and Urry (1983). Wright (1983) has recast some of his leading ideas, but this does not substantially affect the argument of this chapter.

4 Abercromby and Urry (1983), p. 110ff. make this point but follow the Marxist usage of 'class place' rather than using the term 'economic location'.

5 This stress on 'household' rather than 'individual' or 'family' as the basis of class situation cannot be fully defended here. My position owes much to Pahl (1984), though Pahl does not pursue the implications of his analysis of household structure for the reconceptualization of class.

6 Weber's remarks on stratification are insightful but fragmentary. Though he sees property as basic to class analysis, he often tends to treat this only in so far as it is reflected in the market mechanism.

7 It must be emphasized that the distinction between 'core' and 'fringe' members does not correspond to differences in level of wealth. The core households of the class are defined by the

dual fact of their derivation of superior life chances from the operation of the business system and the participation of their members in the strategic control of that system.

8   For a discussion of the problems of drawing class boundaries, see Mackenzie (1982).

9   See Goldthorpe (1982) and also Bechhofer *et al.* (1978) and Goldthorpe (1978). The concept of a service class was in fact first formulated by Renner.

10   Some occupants of service locations may be members of the propertied upper class who have the economic freedom to take such jobs without the risk of downward mobility.

11   A number of such consultants may have accumulated experience and contacts through career employment prior to adopting a self-employed position.

12   Weber adds that the most extreme form of closure is the religious sanctioning of caste distinctions.

13   Critics of official statistics, such as Titmuss (1962), Meade (1964), and Atkinson (1975) have suggested that actual concentration may be somewhat higher than this.

14   Considerable dispute has arisen in recent years over the precise figures on income and wealth distribution in Britain during the 1970s. The disputants have analysed variations in year-to-year proportions and have tried to extrapolate from these. It is still too early to see whether these are minor fluctuations around a long-term constant proportion, whether they indicate a change of trend, or whether they reflect the peculiar economic features of the 1970s. See Atkinson (1972), Polanyi and Wood (1974), Diamond Report (1975a).

15   The calculations on relative purchasing power are based on indices given in Butler and Sloman (1979).

16   Townsend recognizes that his measure understates the value of the assets of the rich and leads to a correspondingly greater apparent significance of income in income net worth.

17   Some sectoral variations have been discovered. Whitt (1981), for example, found that the proportion of directors from top universities in 1970 was lower in the oil industry than the average for manufacturing industry.

18   Perkin (1978), p. 227 shows that, over the period 1880–1970, only one woman became chairman of one of the top 200

enterprises – Lady Pirrie, who succeeded her husband at Harland and Wolff.

19 In Britain the so-called 'public schools' are, in fact, private schools.

20 For some fragmentary evidence on Canada and Australia see Porter (1965), pp. 122, 246–7, 275–8; Clement (1975a), pp. 192, 173–8; Smith and Tepperman (1974); Encel (1970), pp. 391–5.

21 On land and industry in Germany see Koenig (1971), p. 284.

22 Biographical information of this type is complicated by the fact that not all directors were listed in the reference books consulted. It is therefore possible to base estimates on either the proportion of those listed or the proportion of those in the data set. Useem is inconsistent on which is likely to be closer to the actual figure (1984), pp. 65, 209, but it seems clear that what he calls the 'B estimate' (based on the proportion of those in the data set) is the preferable figure. This is confirmed by a statement in Useem and McCormack (1981), p. 389.

23 In Useem (1978) this group is called the 'inner group', the term employed by Zeitlin (1974), and in Useem (1982) they were called the 'dominant segment'.

24 Burch criticizes Silk and Silk (1980).

25 Bourdieu and Boltanski (1978) seems to be a virtual translation of Bourdieu *et al.* (1973), though no indication of this fact is given.

9 The search for an alternative theory

This book has tried to show the ways in which the big business enterprise and its influence on our everyday lives are determined by the patterns of ownership and control in which the enterprise is enmeshed. Neither the theory of industrial society nor the theory of capitalist society have proved able to grasp the complexities of modern industrial capitalism, though a number of their achievements have been recognized. The alternative view which has been presented in this book centres on the transition from personal to impersonal possession and the re-organization of the propertied class which this has entailed. In all the major capitalist economies entrepreneurial capitalists with personal majority or minority control have declined in numbers and significance, though they are by no means unimportant in the modern economy. The prevailing form of ownership is now a de-personalized structure of inter-corporate shareholdings, and the many families that survive as large shareholders become co-opted into a dominant group of finance capitalists with interests throughout the system. The concrete forms taken by this structure of impersonal possession have been shown to vary from one country to another: in the Anglo-American economies it has involved a polyarchic structure of hegemonic financial intermediaries which participate in the controlling constellations of the major enterprises; in Germany an oligarchy of banks retains an important role in the network of connections; in Belgium and France intercorporate shareholdings have been structured into a loose holding system; and in Japan the predominant form of organization is tight combines built from coalitions of aligned participations. In no case has control been divorced from ownership. Strategic control reflects the continuation of proprietary interests. The growing concentration of markets, the internationalization of production, the increased economic role of the state, and internal changes in corporate administration have enhanced the dominance of the large enterprises and their controllers, and have buttressed the continuing power and wealth of the upper-class households who depend on its operations for their superior life chances. The managerial revolution, far from nearing completion, has not yet begun.

The characteristic pattern of capitalist development in Britain, the United States, Australia, and Canada has involved a transition from the personal forms of majority and minority control to the impersonal form of control through a constellation of interests. The management control which emerged in the United States in the 1930s, and to a lesser extent and later elsewhere, was a relatively short-lived response to the dispersal of shareholdings which had begun at the turn of the century and which was markedly reversed with the growth of 'institutional' holdings in the post-war period. Minority and majority control by families and individual entrepreneurs has increasingly operated within an environment structured by the system of impersonal possession. This system can be understood as a system of finance capital, a structuring of capital in manufacturing, commerce, and banking such that there are relatively few obstacles to its free movement from one sector to another. Finance capital involves the existence of an extensive intercorporate network of capital, commercial, and personal relations in which an inner circle of finance capitalists is the embodiment of this network of intercorporate relations. Through their directorships in the hegemonic financial intermediaries the finance capitalists exercise a considerable influence over the mobilization of capital, and hence over the strategies pursued by the enterprises which make up the system. Banks, with their associated spheres of influence, play a key role in this network by providing the important meeting points for finance capitalists and by virtue of the central position of banks in the provision of credit.

This pattern of development has had an important effect on the internal administration and decision-making of enterprises. In the United States a centralized form of large-scale administration emerged in the enterprises created by the investment banks of the 'Money Trust', and this gradually gave way to a decentralized divisional organization as control through a constellation of interests became the predominant mode of control over corporate strategy. The form of relationship between the City and industry in Britain meant that an extremely loose system of decentralized administration emerged in the inter-war years; only in the post-war period, when competition from the more efficient American enterprises threatened to decimate British industry, did divisional organization become at all widespread. Within the multi-divisional enterprise the managers are constrained to meet the requirements set out in the corporate strategy by their acceptance of financial criteria of corporate viability and by their orientation towards success in their career. It is through the interplay of mode of control and mode of administration that the range of market possibilities is narrowed-down to a specific item of corporate behaviour.

The upper class in the Anglo-American societies owes its privileged life chances to the benefits generated by the system of finance capital, though the continuing importance of entrepreneurial capitalists with personal possession of particular units of capital should not be underemphasized. In the stratification system, the impersonal possession of capital is reflected in the managerial re-organization of the propertied class, which is no longer so fragmented into kinecon, ethnic, or regional groups but is organized at a national level through the background and connections which its members have in common. The inner circle of finance capitalists lies at the core of the class and plays an important role in the formulation and representation of the interests of the business world. Finance capitalists have had increasingly to supplement the older informal mechanisms of business representation with mechanisms more appropriate to interventionist states in which formally organized interests play a great role. The finance capitalists in the Anglo-American economies, therefore, appear as key agents in mediating the interests of capitalist property owners 'downwards' into corporate administration and 'outwards' into the realm of politics.

A number of alternative patterns can be discerned outside the Anglo-American world which has figured large in the bulk of the research and theoretical work reviewed in this book. In none of the patterns discussed have insurance companies, pension funds, and the stock exchange played such a central role as they have in the Anglo-American economies; and banks and investment companies have played correspondingly greater roles. Only in the Netherlands was a situation similar to that in Britain and the United States discovered, but here it was overlain by a sharp separation between a bank-dominated domestic sector and a multinational sector independent of the influence of the Dutch banks. In Germany, pre-war Austria, and, at varying points and to a lesser extent, in Switzerland and Italy, a small number of 'universal' banks dominated the availability of share capital and other forms of credit. This 'oligarchic' form of impersonal possession resulted in a distinct, and highly efficient, system of capital mobilization in which bankers play a key role in deciding the major directions of corporate strategy. In France, Belgium, and pre-war Japan, banks have been subordinate to other investment interests and formed parts of more or less cohesive holding systems. The holding system involved the structuring of the economy into competing but overlapping interest groups, allied through mutual shareholdings and interlocks, in which bank capital played its part alongside family capital and the capital mobilized by the investment holding companies. With the replacement of the *zaibatsu* by the *kigyoshudan* in post-war Japan, tighter interest groups emerged with centralized strategic control. Each combine brought together enterprises in a range of industries, and a bank was invariably to be found at the heart of each of the major combines. Entrepreneurial capital has survived as an important element in all the advanced capitalist economies, including Britain and the United States, but small-scale capital has been especially important in Italy, France, and Belgium, where it plays a key role alongside the financial intermediaries and holding companies.

As in Britain, corporate administration in the rest of Western Europe and in Japan has involved a transition from small enterprises to large amorphous organizations in which the bureaucratization of management was inhibited by the perpetuation of dynastic family struggles on the parent board. This pattern prevailed through the inter-war years, though the post-war combines which developed in Japan led to its continuation in a modified form. In Europe, the federal holding company gradually gave way to the divisional organization with its decentralized systems of bureaucratic control. By the post-war period, therefore, divisional organization had become an important feature of the advanced capitalist economies. Operational managers experienced the constraints of de-personalized capital through the strategic control exercised by the finance capitalists and internal capitalists who filled the boardrooms of the large enterprises. As a result, the 'profit motive', far from declining in importance, has become institutionalized in the control systems of the modern enterprise. The upper class in all societies was based around the wealthy corporate controllers who monitored the pursuit of profit and supervised the behaviour of their subordinate managers. The finance capitalists who lie at the heart of this system have, in all societies, had to come to terms with higher levels of state intervention in economic affairs and to adopt more 'technocratic' principles of recruitment and action.

Despite the wide-sweeping implications of these trends in capitalist development, managerialism – especially the non-sectional variant – has been a potent influence on the public legitimations of business practice espoused by businessmen and business commentators. A survey in *The Economist*,[1] Britain's leading business magazine, recently claimed that American managers run their enterprises in a socially responsible way. The new class of professional managers, it argued, is recruited from the business schools and is responsive to the needs of their employees and consumers. They express 'the shift, common to all industrial countries, from blue-collar production of goods to white-collar, knowledge-intensive work; and ... the greater emphasis in advanced industrial societies on creating, rather than distributing, wealth'.[2] This shift has, it is argued, led managers to depart from formal principles of corporate administration and Taylorist scientific management to adopt 'informal systems' relying on a 'human relations' perspective which emphasizes the 'well-being' and 'quality of work life' of its employees. The 'motivation' of employees is all-important, and is encouraged by the greater 'respect' of managers for their workers. This view is widely-shared in the business communities of Britain, the United States, and Japan, and has led to a movement within the accountancy profession for the adoption of 'corporate social accounting'.[3] The auditing of a company, it is held, must take account not only of its financial probity but also of such factors as its health and safety record and its social impact. The modern business enterprise has to be responsive to all the 'stakeholders' with an interest in the company – employees, customers, government, and the public – as well as its shareholders and creditors. The basis for this claim is the supposed separation of ownership from control – professional managers divorced from the constraining influence of corporate shareholders have the freedom to respond to the more pressing constraints of other stakeholders.

The managerialist thesis, therefore, remains an important element in the self-image of the business community. But it has been argued throughout this book that the managerialist position and its associated theory of industrial society can no longer be used in explanation of business behaviour. But neither is the rival theory of capitalist society a feasible alternative, despite its continued use as the intellectual support of political ideology. Researchers must learn to live without the theoretical and political props provided by the two contending perspectives. Both must be rejected in favour of an alternative interpretation of modern capitalist development. The purpose of this book has been to clear the grounds of debate rather than prematurely to offer a systematic alternative to the inadequate theories. Its aim has been to outline what can now be regarded as established knowledge and so to highlight the remaining areas of contention. The question will inevitably be raised, however, of what is to be put in place of the rejected theories. The summary above has not attempted to answer this question, but simply sketched the main facts to be taken into account in any viable alternative. Facts, however, never 'speak for themselves'; they are not theoretically neutral, but draw on a more or less implicit theoretical framework. The framework which underlies the origins of the present book represents, in large part, the legacy of the two contending theories which have now been superseded. The working through of this framework and its development into an alternative theory of general relevance to the advanced capitalist societies with the explanatory scope of its rivals will be the end result of a long process of theoretical and empirical reseach. The ground-clearing carried out in this book is intended as a starting point for this research; its aim has been to set out the major directions in which future research should advance.

The major directions of advance have been drawn in the preceding chapters, but it is perhaps important here to spell out how the argument of this book requires the reconceptualization of particular areas of research. A great deal of basic sociographic research remains to be done in order to fill out the picture which has been presented. Only recently has research in Britain, America, and Japan begun to utilize available documentary evidence on shareholdings and directorships in a more sophisticated way than did the pioneers. In most of Western Europe this is now true for research on board membership and interlocks, but research into shareholdings is all but non-existent. In none of the advanced economies has bank lending been investigated in a systematic way in order to approach the issues involved in the concept of finance capital. Despite the great obstacles in obtaining data on bank

lending and, in countries other than Britain and Japan, on shareholdings, much can be done to complete the description painted in
this book. More fundamentally, a shift in methods and sources of
evidence is required if research is to move more markedly from
descriptive to explanatory concerns. Traditionally, research on the
issues of ownership and control has involved the cross-sectional
correlation of statistical data; new research must be more prepared
to adopt longitudinal case-study material, drawing on a variety of
documentary, observational, and interview material. This point
may be illustrated through two major areas of continuing debate:
the analysis of corporate performance and the investigation of
class power.

Sectional and non-sectional managerialist writings have both
emphasized the likely effect of the separation of ownership from
control on economic performance, though the effects which they
predict have differed. This common concern has stimulated the
considerable but indecisive research which was reviewed in Chapter 6. A major re-orientation of this research must involve more
satisfactory measures of 'control' and 'performance', and a clearer
understanding of the mechanisms which link the two. Previous
research has tended to operate with a simple dichotomous model
of strategic control: 'owner control' is identified on the basis of the
existence of a dominant shareholder with more than a specified
percentage holding, while 'management control' is the label used
to characterize the residual enterprises without dominant shareholders. This approach relies, of course, on an ill-thought-out
notion of management control, ignoring the existence of control
through a constellation of interests, but it also adopts an over-
simplified concept of owner control. The goals of the dominant
shareholder may vary between personal and corporate controllers,
the size of the controlling holding may influence the orientation of
the controller, and the strategy pursued by the controller may vary
according to whether the controlling holding is a newly acquired
block or the residue of an earlier holding. Research has largely
failed to come to grips with these issues, and there has not even
been any plausible and generally accepted specification of the
varying goals of the traditional entrepreneurial capitalist and the
modern pension fund. Similarly, there are problems in both select-
ing the appropriate indicators of corporate performance and arriving at accurate and reliable measures of these indicators. When
these tasks have been carried out it is possible to begin to tease out

the links between control and performance, recognizing that any effects will be mediated through the internal administrative structure of enterprises and constrained by their capital and product market situations. Only then will it be possible to begin to pursue some of the research suggestions of Lawriwsky (1984), who argued that the various modes of control must be seen as imposing distinct limits on the opportunities of action available to those who make up the dominant coalitions of the enterprises. Researchers should not expect to find any simple or clear-cut correlation between 'control' and 'performance', but should be open to more complex relationships. It can further be argued that alternative research strategies may prove more informative in this area. Rather than relying on cross-sectional correlations of economic indicators, researchers might investigate in detail, through case-study methods, responses to corporate failure. An enterprise that runs into serious difficulties and is – or is not – 'rescued' by other enterprises can be regarded as a trace of deeper intercorporate relations. The researcher must investigate which shareholders and banks are active in any reconstruction and which directors are hired or fired to implement the reconstruction. By pursuing such investigations the researcher can catch a glimpse of institutional intervention in action and can gain some understanding of its purposes and limits. There are, of course, considerable problems in implementing such a research strategy, not only the difficulty of obtaining the relevant information from behind 'closed doors', but also in awaiting suitable cases of corporate collapse and deciding on their representativeness. It remains true, however, that such research, using a mixture of documentary, observational, and interview material, offers the only realistic way of obtaining direct evidence on the impact of ownership and control on performance.

The question of class power has, of course, figured centrally in the theory of capitalist society, where the financial oligarchy which dominates industry is depicted as the core of a ruling class which dominates both the political and the ideological spheres. Research on this issue has adopted a 'social background' approach, examining the links between the occupancy of certain 'top' positions in the corporate world and the occupancy of leading roles in the institutions of political decision-making. Such research shades over all too easily into the analysis of 'elites', the anodyne non-Marxist alternative to the concept of ruling class, and the adoption of an elitist perspective by writers such as Miliband (1969) led to the counter-position of Poulantzas (1969).[4] This latter position rejected the emphasis on social background and stressed the structural constraints which operate on all occupants of positions of political power. It has been argued in Chapter 8 that social background research is invaluable in arriving at definitive conclusions on the integration and recruitment of the upper class. Nevertheless, it must be recognized that the issues of the economic power exercised by members of this class and the political power which their participation in the state machine affords them are analytically and empirically distinct from the issues of social background. As has frequently been pointed out, similarity of background and occupancy of institutional position, even if expressed in a consensus of opinion, are not to be equated with the actual exercise of power. Future research in this area must address the latter directly. The economic power available to members of upper-class households must be studied through the opportunities which their presence on company boards affords them for participation in strategic control. To understand this, it is necessary to study the roles of internal, entrepreneurial, and finance capitalists in corporate decision-making and, in particular, to investigate the part played by banks and bank directors in and through bank spheres of influence. To what extent, it must be asked, does the intercorporate network of capital, commercial, and personal relations provide the foundation for the power of the inner circle of finance capitalists to influence decisions taken in particular enterprises and to formulate a generalized conception of business interests? Once again, a case-study approach might best be pursued, combining documentary sources with the observational and interview methods pioneered by Pahl and Winkler (1974).[5] Explanations of economic power must inevitably lead to a direct confrontation with the question of political power exercised by these same people and by those drawn from a similar social background. The potential of the social background approach must initially be pushed to its fullest extent by examining the network of interpersonal connections which link the major political organizations with one another and with economic organizations. But this is only the beginning of an adequate research design. It is important to recognize the value of the pluralist emphasis on the study of key decisions, though it is equally important to see that such a study can yield fruitful results only if the structural context in which decisions are made has already been mapped by different methods. Studying the role of upper-class members in decision-making is, as is by now well-known, seriously limited by the 'behind-the-scenes' processes of non-decision-making which are not generally accessible to observation by the social researcher. Nevertheless, the attempt must be made, using all methods and sources of evidence available.

Through pursuing research in the directions indicated, and in all the other directions suggested in earlier chapters, the alternative theoretical framework which has been glimpsed in this book will begin to be fleshed-out in greater detail. But it is, perhaps, a mistake to expect to find any general theory of social development, as Giddens (1984) has pointed out. Both functionalism and Marxism, the underlying frameworks for the theories of industrial society and capitalist society, depict social development as the immanent unfolding of social mechanisms internal to specific systems of action. Such general theories have involved the assertion that particular clusters of social institutions comprise the 'motor' of social change, both the theories under consideration here emphasizing the pivotal role of economic institutions. Giddens has persuasively argued that these theories cannot be replaced with a theory of a similar form: 'In explaining social change no single and sovereign mechanism can be specified; there are no keys that will unlock the mysteries of human social development, reducing them to a unitary formula, or that will account for the major transitions between societal types in such a way either' (Giddens 1984, p. 243). The alternative theory which underlies the argument of this book draws heavily on recent work within the Marxist tradition, but it must not be assumed that the final result of the theoretical and empirical research programme set out in this book will bear any but the most superficial similarities to the theory of the founding father himself. Much has been made of the concepts of Weber, a writer who was much more aware than was Marx of the pitfalls of general systems of theory. But again, research will advance beyond the ideas of Weber himself. This book has spelt out the starting point of the research programme; the point to which that programme might lead can hardly be glimpsed.

Notes

1   *The Economist*, 4 January 1985.
2   ibid. p. 93.

3 I draw here on Jones (1984).
4 See also Miliband (1970 and 1973).
5 In their research, Pahl and Winkler (1974) studied the roles of inside and outside directors in particular companies. Their approach must be extended to investigate the role of outside directors in inter-company affairs.

Bibliography

In all cases the date of first publication follows the author's name. Occasionally an additional date appears after the publisher's name, and refers to the English language edition or to a reprint.

Aaronovitch, S. (1955), *Monopoly: A Study of British Monopoly Capitalism*, London: Lawrence and Wishart

Aaronovitch, S. (1961), *The Ruling Class*, London: Lawrence and Wishart

Aaronovitch, S. and Sawyer, M. C. (1975), *Big Business*, London: Macmillan ρ 78

Abercromby, N. and Urry, J. (1983), *Capital, Labour, and the Middle Classes*, London: George Allen and Unwin

Adams, T. F. M. and Hoshi, I. (1972), *A Financial History of the New Japan*, Tokyo: Kodansha International

Aitken, H. G. J. (1959a), 'The changing structure of the Canadian economy', in Aitken (1959b)

Aitken, H. G. J. (1959b), *The American Impact on Canada*, Cambridge University Press

Alchian, A. A. (1950), 'Uncertainty, evolution and economic theory', *Journal of Political Economy*, 58/2

Allan, G. (1982), 'Property and family solidarity', in Hollowell (ed.) (1982)

Allard, P., Beaud, M., Bellon, B., Lévy, A-M., and Lienart, S. (1978), *Dictionnaire des groupes industriels et financiers en France* (Dictionary of Industrial and Financial Groups in France), Paris: Editions du Senil

Allen, G. C. (1972), *A Short Economic History of Modern Japan*, third edition, London: George Allen and Unwin

Allen, G. C. (1940), 'The concentration of economic control', in Livingston *et al.* (eds.) (1973a)

Allen, M. P. (1974), 'The structure of interorganizational elite cooptation', *American Sociological Review*, 39

Allen, M. P. (1976), 'Management control in the large corporation', *American Journal of Sociology*, 81/4

Allen, M. P. (1978a), 'Economic interest groups and the corporate elite', *Social Science Quarterly*, 58

Allen, M. P. (1978b), 'Continuity and change within the core corporate elite', *Sociological Quarterly*, 19

Allen, M. P. (1981), 'Power and privilege in the large corporation: corporate control and managerial comensation', *American Journal of Sociology*, 86

Althusser, L. and Balibar, R. (1970), *Reading Capital*, Paris: Maspero

Altvater, E. (1972), 'Notes on some problems of state intervention', *Kapitalistate*, 1 and 2

Amin, S. (1971), *Accumulation on a World Scale*, New York: Monthly Review Press, 1974

Amin, S. (1973), *Unequal Development*, Sussex: Harvester Press, 1976

Anderson, D., *et al.* (1941), *Final Report to the Temporary National Economic Committee on the Concentration of Economic Power in the United States*, Washington: Government Printing Office for the US Senate

Anderson, P. (1964), 'Origins of the present crisis', *New Left Review*, 23

Andrews, J. A. Y. (1982), *The Interlocking Corporate Director: A Case Study in Conceptual Confusion*, MA Dissertation, University of Chicago

Ansoff, H. I. (1965), *Corporate Strategy*, New York: McGraw-Hill

Antitrust Committee (1965), *Interlocks in Corporate Management*, Antitrust Subcommittee of the Committee on the Judiciary, House of Representatives, 89th Congress, 1st session, Washington: Government Printing Office

Archer, M. S. and Giner S. (eds.) (1971), *Contemporary Europe: Class, Status, and Power*, London: Routledge and Kegan Paul

Armstrong, P. (1984), 'Management control strategies and interprofessional competition', Paper to UMIST-Aston Conference on the Labour Process, March 1984

Aron, R. (1960), 'Classe Sociale, classe politique, classe dirigeante' ('Social class, political class, ruling class'), *European Journal of Sociology*, 1/2

Aron, R. (1967), *The Industrial Society*, London: Weidenfeld and Nicolson

Aron, R. (1968), *Progress and Disillusion*, Harmondsworth: Penguin, 1972

Atkinson, A. B. (1972), *Unequal Shares*, Harmondsworth: Penguin, 1974

Atkinson, A. B. (1973a), 'The distribution of income in Britain and the US', in Atkinson (ed.) (1973b)

Atkinson, A. B. (ed.) (1973b), *Wealth, Income and Inequality*, Harmondsworth: Penguin

Atkinson, A. B. (1975), *The Economics of Inequality*, Oxford: Oxford University Press

Averitt, R. (1968), *The Dual Economy*, New York: W. W. Norton

Babeau, A., and Strauss-Kahn, D. (1977), *La richesse des français* (The Wealth of the French), Paris: Presses Universitaires de France

Bacon, J., and Brown, J. K. (1977), *The Board of Directors: Perspectives and Practices in Nine Countries*, New York: The Conference Board

Baldamus, W. (1961), *Efficiency and Effort*, London: Tavistock

Baltzell, E. D. (1958), *Philadelphia Gentlemen*, Glencoe, Ill.: Free Press

Bank of England (1979), 'Composition of company boards', *Bank of England Quarterly Review*, 14

Banks, J. A. (1959), 'Veblen and industrial sociology', *British Journal of Sociology*, 10/3

Baran, P. A. (1957), *The Political Economy of Growth*, Harmondsworth: Penguin

Baran, P. A., and Sweezy, P. M. (1966), *Monopoly Capital*, Harmondsworth: Penguin, 1968

Barratt Brown, M. (1968a), 'The controllers of British industry', in Coates (ed.) (1968) p 58 - 60

Barratt Brown, M. (1968b), 'The limits of the welfare state', in Coates (ed.) (1968)

Barratt Brown, M. (1974), *The Economics of Imperialism*, Harmondsworth: Penguin

Barry, B. (ed.) (1976), *Power and Political Theory*, London: Wiley

Baum, D. J. and Stiles, N. B. (1965), *The Silent Partners: Institutional Investors and Corporate Control*, Syracuse University Press

Baumol, W. J. (1959), *Business Behaviour*, New York: Macmillan

Baumol, W. J. (1962), 'On the theory of expansion of the firm', *American Economic Review*, 52

Bearden, J., Atwood, W., Freitag, P., Hendricks, C., Mintz, B. and Schwartz, M. (1975), 'The nature and extent of bank centrality in corporate networks', Paper to the American Sociological Association

Bearden, J. and Mintz, B. (1985), 'Regionality and integration in the United States interlock network', in Stokman *et al.* (1985)

Bechhofer, F., Elliott, B. and McCrone, D. (1978), 'Structure, consciousness and action: a sociological profile of the British middle class', *British Journal of Sociology*, 29

Becker, G. S. (1962), 'Irrational behaviour and economic theory', *Journal of Political Economy*, 70/1

Becker, L. C. (1977), *Property Rights*, London: Routledge and Kegan Paul

Beed, C. S. (1966), 'The separation of ownership from control', *Journal of Economic Studies*, 1/2

Bell, D. (1953), 'The prospects of American capitalism', in Bell (1961)

Bell, D. (1957), 'The breakup of family capitalism', in Bell (1961)

Bell, D. (1958), 'Is there a ruling class in America?', in Bell (1961)

Bell, D. (1961), *The End of Ideology*, New York: Collier-Macmillan

Bell, D. (1974), *The Coming of Post-Industrial Society*, London: Heinemann

Bellon, B. (1977), 'Méthodologie de délimitation et de reportage des ensembles financiers' (a methodology of delimiting and reporting financial groups), Working Paper, CERCA, Paris

Bendix, R. (1945), 'Bureaucracy and the problem of power', *Public Administration Review*, 5

Bendix, R. (1956), *Work and Authority in Industry*, New York: Wiley

Bendix, R. and Lipset, S. M. (eds.) (1953), *Class, Status and Power*, Glencoe, Ill.: Free Press

Bendix, R. and Lipset, S. M. (eds.) (1967), *Class, Status and Power*, revised edition, London: Routledge and Kegan Paul

Berger, S. (ed.) (1981), *Organizing Interests in Western Europe*, Cambridge: Cambridge University Press

Berkowitz, S. D. (1975), 'The dynamics of elite structure', Thesis for the degree of PhD, Brandeis University

Berle, A. A. (1955), *The Twentieth Century Capitalist Revolution*, London: Macmillan

Berle, A. A. (1960), *Power Without Property*, New York: Harcourt Brace

Berle, A. A. (1963), *The American Economic Republic*, London: Sidgwick and Jackson

Berle, A. A. and Means, G. C. (1932), *The Modern Corporation and Private Property*, New York: Macmillan, 1947

Bertaux, D. (1977), *Destins personnels et structure de classe* (Personal destiny and class structure), Paris: Presses Universitaires de France

Bettelheim, C. (1970), *Economic Calculation and Forms of Property*, London: Routledge and Kegan Paul, 1976

Bieda, K. (1970), *The Structure and Operation of the Japanese Economy*, Sydney: John Wiley

Birnbaum, N. (1969), *The Crisis of Industrial Society*, Oxford: Oxford University Press

Birnbaum, P. (1971), *La structure du pouvoir aux États-Unis* (The structure of power in the United States), Paris: Presses Universitaires de France

Birnbaum, P. (1980), 'The state in contemporary France', in Scase (ed.) (1980)

Blackburn, R. (1965), 'The new capitalism', in Blackburn (ed.) (1972)

Blackburn, R. (1967), 'The unequal society', in Blackburn and Cockburn (eds.) (1967)

Blackburn, R. (ed.) (1972), *Ideology in Social Science*, London: Fontana

Blackburn, R. and Cockburn, A. (eds.) (1967), *The Incompatibles*, Harmondsworth: Penguin

Blank, S. (1973), *Industry and Government in Britain*, Farnborough: Saxon House

Bleton, P. (1966), *Le capitalisme français* (French capitalism), Paris: Editions Ouvrieres

Bleton, P. (1974), 'L'argent: pouvoir ambigu' (Money: ambiguous power), *Economie et Humanisme*, 220

Bleton, P. (1976a), 'Le capitalisme francais a l'ombre de l'université' (French capitalism in the shadow of the university), *Economie et Humanisme*, 229

Bleton, P. (1976b), 'Bons concepts et méchantes realités' (Good concepts and bad realities), *Economie et Humanisme*, 229

Blumberg, P. I. (1975), *The Megacorporation in American Society*, Englewood Cliffs, NJ: Prentice-Hall

Boddy, R. and Crotty, J. (1974), 'Class conflict, Keynesian policies and the business cycle', *Monthly Review*, 26

Booth, A. (1982), 'Corporatism, capitalism, and depression in twentieth century Britain', *British Journal of Sociology*, 33

Bottomore, T. B. (1965), *Classes in Modern Society*, London: George Allen and Unwin

Bourdieu, P. (1971), 'Cultural reproduction and social reproduction', in Brown (ed.) (1973)

Bourdieu, P. (1974), 'Avenir de classe et causalité du probable' (Class future and the causality of the probable), *Revue française de sociologie*, 15/1

Bourdieu, P. and Boltanski, L. (1978), 'Changes in social structure and changes in the demand for education', in Giner and Archer (eds.) (1978)

Bourdieu, P. and De St Martin, M. (1978), 'Le patronat' (The directors), *Actes de la Récherche en Sciences Sociales*, 20–21

Bourdieu, P. and Passeron, J. C. (1970), *Reproduction in Education. Society and Culture*, London: Sage, 1977

Bourdieu, P. *et al.* (1973), 'Les stratégies de reconversion: Les classes sociales et le systeme d'enseignement' (Reconversion strategies: social classes and the system of education), *Social Science Information*, 12/5

Boyd, D. (1973), *Elites and their Education*, Windsor: NFER

Brady, R. A. (1943), *Business as a System of Power*, New York: Columbia University Press

Brandeis, L. D. (1914), *Other People's Money and How the Bankers Use It*, New York: Harper and Row, 1967

Brash, D. T. (1970), 'Australia as host to the international corporation', in Kindleberger (ed.) (1970)

Braverman, H. (1974), *Labour and Monopoly Capital*, New York: Monthly Review Press

Briston, R. J. and Dobbins, R. (1878), *The Growth and Impact of Institutional Investors*, London: Institute of Chartered Accountants

Broadbridge, S. (1966), *Industrial Dualism in Japan*, London: Frank Cass

Brooke, M. Z. and Remmers, A. L. (1970), *The Strategy of Multinational Enterprise*, London: Longman

Brooke, M. Z. and Remmers, A. L. (1972), *The Multinational Corporation in Europe*, London: Longman

Brown, G. (ed.) (1975), *The Red Paper on Scotland*, Edinburgh: Edinburgh University Student Publications Board

Brown, R. (ed.) (1973), *Knowledge, Education and Cultural Change*, London: Tavistock

Bukharin, N. (1915), *Imperialism and World Economy*, London: Merlin Press, 1972

Bukharin, N. and Preobrazhensky, E. (1920), *The ABC of Communism*, Harmondsworth: Penguin, 1962

Bunting, D. (1976), 'Corporate interlocks', parts 1–4, *Directors and Boards*, 1

Bunting, D. (1983), 'Origins of the American corporate network', *Social Science History*, 7

Bunting, D. and Barbour, J. (1971), 'Interlocking directorates in large American corporations, 1896–1964', *Business History Review*, 45/3

Burch, P. H. (1972), *The Managerial Revolution Reassessed*, Massachusetts: Lexington Books

Burch, P. H. (1983), 'The American establishment: its historical development and major economic components', *Research in Political Economy*, 6

Burcke, C. G. (1976), 'A group profile of the Fortune 500 chief executive', *Fortune*, 93 (May)

Burnham, J. (1941), *The Managerial Revolution*, Harmondsworth: Penguin, 1945

Burns, T. R. and Buckley, W. (eds.) (1976), *Power and Control*, London: Sage

Burt, R. (1980), 'Corporate profits and cooptation: a network analysis of market constraints and directorate ties in the 1967 American economy', Working Paper, Survey Research Center, Department of Sociology, University of California at Berkeley

Butler, D. and Sloman, A. (1979), *British Political Facts 1900–79*, London: Macmillan

Cafagna, L. (1971), 'Italy, 1830–1914', in Cipolla (ed.) (1973b)

Cairncross, A. K. (1953), *Home and Foreign Investment*, Cambridge: Cambridge University Press

Carchedi, G. (1975), 'On the economic identification of the new middle class', *Economy and Society*, 4/1

Carchedi, G. (1983), *Problems in Class Analysis*, London: Routledge and Kegan Paul

Carrington, J. C. and Edwards, G. T. (1979), *Financing Industrial Investment*, London: Macmillan

Carrington, P. J. (1981), 'Anticompetitive effects of directorship interlocks', Research Paper no. 27, Structural Analysis Programme, University of Toronto

Carosso, V. P. (1970), *Investment Banking in America*, Cambridge, Mass.: Harvard University Press

Carroll, W. K. (1982), 'The Canadian corporate elite: financiers or finance capitalists', *Studies in Political Economy*, 8

Castells, M. (1976), *La Crise économique et la société américane* (The economic crisis and American society), Paris: Presses Universitaires de France

Causer, G. (1978), *Private Capital and the State in Western Europe*, in Giner and Archer (1978)

Causer, G. (1982), 'Some aspects of property distribution and class structure', in Hollowell (ed.) (1982)

Caves, R. E. and Uekusa, M. (1976), *Industrial Organization in Japan*, Washington: Brookings Institution

Cawson, A. and Saunders, P. (1983), 'Corporatism, competitive politics and class struggle', in King (ed.) (1983)

CDE (1980a), 'Banking and finance', *CDE Stock Ownership Directory*, no. 3, New York: Corporate Data Exchange

CDE (1980b), *Banking and Finance: The Hidden Cost*, New York: Corporate Data Exchange

CDE (1981), *Fortune 500. CDE Stock Ownership Directory*, no. 5, New York: Corporate Data Exchange

Chamberlin, E. (1933), *The Theory of Monopolistic Competition*, Cambridge, Mass.: Harvard University Press

Chandler, A. D. (1962), *Strategy and Structure*, Cambridge, Mass.: MIT Press

Chandler, A. D. (1969), 'The structure of American industry in the twentieth century: an historical overview', *Business History Review*, 43

Chandler, A. D. (1976), 'The development of modern management structure in the US and UK', in Hannah (1979)

Chandler, A. D. (1977), *The Visible Hand*, Cambridge, Mass.: Belknap Press

Chandler, A. D. and Daems, H. (1974), 'Introduction', in Daems and Van der Wee (eds.) (1974)

Chandler, A. D. and Daems, H. (eds.) (1980), *Managerial Hierarchies*, Cambridge, Mass.: Harvard University Press

Channon, D. F. (1973), *The Strategy and Structure of British Enterprise*, London: Macmillan

Channon, D. F. (1977), *British Banking Strategy and the International*

Challenge, London: Macmillan

Chevalier, J. M. (1969), 'The problem of control in large American corporations', *The Antitrust Bulletin*, 14

Chevalier, J. M. (1970), *La structure financière de l'industrie américaine* (The financial structure of American industry), Paris: Cujas

Chiesi, A. M. (1982), 'L'Elite finanziaria Italiana' (The Italian financial elite), *Rassegna Italiana Di Sociologia*, 23

Chiesi, A. M. (1985), 'Property, capital, and network structure in the Italian case', in Stokman *et al.* (eds.) (1985)

Child, J. (1969a), *The Business Enterprise in Modern Industrial Society*, London: Collier-Macmillan

Child, J. (1969b), *British Management Thought*, London: George Allen and Unwin

Child, J. (1972), 'Organisational structure, environment and performance: The role of strategic choice', *Sociology*, 6

Child, J. (ed.) (1973), *Man and Organisation*, London: George Allen and Unwin

Cipolla, C. (ed.) (1973a), *The Fontana Economic History of Europe, Volume 3*, London: Fontana

Cipolla, C. (ed.) (1973b), *The Fontana Economic History of Europe, Volume 4*, London: Fontana

Citoleux, Y., Encaoua, D., Franck, B. and Héon, M. (1977), 'Les groupes de sociétés en 1974: une methode d'analyse' (Company groups in 1974: a method of analysis), *Economie et Statistique*, 87

Clark, R. (1979), *The Japanese Company*, New Haven: Yale University Press

Clarke, W. (1889), 'Industrial [Basis of Socialism]', in Shaw (ed.) (1889).

Clarke, W. M. (1967), *The City in the World Economy*, Harmondsworth: Penguin

Clement, W. (1975a), *The Canadian Corporate Elite*, Toronto: McClelland and Stewart

Clement, W. (1975b), *Continental Corporate Power*, Toronto: McClelland and Stewart

Clements R. V. (1958), *Managers: A Study of their Careers in Industry*, London: George Allen and Unwin

Coates, K. (ed.) (1968), *Can the Workers Run Industry?*, London: Sphere

Cole, G. D. H. (1948), *The Meaning of Marxism*, University of Michigan Press, 1964

Cole, G. D. H. (1955), *Studies in Class Structure*, London: Routledge and Kegan Paul

Collett, D. and Yarrow, G. (1976), 'The size distribution of large shareholdings in some leading British companies', *Oxford Bulletin of Economics and Statistics*

Commission on Concentration (1968), 'Ownership and influence in the economy', Extract from Commission on Industrial and Economic Concentration, Stockholm: Government Publications Office, in Scase (1976)

Connell, R. (1976), *Ruling Class, Ruling Culture*, Cambridge: Cambridge University Press

Copeman, G. H. (1955), *Leaders of British Industry*, London: Gee

Cottrell, P. L. (1975), *British Overseas Investment in the Nineteenth Century*, London: Macmillan

Cox, E. B. (1963), *Trends in the Distribution of Stock Ownership*, University of Pennsylvania Press

Crewe, I. (ed.) (1974), *British Political Sociology Yearbook, Volume 1*, London: Croom Helm

CRISP (1962), *Morphologie des groupes financiers belges* (Morphology of Belgian financial groups), Bruxelles: CRISP

Cronjé, S. *et al.* (1976), *Lonrho*, Harmondsworth: Penguin

Crosland, C. A. R. (1956), *The Future of Socialism*, London: Jonathan Cape

Crosland, C. A. R. (1962), *The Conservative Enemy*, London: Cape

Crouch, C. (1977), *Class Conflict and the Industrial Relations Crisis*, London: Heinemann

Crouch, C. (ed.) (1978), *British Political Sociology Yearbook, Volume 5*, London: Croom Helm

Crouch, C. (ed.) (1979), *State and Economy in Contemporary Capitalism*, London: Croom Helm

Crough, G. (1980), 'Small is beautiful but disappearing: a study of share ownership in Australia', *Journal of Australian Political Economy*, 8

Cubbin, J. and Leech, D. (1983), 'The effect of shareholder dispersion on the degree of control in British companies: theory and measurement', *Economic Journal*, 93

Cutler, A. *et al.* (1977), *Marx's 'Capital' and Capitalism Today, Volume 1*, London: Routledge and Kegan Paul

Cutler, A. *et al.* (1978), *Marx's 'Capital' and Capitalism Today, Volume 2*, London: Routledge and Kegan Paul

Cuyvers L. and Meeusen, W. (1976), 'The structure of personal influence of the Belgian holding companies', *European Economic Review*, 8/1

Cuyvers, L. and Meeusen, W. (1978), 'A time-series analysis of concentration in Belgian banking and holding companies', Paper to European Consortium for Political Research, Grenoble

Cuyvers, L. and Meeusen, W. (1985), 'Financial groups in the Belgian network of interlocking directorships', in Stokman *et al.* (eds.) (1985)

Daems, H. (1978), *The Holding Company and Corporate Control*, Leiden: Martinus Nijhoff

Daems, H. (1980), 'The rise of the modern industrial enterprise: a new perspective', in Chandler and Daems (eds.) (1980)

Daems, H. and Van der Wee, H. (eds.) (1974), *The Rise of Managerial Capitalism*, The Hague: Martinus Nijhoff

Dahrendorf, R. (1959), *Class and Class Conflict in an Industrial Society*, London: Routledge and Kegan Paul

Daumard, A. (1980), 'Wealth and affluence in France since the beginning of the nineteenth century', in Rubinstein (ed.) (1980)

Davis, K. and Moore, W. E. (1945), 'Some principles of stratification', *American Sociological Review*, 10/2

De Alessi, L. (1973), 'Private property and dispersion of ownership in large corporations', *Journal of Finance*, 28/4

De Vries, J. (1978), *The Netherlands Economy in the Twentieth Century*, Assen: Van Gorcum

De Vroey, M. (1973), *Propriété et pouvoir dans les grandes enterprises* (Property and power in large enterprises), Brussels: CRISP

De Vroey, M. (1975a), 'The separation of ownership and control in large corporations', *Review of Radical Political Economics*, 7/2

De Vroey, M. (1975b), 'The owners' interventions in decision-making on large corporations', *European Economic Review*, 6

De Vroey, M. (1976), 'The measurement of ownership and control in large corporations: a critical review', Document de travail, no. 718, CRIDE

Department of Industry (1979), *The Ownership of Company Shares: A survey for 1975*, London, HMSO for the Central Statistical Office

Dhondt, J. and Bruwier, M. (1970), 'The low countries, 1700–1914', in Cipolla (ed.) (1973b)

Diamond Report (1975a), *Royal Commission on the Distribution of Income and Wealth Report No. 1*, Cmnd 6172, London: HMSO

Diamond Report (1975b), *Royal Commission on the Distribution of Income and Wealth, Report No. 2*, Cmnd 6173, London: HMSO

Dodwell (1975), *Industrial Groupings in Japan*, Tokyo: Dodwell

Dodwell (1980), *Industrial Groupings in Japan, 1980–81*, Tokyo: Dodwell

Domhoff, G. W. (1967), *Who Rules America?*, Englewood Cliffs, NJ: Prentice-Hall

Domhoff, G. W. (1971), *The Higher Circles: The Governing Class in America*, New York: Vintage Books

Domhoff, G. W. (1974), *The Bohemian Grove*, New York: Harper and Row

Domhoff, G. W. (1975), 'Social clubs, policy-planning groups and corporations', *Insurgent Sociologist*, 5/3

Donolo, C. (1980), 'Social change and transformation of the state in Italy', in Scase (ed.) (1980)

Dooley, P. C. (1969), 'The interlocking directorate', *American Economic Review*, 59

Dore, R. (1973), *British Factory, Japanese Factory*, London: George Allen and Unwin

Drache, D. (1970), 'The Canadian bourgeoisie and its national consciousness', in Lumsden (ed.) (1970)

Drucker, P. F. (1951), *The New Society: The Anatomy of the Industrial Order*, London: Heinemann

Drucker, P. (1976), *The Unseen Revolution: How Pension Fund Socialism Came to America*, New York: Harper and Row

Dunkerley, D. and Salaman, G. (eds.) (1979), *International Yearbook of Organisation Studies 1979*, London: Routledge and Kegan Paul

Dunkerley, D. and Salaman, G. (eds.) (1980), *International Yearbook of Organisation Studies 1980*, London: Routledge and Kegan Paul

Dunning, J. H. (1970), *Studies in International Investment*, London: George Allen and Unwin

Dyas, G. P. and Thanheiser, H. T. (1976), *The Emerging European Enterprise*, London: Macmillan

Eaton, J. (1963), *Political Economy*, New York: International Publishers

Edwards, G. W. (1938), *The Evolution of Finance Capitalism*, London: Longmans Green

Edwards, R. (1979), *Contested Terrain*, London: Heinemann

Eisenberg, M. A. (1969), 'The legal roles of shareholder and management in modern corporate decision-making', *California Law Review*, 57/1

Encel, S. (1970), *Equality and Authority*, London: Tavistock

Erritt, M. J. and Alexander, J. C. D. (1977), 'Ownership of company shares', *Economic Trends*, September

Evely, R. and Little, I. M. D. (1960), *Concentration in British Industry*, Cambridge: Cambridge University Press

Fay, B. (1975), *Social Theory and Political Practice*, London: George Allen and Unwin

Feldman, G. D. (1981), 'German interest group alliances in war and inflation, 1914–23', in Berger (ed.) (1981)

Fennema, M. (1982), *International Networks of Banks and Industry*, The Hague: Martinus Nijhoff

Fennema, M. and Schijf, H. (1978), 'Analysing interlocking directorates', *Social Networks*, 1

Fennema, M. and Schijf, H. (1985), 'The transnational network', in Stokman *et al.* (eds.) (1985)

Fidler, J. (1981), *The British Business Elite*, London: Routledge and Kegan Paul

Field, F. (ed.) (1979), *The Wealth Report*, London: Routledge and Kegan Paul

Financial Times (1982), 'The F.T. European 500', Supplement to *Financial Times*, 21 October

Fine, B. and Harris, L. (1976), 'State expenditure in advanced capitalism: a critique', *New Left Review*, 98

Finer, S. (1955), 'The political power of private capital', part I, *Sociological Review*, 3

Finer, S. (1956), 'The political power of private capital', part II, *Sociological Review*, 4

Firn, J. (1975), 'External control and regional policy', in Brown (ed.) (1975)

Fitch, R. (1971), 'Reply to James O'Connor', *Socialist Revolution*, 7

Fitch, R. (1972), 'Sweezy and corporate fetishism', *Socialist Revolution*, 12

Fitch, R. and Oppenheimer, M. (1970a), 'Who rules the corporations?', part I, *Socialist Revolution*, 4

Fitch, R. and Oppenheimer, M. (1970b), 'Who rules the corporations?', part II, *Socialist Revolution*, 5

Fitch, R. and Oppenheimer, M. (1970c), 'Who rules the corporations?', part III, *Socialist Revolution*, 6

Florence, P. S. (1947), 'The statistical analysis of joint stock company control', *Statistical Journal*, part 1

Florence, P. S. (1953), *The Logic of British and American Industry*, London: Routledge and Kegan Paul, revised edition, 1961

Florence, P. S. (1961), *Ownership, Control, and Success of Large Companies*, London: Sweet and Maxwell

Fohlen, C. (1978), 'Entrepreneurship and management in France in the nineteenth century', in Mathias and Postan (eds.) (1978a)

Fournier, P. (1978), *The Quebec Establishment*, Montreal: Black Rose Books

Fox, A. (1973), 'Industrial relations: a socialist critique of pluralist ideology', in Child (ed.) (1973)

Fox, A. (1974), *Beyond Contract*, London: Faber and Faber

Francis, A. (1980a), 'Families, firms, and finance capital', *Sociology*, 14

Francis, A. (1980b), 'Company objectives, managerial motivations and the behaviour of large firms', *Cambridge Journal of Economics*

Frankel, H. (1970), *Capitalist Society and Modern Sociology*, London: Lawrence and Wishart

Francko, L. G. (1976), *The European Multinationals*, London: Harper and Row

Freitag, P. J. (1975), 'The Cabinet and big business: a study of interlocks', *Social Problems*, 23/2

Friedmann, A. (1977), *Industry and Labour*, London: Macmillan

Futatsugi, Y. (1969), 'The measurement of interfirm relationships', *Japanese Economic Studies*, 1973

Galaskiewicz, J. and Wasserman, S. (1981), 'A dynamic study of change in a regional corporate network', *American Sociological Review*, 46

Galbraith, J. K. (1952), *American Capitalism*, Massachusetts: Riverside Press

Galbraith, J. K. (1954), *The Great Crash*, Harmondsworth: Penguin, 1961

Galbraith, J. K. (1967), *The New Industrial State*, London: Hamish Hamilton

Gallino, L. (1971), 'Italy', in Archer and Giner (eds.) (1971)

George, K. D. and Ward, T. S. (1975), *The Structure of Industry in the EEC*, Cambridge: Cambridge University Press

Gershenkron, A. (1962), *Economic Backwardness in Historical Perspective*, Cambridge, Mass.: Belknap Press

Gerstenberger, H. (1976), 'Theory of the state', *German Political Studies*, 2

Gerth, H. and Mills, C. W. (1954), *Character and Social Structure*, London: Routledge and Kegan Paul

Gessell, G. A. and Howe, E. J. (1941), *A Study of Legal Reserve Life Insurance Companies*, Monographs of the Temporary National Economic Committee, no. 28, Washington: Government Printing Office for the US Senate

Giddens, A. (1971), *Capitalism and Modern Social Theory*, Cambridge: Cambridge University Press

Giddens, A. (1973), *The Class Structure of the Advanced Societies*, London: Hutchinson

Giddens, A. (1976), 'Classical social theory and the origins of modern sociology', *American Journal of Sociology*, 81/4

Giddens, A. (1984), *The Constitution of Society*, Cambridge: Polity Press

Giddens, A. and Mackenzie, G. (eds.) (1982), *Social Class and the Division of Labour*, Cambridge: Cambridge University Press

Gille, B. (1970), 'Banking and industrialisation in Europe, 1730–1914', in Cipolla (ed.) (1973a)

Giner, S. (1971), 'Spain', in Archer and Giner (eds.) (1971)

Giner, S. and Archer, M. S. (eds.) (1978), *Contemporary Europe: Social Structures and Cultural Patterns*, London: Routledge and Kegan Paul

Glasberg, D. A. (1981), 'Corporate power and control: the case of Leasco Corporation and Chemical Bank', *Social Problems*, 29

Glasberg, D. A. and Schwartz, M. (1983), 'Ownership and control of corporations', *Annual Review of Sociology*, 9

Glyn, A. and Sutcliffe, B. (1972), *British Capitalism, Workers and the Profit Squeeze*, Harmondsworth: Penguin

Gogel, R. and Koenig, T. (1981), 'Commercial banks, interlocking directorates and economic power: an analysis of the primary metals industry', *Social Problems*, 29

Goldsmith, R. W. (1958), *Financial Intermediaries in the American Economy since 1900*, Princeton University Press

Goldsmith, R. W. and Parmelee, R. C. (1940), *The Distribution of*

Ownership in the 200 Largest Non-financial Corporations, Monographs of the Temporary National Economic Committee, no. 29, Washington: Government Printing Office for the US Senate

Goldthorpe, J. H. (1964), 'Social stratification in industrial societies', in Halmos (ed.) (1964)

Goldthorpe, J. H. (1972), 'Class, status and party in modern Britain', *European Journal of Sociology*, 13

Goldthorpe, J. H. (1974), 'Theories of industrial society', *European Journal of Sociology*, 12/2

Goldthorpe, J. (1978), 'Comment', *British Journal of Sociology*, 29

Goldthorpe, J. (1982), 'On the service class, its formation and future', in Giddens and Mackenzie (eds.) (1982)

Gollan, J. (1956), *The British Political System*, London: Lawrence and Wishart

Gonick, C. W. (1970), 'Foreign ownership and political decay', in Lumsden (ed.) (1970)

Gordon, R. A. (1936), 'Stockholdings of officers and directors in American industrial corporations', *Quarterly Journal of Economics*, 50

Gordon, R. A. (1938), 'Ownership by management and control groups in the large corporations', *Quarterly Journal of Economics*, 52

Gordon, R. A. (1945), *Business Leadership in Large Corporations*, Washington: Brookings Institution

Gospel, H. (1983a), 'Management structure and strategies: an introduction', in Gospel and Littler (eds.) (1983)

Gospel, H. (1983b), 'The development of management organisation in industrial relations', in Thurley and Wood (eds.) (1983)

Gospel, H. and Littler, C. R. (eds.) (1983), *Management Strategy and Industrial Relations*, London: Heinemann

Gough, I. (1975), 'State expenditure in advanced capitalism', *New Left Review*, 92

Granick, D. (1962), *The European Executive*, New York: Doubleday

Granovetter, M. (1973), 'The strength of weak ties', *American Journal of Sociology*, 78

Grant, W. (1983), 'Representing capital: the role of the CBI', in King (ed.) (1983)

Grant, W. and Marsh, D. (1977), *The Confederation of British Industry*, London: Hodder and Stoughton

Grou, P. (1983), *La structure financière du capitalisme multi-national* (The financial structure of multinational capital-ism), Paris: Presses de la Fondation Nationale des Sciences Politiques

Grossfeld, B. and Ebke, W. (1978), 'Controlling the modern corporation: a comparative view of corporate power in the US and Europe', *American Journal of Comparative Law*, 26

Gustavsen, B. (1976), 'The social context of investment decisions', *Acta Sociologica*, 19

Guttsman, W. L. (1963), *The British Political Elite*, London: McGibbon and Kee

Guttsman, W. L. (1974), 'The British political elite and the class structure', in Stanworth and Giddens (eds.) (1974b)

Habermas, J. (1973), *Legitimation Crisis*, London: Hutchinson, 1976

Habermas, J. (1976), *Zur Rekonstruktion des historischen Materialismus* (The reconstruction of historical materialism), Frankfurt: Suhrkamp

Hadden, T. (1977), *Company Law and Capitalism*, London: Weidenfeld and Nicolson

Hadley, E. M. (1970), *Antitrust in Japan*, Princeton University Press

Hague, D. C. and Wilkinson, G. (1983), *The IRC: An Experiment in Industrial Intervention*, London: George Allen and Unwin

Hall, D., De Bettignies, H-C. and Amado-Fischgrund, G. (1969), 'The European business elite', *European Business*, 32

Hall, S. *et al.* (1957), 'The insiders', *Universities and Left Review*, 1/3

Halliday, J. (1975), *A Political History of Japanese Capitalism*, New York: Pantheon Books

Halliday, J. and McCormack, G. (1973), *Japanese Imperialism Today*, Harmondsworth: Penguin

Halmos, P. (ed.) (1964), *The Development of Industrial Societies*, Sociological Review Monograph, no. 8

Hannah, L. (1974), 'Managerial innovation and the rise of the large-scale company in interwar Britain', *Economic History Review*, 27

Hannah, L. (ed.) (1976a), *Management Strategy and Business Development*, London: Macmillan

Hannah, L. (1976b), 'Strategy and structure in the manufacturing sector', in Hannah (ed.) (1976a)

Hannah, L. (1976c), *The Rise of the Corporate Economy*, London: Methuen

Hannah, L. (1980), 'Visible and invisible hands in Great Britain', in Chandler and Daems (eds.) (1980)

Harbury, C. D. (1962), 'Inheritance and the distribution of personal wealth in Britain', in Atkinson (ed.) (1973b)

Harbury, C. D. and Hitchens, D. M. W. N. (1979), *Inheritance and Wealth Inequality in Britain*, London: George Allen and Unwin

Harbury, C. D. and McMahon, P. C. (1974), 'Intergenerational wealth transmission and the characteristics of top wealth leavers in Britain', in Stanworth and Giddens (1974b)

Harré, R. and Madden, E. (1975), *Causal Powers*, Oxford: Basil Blackwell

Harvey, J. and Hood, K. (1958), *The British State*, London: Lawrence and Wishart

Heath, A. (1981), *Social Mobility*, London: Fontana

Heilbronner, R. L. (1976), *Business Civilization in Decline*, Harmondsworth: Penguin

Helmers, H. M. *et al.* (1975), *Graven naur Macht* (Digging for power), Amsterdam: Van Gennep

Henderson, W. O. (1961), *The Industrial Revolution in Europe*, Chicago: Quadrangle

Herman, E. S. (1973), 'Do bankers control corporations', *Monthly Review*, 25/2

Herman, E. S. (1981), *Corporate Control, Corporate Power*, Cambridge: Cambridge University Press

Higley, J. *et al.* (1976), *Elite Structure and Ideology*, Oslo: Universitets-forlaget

Hilferding, R. (1910), *Finance Capital*, London: Routledge and Kegan Paul, 1981

Hirsch, J. (1977), 'Remarques théoriques sur l'état bourgeois et sa crise' (Theoretical remarks on the bourgeois state and its crisis), in Poulantzas (ed.) (1977)

Hirsch, J. (1980), 'Developments in the political system of Western Germany since 1945', in Scase (ed.) (1980)

Hirst, P. (1979), *On Law and Ideology*, London: Macmillan

Hobsbawm, E. J. (1968), *Industry and Empire*, Harmondsworth: Penguin, 1969

Hobson, J. A. (1906), *The Evolution of Modern Capitalism*, London: George Allen and Unwin, 1926

Hodges, M. (1974), *Multinational Corporations and National Government*, Farnborough: Saxon House

Holl, P. (1977), 'Control type and the market for corporate control in large US corporations', *Journal of Industrial Economics*, 25

Holl, P. (1980), 'Control type and the market for corporate control: reply', *Journal of Industrial Economics*, 28

Holland, S. (1975), *The Socialist Challenge*, London: Quartet

Holland, S. (1976), *Capital Versus the Regions*, London: Macmillan

Hollowell, P. G. (ed.) (1982), *Property and Social Relations*, London: Heinemann

Hollowell, P. G. (1982), 'On the operationalisation of property', in Hollowell (ed.) (1982)

Homburg, H. (1983), 'Scientific management and personnel policy in the modern German enterprise, 1918–39', in Gospel and Littler (eds.) (1983)

Hood, N. and Young, S. (1979), *The Economics of Multinational Enterprise*, London: Longman Group

Hoogvelt, A. (1976), *The Sociology of the Developing Societies*, London: Macmillan

Hoselitz, B. F. (1960), *Sociological Aspects of Economic Growth*, Glencoe, Ill.: Free Press

Hoselitz, B. F. and Moore, W. E. (1966), *Industrialisation and Society*, Paris: Mouton

House, J. D. (1977), 'The social organisation of multinational corporations: Canadian subsidiaries in the oil industry', *Canadian Review of Sociology and Anthropology*, 14/1

Hughes, M. D. (1973), 'American investment in Britain', in Urry and Wakeford (eds.) (1973)

Hunt, A. (ed.) (1977), *Class and Class Structure*, London: Lawrence and Wishart

Hussain, A. (1976), 'Hilferding's finance capital', *Bulletin of the Conference of Socialist Economists*, 13

Hussain, A. (1977), 'Crises and tendencies of capitalism', *Economy and Society*, 6/4

Hymer, S. (1972), 'The multinational corporation and the law of uneven development', in Radice (ed.) (1975)

Ingham, G. (1982), 'Divisions within the dominant class and British "exceptionalism"', in Giddens and Mackenzie (eds.) (1982)

Ingham, G. (1984), *Capitalism Divided?*, London: Macmillan

Israel, J. (1974), 'The welfare state: a manifestation of advanced capitalism', *Acta Sociologica*, 17/4

Jackson, P. M. (1982), *The Political Economy of Bureaucracy*, Oxford: Philip Allan Publisher

Jacquemin, A. P. and De Jong, H. W. (1977), *European Industrial Organisation*, London: Macmillan

Jacquemin, A. and Gellinck, E. de (1980), 'Familial control, size and performance in the largest French firms', *European Economic Review*, 13

Jancovici, E. (1972), 'Informatique et entreprise' (Information and enterprise), *Sociologie du travail*, 14/1

Jeidels, O. (1905), *Das Verhaltnis der deutschen Grossbanken zur Industrie mit besonderer Berucksichtigung der Eisenindustrie* (The relation of the large German banks to industry with particular reference to the steel industry), Leipzig

Jessop, B. (1978), 'Remarks on some recent theories of the capitalist state', *Cambridge Journal of Economics*, 1/4

Jessop, B. (1980), 'The transformation of the state in post-war Britain', in Scase (ed.) (1980)

Jewkes, J. (1977), *Delusions of Dominance*, London: Institute of Economic Affairs

Johnson, R. W. (1973), 'The British political elite, 1955–1972', *European Journal of Sociology*, 14/2

Johnson, T. (1982), 'The state and the professions: peculiarities of the British', in Giddens and Mackenzie (eds.) (1982)

Jones, C. (1984), 'Corporate social accounting: the conflict between theory and practice', Unpublished paper, Department of Economics and Social Science, Bristol Polytechnic

Jones, K. (1982), *Law and Economy*, London: Academic Press

Juran, J. and Louden, J. K. (1966), *The Corporate Director*, New York: American Management Association

Kamerschen, D. R. (1968), 'The influence of ownership and control on profit rates', *American Economic Review*, 58

Kania, J. J. and McKean, J. R. (1976), 'Ownership, control and the contemporary corporation', *Kyklos*, 29

Kania, J. J. and McKean J. R. (1978), 'Ownership, control, and the contemporary corporation: a reply', *Kyklos*, 31

Karpik, L. (1972), 'Les politiques et les logiques d'action de la grande entreprise industrielle' (The policies and logics of action of the large industrial enterprise), *Sociologie du travail*, 14/1

Kautsky, K. (1902), *The Social Revolution*, New York: Dial Press, 1925

Kaysen, C. (1957), 'The social significance of the modern corporation', *American Economic Review*, 47

Keller, S. (1963), *Beyond the Ruling Class*, New York: Random House

Kennedy, W. P. (1976), 'Institutional responses to economic growth: capital markets in Britain to 1814', in Hannah (1976a)

Kerr, C. *et al.* (1960), *Industrialism and Industrial Man*, Harmondsworth: Penguin, 1973

Kiernan, V. G. (1974), *Marxism and Imperialism*, London: Edward Arnold

Kindleberger, C. P. (ed.) (1970), *The International Corporation*, Massachusetts: MIT Press

Kindleberger, C. P. (1984), *A Financial History of Western Europe*, London: George Allen and Unwin

King, R. (ed.) (1983), *Capital and Politics*, London: Routledge and Kegan Paul

Kinsey, R. (1983), 'Karl Renner on socialist legality', in Sugarman (1983)

Kitahara, I. (1980), 'Ownership and control in the large corporation', *Keio Economic Studies*, 17/2

Kiyonari, T. and Nakamura, H. (1977), 'The establishment of the big business system', in Sato (ed.) (1980)

Klein, L. R. *et al.* (1956), 'Savings and finances of the upper income classes', *Oxford Institute of Statistics Bulletin*, 18

Knowles, J. C. (1973), *The Rockefeller Financial Group*, MSS Modular Publications, Module 343

Kocka, J. (1978), 'Entrepreneurs and managers in German industrialisation', in Mathias and Postan (eds.) (1978a)

Kocka, J. (1980), 'The rise of the modern industrial enterprise in Germany', in Chandler and Daems (eds.) (1980)

Koenig, R. (1971), 'Western Germany', in Archer and Giner (eds.) (1971)

Koenig, T. and Gogel, R. (1981), 'Interlocking corporate directorships as a social network', *American Journal of Economics and Sociology*, 40

Koenig, T., Gogel, R. and Sonquist, J. (1979), 'Models of the significance of interlocking corporate directorates', *American Journal of Economics and Sociology*, 38

Kolko, G. (1962), *Wealth and Power in America*, London: Thames and Hudson

Komiya, R. (1961), '"Monopoly capital" and income redistribution policy', in Sato (ed.) (1980)

Korpi, W. (1978), *The Working Class in Welfare Capitalism*, London: Routledge and Kegan Paul

Kotz, D. M. (1978), *Bank Control of Large Corporations in the United States*, Berkeley: University of California Press

Kozlov, G. A. (1977), *Political Economy: Capitalism*, Moscow: Progress

Krejci, J. (1976), *Social Structure in Divided Germany*, London: Croom Helm

Kriesi, H. (1982), 'The structure of the Swiss political system', in Lehmbruch and Schmitter (eds.) (1982)

Kumar, K. (1978), *Prophecy and Progress*, Harmondsworth: Penguin

Kurth, J. R. (1975), 'The international politics of post-industrial societies', in Lindberg (1975)

Kuusinen, O. V. *et al.* (eds.) (1959), *Fundamentals of Marxism–Leninism*, New York: Crowell-Collier and Macmillan, n.d

Kuznets, S. (1953), *Shares of Upper Income Groups in Incomes and Savings*, New York: National Bureau of Economic Research

Kuznets, S. (1961), *Capital in the American Economy*, Princeton University Press

Lampman, R. (1959), 'The share of top wealth holders in the United States', in Atkinson (ed.) (1973b)

Lampman, R. (1962), *The Share of Top Wealth Holders in National Wealth*, Princeton University Press

Landes, D. S. (1951), 'French business and the businessman: a social and cultural analysis', Bobbs Merrill Reprint no. 159

Larner, R. J. (1966), 'Ownership and control in the 200 largest non-financial corporations: 1929 and 1963', *American Economic Review*, 56

Larner, R. J. (1970), *Management Control and the Large Corporation*, New York: Dunellen

Lash, S. (1984), 'The end of neo-corporatism?: the breakdown of centralised bargaining in Sweden', Paper presented to ESRC Seminar on Social Stratification, University of Cambridge, September 1984

Lawrence, P. A. (1980), *Managers and Management in West Germany*, London: Croom Helm

Lawriwsky, M. L. (1980), 'Control type and the market for corporate control: a note', *Journal of Industrial Economics*, 28

Lawriwsky, M. L. (1982), 'Some issues in foreign relations and the control of Australia's mineral resources', *Australian Quarterly*

Lawriwsky, M. L. (1984), *Corporate Structure and Performance*, London: Croom Helm

Layton, E. T. (1971), *The Revolt of the Engineer*, Cleveland: Case Western Reserve University

Lehmbruch, G. (1982), 'Introduction: neo-corporatism in comparative perspective', in Lehmbruch and Schmitter (eds.) (1982)

Lehmbruch, G. and Schmitter, P. C. (eds.) (1982), *Patterns of Corporatist Policy Making*, Beverly Hills: Sage Publications

Leinhardt, S. (ed.) (1977), *Symposium on Social Networks*, New York: Academic Press

Lenin, V. I. (1917a), *Imperialism: The Highest Stage of Capitalism*, Moscow: Progress Publishers, 1966

Lenin, V. I. (1917b), *The State and Revolution*, Moscow: Progress, 1969

Lenski, G. (1966), *Power and Privilege*, New York: McGraw-Hill

Levine, J. (1972), 'Spheres of influence', *American Sociological Review*, 37

Levine, J. (1978), 'The theory of bank control: comment on Moriolis's test of the theory', *Social Science Quarterly*, 58

Levine, J. H. and Roy, W. S. (1977), 'A study of interlocking directorates', in Leinhardt (ed.) (1977)

Levitt, K. (1970), *Silent Surrender: The Multinational Corporation in Canada*, Toronto: Macmillan

Levy, A. B. (1950), *Private Corporations and their Control*, London: Routledge and Kegan Paul

Levy-Leboyer, M. (1980), 'The large corporation in modern France', in Chandler and Daems (eds.) (1980)

Lieberson, S. and O'Connor, J. R. (1972), 'Leadership and organizational performance: a study of large corporations', *American Sociological Review*, 37/2

Lindberg, L. *et al.* (1975), *Stress and Contradiction in Modern Capitalism*, London: D. C. Heath

Lintner, J. (1959), 'The financing of corporations', in Mason (ed.) (1959)

Lipset, S. M. (1960), *Political Man*, London: Heinemann

Lisle-Williams, M. (1984), 'Beyond the market: the survival of family capitalism in the English merchant banks', *British Journal of Sociology*, 35

Littler, C. (1982), *The Development of the Labour Process in Capitalist Societies*, London: Heinemann

Littler, C. R. and Salaman, G. (1984), *Class at Work*, London: Batsford

Livingston, J., Moore, J. and Oldfather, F. (eds.) (1973a and b), *The Japan Reader*, Volumes I and II, Harmondsworth: Penguin, 1976

Lockwood, D. (1958), *The Blackcoated Worker*, London: George Allen and Unwin

Lockwood, W. W. (1965a), 'Japan's "new capitalism"', in Lockwood (1965b)

Lockwood, W. W. (1965b), *The State and Economic Enterprise in Japan*, Princeton University Press

Lockwood, W. W. (1968), *The Economic Development of Japan*, Princeton University Press

Longstreth, F. (1979), 'The City, industry and the state', in Crouch (ed.) (1979)

Lumsden, I. (ed.) (1970), *Close the 49th Parallel: The Americanization of Canada*, University of Toronto Press

Lundberg, F. (1937), *America's Sixty Families*, New York: Vanguard Press

Lundberg, F. (1969), *The Rich and the Super Rich*, London: Nelson

Lupton, C. and Wilson, C. (1959), 'The social background and connections of top decision-makers', in Urry and Wakeford (eds.) (1973)

Luxemburg, R. (1913), *The Accumulation of Capital*, London: Routledge and Kegan Paul, 1951

Lydall, H. F. (1959), 'The long-term trend in the size distribution of income', *Journal of the Royal Statistical Society*, Series A, 122/1

Lydall, H. F. and Tipping, D. G. (1961), 'The distribution of personal wealth in Britain', in Atkinson (ed.) (1973b)

Mace, M. L. (1971), *Directors: Myth and Reality*, Harvard University Press

McClelland, D. C. (1961), *The Achieving Society*, New York: Van Nostrand

McEachern, W. A. (1975), *Managerial Control and Performance*, Lexington: Lexington Books

McEachern, W. A. (1978), 'Corporate control and growth: an alternative', *Kyklos*, 31/3

Mackenzie, G. (1982), 'Class boundaries and the labour process', in Giddens and Mackenzie (eds.) (1982)

Macpherson, C. B. (1973), *Democratic Theory*, Oxford: Clarendon Press

Macrosty, H. W. (1901), *Trusts and the State*, Fabian Series no. 1, London: Grant Richards

Mandel, E. (1970), *Europe Versus America*, London: New Left Books

Mandel, E. (1972), *Late Capitalism*, London: New Left Books, 1975

Mankoff, M. (ed.) (1972), *The Poverty of Progress*, New York: Holt, Rinehart and Winston

Mannari, H. (1974), *The Japanese Business Leaders*, University of Tokyo Press

Marceau, J. (1977), *Class and Status in France*, Oxford: Oxford University Press

March, J. G. and Simon, H. A. (1963), *Organizations*, New York: John Wiley

Marchak, P. (1979), *In Whose Interest*, Toronto: McClelland and Stewart

Marcuse, H. (1964), *One Dimensional Man*, London: Sphere Books, 1968

Mariolis, P. (1975), 'Interlocking directorates and control of corporations', *Social Science Quarterly*, 56/3

Mariolis, P. (1978), 'Type of corporation, size of firm, and interlocking directorates: a reply to Levine', *Social Science Quarterly*, 58

Marris, R. (1964), *The Economic Theory of 'Managerial' Capitalism*, London: Macmillan

Marx, K. (1857), 'introduction' to *Grundrisse*, Harmondsworth: Penguin, 1973

Marx, K. (1885), *Capital*, Volume 2, London: Lawrence and Wishart, 1974

Marx, K. (1894), *Capital*, Volume 3, London: Lawrence and Wishart, 1959

Mason, E. S. (ed.) (1959), *The Corporation in Modern Society*, New York: Atheneum Press

Mathias, P. (1969), *The First Industrial Nation*, London: Methuen

Mathias, P. and Postan, M. M. (1978a and b), *Cambridge*

Economic History of Europe, Volumes 7 and 8, Cambridge: Cambridge University Press

Mayo, E. (1949), *The Social Problems of an Industrial Civilization*, London: Routledge and Kegan Paul

Meade, J. E. (1964), *Efficiency, Equality, and the Ownership of Property*, London: George Allen and Unwin

Means, G. C. (1964), 'Economic concentration', Report to Senate Hearings, in Zeitlin (ed.) (1970)

Means, G. C. *et al.* (1939), 'The structure of controls', Chapter IX in *The Structure of the American Economy*, National Resources Committee of the US Senate, Washington: Government Printing Office

Meeks, G. and Whittington, G. (1975), 'Giant companies in the United Kingdom', *Economic Journal*, 85

Meeks, G. and Whittington, G. (1976), *The Financing of Quoted Companies*, Background Paper no. 1, Royal Commission on the Distribution of Income and Wealth, London: HMSO

Meier, H. P. (1976), 'Ideology and control of crisis in highly developed capitalist societies', in Burns and Buckley (1976)

Menshikov, S. (1969), *Millionaires and Managers*, Moscow: Progress Publishers

Meeusen, W. and Cuyvers, L. (1985), 'The interaction between interlocking directorships and the economic behaviour of companies', in Stokman *et al.* (eds.) (1985)

Michalet, C. A. (1976), *Le capitalisme mondial* (World capitalism), Paris: Presses Universitaires de France

Middlemas, K. (1979), *Politics in Industrial Society*, London: Andre Deutsch

Miliband, R. (1968), 'Professor Galbraith and American capitalism', in Mankoff (ed.) (1972)

Miliband, R. (1969), *The State in Capitalist Society*, London: Quartet edition, 1973

Miliband, R. (1970), 'The capitalist state', *New Left Review*, 59

Miliband, R. (1973), 'Poulantzas and the capitalist state', *New Left Review*, 82

Miliband, R. (1977), *Marxism and Politics*, Oxford: Oxford University Press

Miller, H. P. (1966), 'Income distribution in the United States', in Atkinson (ed.) (1973b)

Miller, S. M. (1975), 'Notes on neo-capitalism', *Theory and Society*, 2/1

Mills, C. W. (1940), 'Situated actions and vocabularies of motive', *American Sociological Review*, 5

Mills, C. W. (1942), 'A Marx for the managers', *Ethics*, 52

Mills, C. W. (1956), *The Power Elite*, New York: Oxford University Press

Minns, R. (1980), *Pension Funds and British Capitalism*, London: Heinemann

Minns, R. (1982), 'Management of shareholdings in large manufacturing companies', Social Science Working Papers, The Open University

Mintz, B. (1975), 'The president's cabinet, 1897–1972', *Insurgent Sociologist*, 5/3

Mintz, B. and Schwartz, M. (1981a), 'Interlocking directorates and interest group formation', *American Sociological Review*, 46

Mintz, B. and Schwartz, M. (1981b), 'The structure of intercorporate unity in American Business', *Social Problems*, 29

Mintz, B. and Schwartz, M. (1983), 'Financial interest groups and interlocking directorates', *Social Science History*, 7

Mishima, Y. (1977), 'Comments [on Morikawa]', in Nakagawa (ed.) (n.d.)

Miyazaki, Y. (1967), 'Excessive competition and the formation of Keiretsu', in Sato (ed.) (1980)

Miyazaki, Y. (1973), 'The Japanese-type structure of big business', in Sato (ed.) (1980)

Mizruchi, M. S. (1982), *The American Corporate Network, 1900–74*, London: Sage

Mizruchi, M. S. (1983), 'Relations among large American corporations, 1904–74', *Social Science History*, 7

Mokken, R. J. and Stokman, F. N. (1974), 'Interlocking directorates between large corporations', Paper to European Consortium for Political Research, Strasbourg

Mokken, R. J. and Stokman, F. N. (1976), 'Power and influence as political phenomena', in Barry (1976)

Monjardet, D. (1972), Carrière des dirigeants et controle de l'entreprise' (Managerial careers and the control of enterprises), *Sociologie du travail*, 14/2

Monsen, R. J. and Downs, A. (1965), 'A theory of large managerial firms', *Journal of Political Economy*, 73

Monsen, R. J., Chiu, J. S. and Cooley, D. E. (1968), 'The effect of separation of ownership and control on the performance of the large firm', *Quarterly Journal of Economics*, 82/1

Moody, J. (1904), *The Truth About the Trusts*, Chicago: Moody Publishing

Moody, J. (1919), *The Masters of Capital*, New Haven: Yale University Press

Moran, M. (1983), 'Power, policy and the City of London', in King (ed.) (1983)

Morikawa, H. (1977), 'Managerial structure and control devices for diversified zaibatsu business', in Nakagawa (ed.) (n.d.)

Morin, F. (1974a), *La structure financière du capitalisme français* (The financial structure of French capitalism), Paris: Calmann-Levy

Morin, F. (1974b), 'Qui détient le pouvoir financier en France?' (Who holds financial power in France?), *Economie et Humanisme*, 220

Morin, F. (1976), 'Ombres et lumières du capitalisme français' (Shadows and illuminations of French capitalism), *Economie et Humanisme*, 229

Morin, F. (1977), *La banque et les groupes industriels à l'heure des nationalisations* (Banking and industrial groups on the eve of nationalization), Paris: Calmann-Levy

Morrison, R. J. (1967), 'Financial intermediaries and economic development: the Belgian case', *Scandinavian Economic History Review*, 15

Morvan, Y. (1972), *La Concentration de l'industrie en France* (The concentration of industry in France), Paris: Librairie Armand Colin

Mullins, N. (1973), *Theory and Theory Groups in Contemporary American Sociology*, New York: Harper and Row

Murray, R. (1971), 'The internationalization of capital and the nation state', in *Multinational Companies and Nation States*, Nottingham: Spokesman Books

Nairn, T. (1972), *The Left Against Europe*, Harmondsworth: Penguin, 1973

Nairn, T. (1977), *The Breakup of Britain*, London: New Left Books

Nakagawa, K. (ed.) (n.d.) (1977), *Strategy and Structure of Big Business*, University of Tokyo Press

Nakagawa, K. (1977), 'Business strategy and industrial structure in pre-World War II Japan', in Nakagawa (ed.) (n.d.)

Neumann, F. (1942), *Behemoth*, New York: Oxford University Press

Nichols, T. (1969), *Ownership, Control, and Ideology*, London: George Allen and Unwin

Nicholson, R. J. (1967), 'The distribution of personal income in the UK', in Urry and Wakeford (eds.) (1973)

Nicolaus, M. (1967), 'Proletariat and middle class in Marx: Hegelian choreography and the capitalist dialectic', *Studies on the Left*, 7

Niosi, J. (1978), *The Economy of Canada*, Montreal: Black Rose Books

Niosi, J. (1981), *Canadian Capitalism*, Toronto: Jas. Lorimer

Noble, T. (1975), *Modern Britain*, London: Batsford

Noguchi, T. (1973), 'Japanese monopoly capital and the state', *Kapitalistate*, 1

Nyman, S. and Silberston, A. (1978), 'The ownership and control of industry', *Oxford Economic Papers*, 30/1

O'Connor, J. (1971), 'Who rules the corporations? The ruling class', *Socialist Revolution*, 7

O'Connor, J. (1973), *The Fiscal Crisis of the State*, New York: St Martins Press

Offe, C. (1970), *Industry and Inequality*, London: Edward Arnold, 1976

Offe, C. (1972), *Strukturprobleme des kapitalistischen Staates* (Structural problems of the capitalist state), Frankfurt: Suhrkamp

Offe, C. (1981), 'The attribution of public status to interest groups: observations on the West German case', in Berger (1981)

O'Hara, M. (1981), 'Property rights and the financial firm', *Journal of Law and Economics*, 24

Ohtani, K. (1984), *Securities Market in Japan*, Tokyo: Japan Securities Research Institute

Okayama, R. (1983), 'Japanese employer labour policy: the heavy engineering industry in 1900–39', in Gospel and Littler (eds.) (1983)

Okumura, H. (1975), *Hojin shinonshugi no kozo* (The structure of corporate capitalism), Tokyo: Nihon Hyoronsha

Okumura, H. (1983), 'Enterprise groups in Japan', unpublished paper, Osaka: Japan Securities Research Institute

Ornstein, M. D. (1982), 'Interlocking directorates in Canada: evidence from replacement patterns', *Social Networks*, 4

Pahl, J. M. and Pahl, R. E. (1971), *Managers and their Wives*, Harmondsworth: Allen Lane The Penguin Press

Pahl, R. E. (1977a), 'Stratification, the relation between states and urban and regional development', *International Journal of Urban and Regional Research*, 1/1

Pahl, R. E. (1977b), '"Collective consumption" and the state in capitalist and state socialist societies', in Scase (ed.) (1977)

Pahl, R. E. (1984), *Divisions of Labour*, Oxford: Basil Blackwell

Pahl, R. E. and Winkler, J. (1974), 'The economic elite: theory and practice', in Stanworth and Giddens (eds.) (1974b)

Palmade, G. P. (1961), *French Capitalism in the Nineteenth Century*, Newton Abbott: David and Charles, 1972

Palmer, D. (1983a), 'Broken ties: interlocking directorates and intercorporate coordination', *Administrative Science Quarterly*, 28

Palmer, D. (1983b), 'Interpreting corporate interlocks from broken ties', *Social Science History*, 7

Palmer, J. P. (1972), 'The separation of ownership from control in large US industrial corporations', *Quarterly Review of Economics and Business*, 12/3

Palmer, J. P. (1973), 'The profit-performance effects of the separation of ownership from control in large US industrial corporations', *Bell Journal of Economics and Management Science*

Papandreou, A. G. (1973), 'Multinational corporations and empire', *Social Praxis*, 1/2

Parkin, F. (1979), *Marxism and Class Theory*, London: Tavistock

Parkinson, H. (1951), *Ownership of Industry*, London: Eyre and Spottiswoode

Parry, G. (1969), *Political Elites*, London: George Allen and Unwin

Parsons, T. (1940), 'The motivation of economic activity', in Parsons (1954b)

Parsons, T. (1954a), 'A revised analytical approach to the theory of social stratification', in Parsons (1954b)

Parsons, T. (1954b), *Essays in Sociological Theory*, Glencoe, Ill.: Free Press

Parsons, T. (1956), 'A sociological approach to the theory of organizations', in Parsons (1960)

Parsons, T. (1958), 'The institutional framework of economic development', in Parsons (1960)

Parsons, T. (1960), *Structure and Process in Modern Societies*, Glencoe, Ill.: Free Press

Parsons, T. and Smelser, N. J. (1957), *Economy and Society*, London: Routledge and Kegan Paul

Pastré, O. (1979), *La stratégie internationale des groupes financiers americains* (The international strategy of American financial groups), Paris: Economica

Patman Report (1966), *Bank Stock Ownership and Control*, Reprinted in Patman Report (1968)

Patman Report (1967), *Control of Commercial Banks and Interlocks Among Financial Institutions*, Reprinted in Patman Report (1968)

Patman Report (1968), *Commercial Banks and Their Trust Activities*, Staff Report for the Subcommittee on Domestic Finance, Committee on Banking and Currency, House of Representatives, 90th Congress, 2nd Session, Washington: Government Printing Office. Includes reprints of Patman Report (1966) and Patman Report (1967)

Pavitt, K. and Worboys, M. (1977), *Science, Technology and the Modern Industrial State*, London: Butterworth

Payne, P. L. (1967), 'The emergence of the large-scale company in Great Britain', *Economic History Review*, 20

Payne, P. L. (1974), *British Entrepreneurship in the Nineteenth Century*, London: Macmillan

Payne, P. L. (1978), 'Industrial entrepreneurship and management in Great Britain', in Mathias and Postan (eds.) (1978b)

Pennings, J. M. (1980), *Interlocking Directorates*, San Francisco: Jossey Bass

Perkin, H. (1969), *The Origins of Modern English Society*, London: Routledge and Kegan Paul

Perkin, H. (1978), 'The recruitment of elites in British society since 1800', *Journal of Social History*, 12

Perlo, V. (1957), *The Empire of High Finance*, New York: International Publishers

Perlo, V. (1958), '"Peoples Capitalism" and stock ownership', *American Economic Review*, 48. References are to the reprint in Mankoff (1972)

Peterson, S. (1965), 'Corporate control and capitalism', *Quarterly Journal of Economics*, 79/1

Pfeffer, J. (1972), 'Size and composition of corporate boards of directors', *Administrative Science Quarterly*, 17

Picciotto, S. and Radice, H. (1973), 'Capital and state in the world economy', *Kapitalistate*, 1

Pickvance, C. G. (ed.) (1976), *Urban Sociology*, London: Methuen

Piedalue, G. (1976), 'Les groupes financiers au Canada, 1900–1930' (Financial groups in Canada), *Revue d'Histoire de l'Amerique Française*, 30

Pitelis, C. N. and Sugden, R. (1983), 'The alleged separation of ownership and control in the theory of the firm', *Warwick Economic Research Papers*, 238

Pitelis, C. N. (1983), '"Contractual" savings and underconsumption', *Warwick Economic Research Papers*, 236

Poland, E. (1939), 'Interlocking directorates among the largest American corporations, 1935', Appendix 12 to The Structure of the American Economy. National Resources Committee of the US Senate, Washington: Government Printing Office

Polanyi, G. and Wood, J. B. (1974), *How Much Inequality?*, London: Institute of Economic Affairs

Pollard, S. (1962), *The Development of the British Economy*, London: Edward Arnold

Pollard, S. (1965), *The Genesis of Modern Management*, Cambridge, Mass.: The Belknap Press, 1977 .

Porter, J. (1965), *The Vertical Mosaic*, University of Toronto Press

Poulantzas, N. (1968), *Political Power and Social Classes*, London: New Left Books, 1973

Poulantzas, N. (1969), 'The problem of the capitalist state', *New Left Review*, 58

Poulantzas, N. (1974), *Classes in Contemporary Capitalism*, London: New Left Books, 1975

Prais, S. J. (1976), *The Evolution of Giant Firms in Britain*, Cambridge: Cambridge University Press

Pratt, S. S. (1905), 'Our financial oligarchy', *Worlds Work*, 10

Presthus, R. (1973), *Elites in the Policy Process*, Cambridge: Cambridge University Press

Pujo Report (1913), *Money Trust Investigation*, House Subcommittee on Banking and Currency, Washington: Government Printing Office

Radcliffe Report (1959), *Report of the Committee on the Working of the Monetary System*, Cmnd 827, London: HMSO

Radice, H. (1971), 'Control type, profitability and growth in large firms: an empirical study', *Economic Journal*, 81

Radice, H. (ed.) (1975), *International Firms and Modern Imperialism*, Harmondsworth: Penguin

Ramsoy, N. (ed.) (1968), *Norwegian Society*, London: Hurst, 1974

Ratcliff, R. E. (1980), 'Banks and corporate lending: an analysis of the impact of the interlock structure of the capitalist class on the lending behaviour of banks', *American Sociological Review*, 45

Raw, C., Page, B. and Hodgson, G. (1971), *Do You Sincerely Want To Be Rich?*, London: Andre Deutsch

Readman, P., Davies, J., Hoare, M. and Poole, D. (1973), *The European Monetary Puzzle*, London: Michael Joseph

Reder, M. (1947), 'A reconsideration of the marginal productivity theory', *Journal of Political Economy*, 55

Reeder, J. A. (1975), 'Corporate ownership and control: a synthesis of recent findings', *Industrial Organisation Review*, 3

Regini, M. (1982), 'Changing relationships between labour and the state in Italy', in Lehmbruch and Schmitter (eds.) (1982)

Renner, K. (1904), *The Institutions of Private Law and their Social Function*, London: Routledge and Kegan Paul, 1949. A translation of the 1928 revised edition

Revell, J. R. (1960), 'An analysis of personal holders of wealth', *British Association for the Advancement of Science*, 17

Revell, J. R. (1965), 'Changes in the social distribution of property in Britain during the twentieth century', *Actes du Troisième Congrès International d'Histoire Economique*, Munich

Rex, J. A. (1974), 'Capitalism, elites and the ruling class', in Stanworth and Giddens (eds.) (1974)

Rifkin, J. and Barber, R. (1978), *The North Will Rise Again*, Boston: Beacon Press

Robinson, J. (1933), *The Economics of Imperfect Competition*, London: Macmillan

Rochester, A. (1936), *Rulers of America*, New York: International Publishers

Rolfe, H. (1967), *The Controllers*, Melbourne: Cheshire

Rose, A. (1967), *The Power Structure*, New York: Oxford University Press

Rostow, W. W. (1960), *The Stages of Economic Growth*, Cambridge: Cambridge University Press

Rowthorn, R. (1971), *International Big Business*, Cambridge: Cambridge University Press

Rowthorn, R. (1976), 'Late capitalism', *New Left Review*, 98

Roy, W. G. (1983a), 'The unfolding of the interlocking directorate structure of the United States', *American Sociological Review*, 48

Roy, W. G. (1983b), 'Interlocking directorates and the corporate revolution', *Social Science History*, 7

Rubinstein, W. D. (1976), 'Wealth, elites, and the class structure of modern Britain', *Past and Present*, 70

Rubinstein, W. D. (ed.) (1980), *Wealth and the Wealthy in the Modern World*, London: Croom Helm

Rubinstein, W. D. (1981), *Men of Property*, London: Croom Helm

Rusterholz, P. (1985), 'The banks in the centre: integration in decentralised Switzerland', in Stokman *et al.* (eds.) (1985)

Ryndina, M. and Chernikov, G. (eds.) (1974), *The Political Economy of Capitalism*, Moscow: Progress Publishers

Safarian, A. E. (1966), *Foreign Ownership of Canadian Industry*, Toronto: McGraw Hill

Salaman, G. (1982), 'Managing the frontier of control', in Giddens and Mackenzie (eds.) (1982)

Sampson, A. (1973), *The Sovereign State*, London: Hodder and Stoughton

Sampson, A. (1975), *The Seven Sisters*, London: Hodder and Stoughton

Sato, K. (ed.) (1980), *Industry and Business in Japan*, London: Croom Helm

Savage, D. (1979), *Founders, Heirs and Managers*, London: Sage

Scase, R. (ed.) (1976), *Readings in the Swedish Class Structure*, London: Pergamon

Scase, R. (ed.) (1977), *Industrial Society: Class, Cleavage and Control*, London: George Allen and Unwin

Scase, R. (ed.) (1980), *The State in Western Europe*, London: Croom Helm

Scase, R. (1982), 'The petty bourgeoisie and modern capitalism', in Giddens and Mackenzie (eds.) (1982)

Schijf, H. (1979), 'Networks of interlocking directorates at the turn of the century in the Netherlands', Paper for Research Workshop, European Consortium for Political Research, Brussels

Schmitter, P. C. (1974), 'Still the century of corporatism', in Schmitter and Lehmbruch (eds.) (1979)

Schmitter, P. C. (1977), 'Modes of interest intermediation and models of societal change in Western Europe', in Schmitter and Lehmbruch (eds.) (1979)

Schmitter, P. C. (1981), 'Interest intermediation and regime governability in contemporary Western Europe and North America', in Berger (ed.) (1981)

Schmitter, P. C. (1982), 'Reflections on where the theory of neo-corporatism has gone and where the praxis of neo-corporatism may be going', in Lehmbruch and Schmitter (eds.) (1982)

Schmitter, P. C. and Lehmbruch, G. (eds.) (1979), *Trends Towards Corporatist Intermediation*, Beverly Hills: Sage Publications

Schönwitz, D. and Weber, H-J. (1980), 'Personelle Verflechtungen zwischen Unternehmen' (Interlocking directorships between enterprises), *Zeitschrift für die gesamte Staatswissenschaft*, 136

Schreiner, J-P. (1984), 'Finance capital and the network of interlocking directorates among major corporations in Switzerland', unpublished paper, Aix-en-Provence

Schuller, T. and Hyman, J. (1984), 'Forms of ownership and control: decision making within a financial institution', *Sociology*, 18/1

Scott, J. P. (1978), 'Critical social theory: an introduction and critique', *British Journal of Sociology*, 29/1

Scott, J. P. (1982a), 'Property and control: some remarks on the British propertied class', in Giddens and Mackenzie (eds.) (1982)

Scott, J. P. (1982b), *The Upper Classes*, London: Macmillan

Scott, J. P. (1985), 'Theoretical framework and research design', in Stokman *et al.* (eds.) (1985)

Scott, J. P. and Griff, C. (1984), *Directors of Industry: The British Corporate Network, 1904–1976*, Cambridge: Polity Press

Scott, J. P. and Griff, C. (1985), 'Bank spheres of influence in the British corporate network', in Stokman *et al.* (eds.) (1985)

Scott, J. P. and Hughes, M. D. (1976), 'Ownership and control in a satellite economy: a discussion from Scottish data', *Sociology*, 10/1

Scott, J. P. and Hughes, M. D. (1980a), 'Capital and Communication in Scottish Business', *Sociology*, 13

Scott, J. and Hughes, M. D. (1980b), *The Anatomy of Scottish Capital*, London: Croom Helm

Seierstad, S. (1968), 'The Norwegian economy', in Ramsoy (ed.) (1968)

Servan-Schreiber, J. J. (1967), *The American Challenge*, London: Hamish Hamilton, 1968

Shaw, G. B. (ed.) (1889), *Fabian Essays in Socialism*, London: Fabian Society

Shaw, G. B. (1928), *The Intelligent Woman's Guide To Socialism, Capitalism, Sovietism and Fascism*, Harmondsworth: Penguin, 1937

Sheehan, R. (1967), 'Proprietors in the world of big business', *Fortune*, 15 June

Shonfield, M. (1965), *Modern Capitalism*, Oxford: Oxford University Press

Silk, L. and Silk, M. (1980), *The American Establishment*, New York: Basic Books

Simon, H. A. (1945), *Administrative Behaviour*, New York: Macmillan, 1961

Simons, A. J. (1927), *Holding Companies*, London: Pitman

Skidelsky, R. (1979), 'The decline of Keynesian politics', in Crouch (ed.) (1979)

Smith, D. and Tepperman, L. (1974), 'Changes in the Canadian business and legal elites', *Canadian Review of Sociology and Anthropology*, 11

Smith, E. O. (1983), *The West German Economy*, London: Croom Helm

Smith, E. P. (1970), 'Interlocking directorates among the "Fortune 500"', *Antitrust, Law and Economic Review*, 3

Smith, E. P. and Desfosses, L. R. (1972), 'Interlocking directorates: a study of influence', *Mississippi Valley Journal of Business and Economics*, 7

Smith, J. D. and Calvert, S. K. (1965), 'Estimating the wealth of top wealth-holders from estate tax returns', *Proceedings of the American Statistical Association*

Smith, R. J. (1983), *Japanese Society*, Cambridge: Cambridge University Press

Solgow, L. (1968), 'Long run changes in British income inequality', in Atkinson (ed.) (1973b)

Sonquist, J. A. *et al.* (1975), 'Interlocking directorships in the top US corporations', *Insurgent Sociologist*, 5/3

Sonquist, J. A. *et al.* (1976), 'Examining corporate interconnections through interlocking directorates', in Burns and Buckley (eds.) (1976)

Soref, M. (1976), 'Social class and a division of labour within the corporate elite', *Sociological Quarterly*, 17/3

Soref, M. (1980), 'The finance capitalists', in Zeitlin (ed.) (1980)

Stano, M. (1976), 'Monopoly power, ownership control, and corporate performance', *Bell Journal of Economics*, 2

Stanworth, P. (1974), 'Property, class and the corporate elite', in Crewe (ed.) (1974)

Stanworth, P. and Giddens, A. (1974a), 'An economic elite: a demographic profile of company chairmen', in Stanworth and Giddens (eds.) (1974b)

Stanworth, P. and Giddens, A. (eds.) (1974b), *Elites and Power in British Society*, Cambridge: Cambridge University Press

Stanworth, P. and Giddens, A. (1975), 'The modern corporate economy', *Sociological Review*, 23/1

Steer, P. and Cable, J. (1978), 'Internal organization and profit: an emperical analysis of large UK companies', *Journal of Industrial Economics*, 27

Steuer, M. D. *et al.* (1973), *The Impact of Foreign Direct Investment on the United Kingdom*, London: HMSO

Steven, R. (1983), *Classes in Contemporary Japan*, Cambridge: Cambridge University Press

Stewart, A. (ed.) (1982), *Contemporary Britain*, London: Routledge and Kegan Paul

Stock Exchange (1977), *The Provision of Funds for Industry and Trade*, London: Stock Exchange

Stock Exchange (1983), *The Stock Exchange Survey of Share Ownership*, London: Stock Exchange

Stokes, H. (n.d. *c.* 1977), *The Japanese Competitors*, London: *Financial Times*

Stokman, F. N. and Wasseur, F. (1985), 'National networks in 1976: a structural comparison', in Stokman *et al.* (eds.) (1985)

Stokman, F. N., Wasseur, R. and Elsas, D. (1985), 'The Dutch network: types of interlocks and network structure', in Stokman *et al.* (eds.) (1985)

Stokman, F. N., Ziegler, R. and Scott, J. P. (eds.) (1985), *Networks of Corporate Power: A Comparative Study of Ten Countries*, Cambridge: Polity Press

Stone, R. *et al.* (1966), *The Owners of Quoted Ordinary Shares*, London: Chapman and Hall

Storey, J. (1980), *The Challenge to Management Control*, London: Kogan Page

Storey, J. (1983), *Managerial Prerogative and the Question of Control*, London: Routledge and Kegan Paul

Streeck, W. (1982), 'Organizational consequences of neo-corporatist cooperation in West German labour unions', in Lehmbruch and Schmitter (eds.) (1982)

Strinati, D. (1982), 'State intervention, the economy, and the crisis', in Stewart (ed.) (1982)

Sugarman, D. (ed.) (1983), *Legality, Ideology and the State*, London: Academic Press

Swartz, D. (1985), 'French interlocking directorships: financial and industrial groups', in Stokman *et al.* (eds.) (1985)

Sweezy, P. M. (1939), 'Interest groups in the American economy', in Sweezy (1953)

Sweezy. P. M. (1940), 'The heyday of the investment banker', in Sweezy (1953)

Sweezy, P. M. (1941), 'The decline of the investment banker', in Sweezy (1953)

Sweezy, P. M. (1942), *The Theory of Capitalist Development*, London: Dennis Dobson

Sweezy, P. M. (1951), 'The American ruling class', in Sweezy (1953)

Sweezy, P. M. (1953), *The Present as History*, New York: Monthly Review Press

Sweezy, P. M. (1971), 'The resurgence of financial control: fact or fancy', *Monthly Review*, 23/6

Szymanski, A. (1973), 'Marx and the laws of competitive and monopoly capitalism', *Social Praxis*, 1/3

Taussig, F. W. and Joslyn, C. S. (1932), *American Business Leaders*, New York: Macmillan

Tawney, R. H. (1920), *The Acquisitive Society*, London: Bell

Tawney, R. H. (1931), *Equality*, 4th ed., London: George Allen and Unwin, 1952

Teulings, A. (1984), 'The power of corporate management: powerlessness of the manager', Paper to UMIST/Aston Conference on the Organisation and Control of the Labour Process, University of Aston, March 1984

Therborn, G. (1976), 'The Swedish class structure, 1930–65: a Marxist analysis', in Scase (1976)

Thomas, A. B. (1978), 'The British business elite: the case of the retail sector', *Sociological Review*, 26

Thomas, A. B. (1981), 'Managerial careers and the problem of control', Paper to EGOS Conference on Capital and Control, York.

Thomas, C. (1979), 'Family and kinship in Eaton Square', in Field (ed.) (1979)

Thomas, W. A. (1978), *The Financing of British Industry, 1918–76*, London: Methuen

Thompson, D. N. (1978), 'Mergers and acquisitions: motives and effects', London: Canada House Lecture Series, no. 3

Thompson, G. (1977), 'The relationship between the financial and industrial sector of the United Kingdom economy', *Economy and Society*, 6/3

Thompson, P. (1983), *The Nature of Work*, London: Macmillan

Thonet, P. J. and Poensgen, O. H. (1979), 'Management control and economic performance in Western Germany', *Journal of Industrial Economics*, 28

Thurley, K. and Wood, S. (eds.) (1983), *Industrial Relations and Management Strategy*, Cambridge: Cambridge University Press

Titmuss, R. (1962), *Income Distribution and Social Change*, London: George Allen and Unwin

Tomkins, C. and Lovering, J. (1973), *Location, Size, Ownership and Control Tables For Welsh Industry*, Cardiff: Welsh Council

Tomlinson, J. (1982), *The Unequal Struggle: British Socialism and the Capitalist Enterprise*, London: Methuen

Townsend, P. (1979), *Poverty in the United Kingdom*, Harmondsworth: Penguin

Tsuchiya, M. (1977), 'Management structure of vertically integrated non-zaibatsu business', in Nakagawa (ed.) (n.d.)

Turner, B. (1975), *Industrialism*, Harlow: Longman

Turner, L. (1970), *Invisible Empires*, London: Hamish Hamilton

Ueda, Y. (1983), 'A quantitative analysis of interlocking directorates in Japanese firm groups' (in Japanese), *Shokan Keizai*, 146

Urry, J. (1973), 'Towards a structural theory of the middle class', *Acta Sociologica*, 16

Urry, J. (1977), 'Capital and the state', Paper to the British Sociological Association, Sheffield

Urry, J. and Wakeford, J. (eds.) (1973), *Power in Britain*, London: Heinemann

Useem, M. (1978), 'The inner group of the American capitalist class', *Social Problems*, 25

Useem, M. (1980), 'Corporations and the corporate elite', *Annual Review of Sociology*, 6

Useem, M. (1982), 'Classwide rationality in the politics of managers and directors of large corporations in the United States and Great Britain', *Administrative Science Quarterly*, 27

Useem, M. (1984), *The Inner Circle*, New York: Oxford University Press

Useem, M. and McCormack, A. (1981), 'The dominant segment of the British business elite', *Sociology*, 15

Utton, M. A. (1982), *The Political Economy of Big Business*, Oxford: Martin Robertson

Varga, E. (1928), *The Decline of Capitalism*, London: Dorrit Press

Veblen, T. (1904), *The Theory of Business Enterprise*, New York: Scribner, 1915

Veblen, T. (1919), *The Industrial System and the Captains of Industry*, New York: Oriole Chapbooks

Veblen, T. (1924), *Absentee Ownership and Business Enterprise in Recent Times*, London: George Allen and Unwin

Vernon, J. R. (1970), 'Ownership and control among large member banks', *Journal of Finance*, 25

Vernon, R. (1971a), *Sovereignty at Bay*, New York: Basic Books

Vernon, R. (1971b), 'Multinational business and national economic goals', *International Organization*, 25/3

Vernon, R. (ed.) (1976), *The Oil Crisis*, New York: W. W. Norton

Vernon, R. (1977), *Storm over the Multinationals*, London: Macmillan

Villarejo, D. (1961a), 'Stock ownership and the control of corporations', Parts I and II, *New University Thought*, 2/1

Villarejo, D. (1961b), 'Stock ownership and the control of corporations', Part III, *New University Thought*, 2/2

Vogl, E. (1973), *German Business After the Economic Miracle*, London: Macmillan

Von Mehren, A. T. (ed.) (1963), *Law in Japan*, Cambridge, Mass.: Harvard University Press

Von Otter, C. (1980), 'Swedish welfare capitalism: the role of the state', in Scase (ed.) (1980)

Warner, W. L. (1959), 'The corporation man', in Mason (ed.) (1959)

Warner, W. L. (ed.) (1967), *The Emergent American Society*, Volume 1, Yale University Press

Warner, W. L. and Abegglen, J. C. (1955), *Big Business Leaders in America*, New York: Harper Brothers

Warner, W. L. and Unwalla, D. B. (1967), 'The system of interlocking directorates', in Warner (ed.) (1967)

Warren, B. (1971), 'How international is capital?', in Radice (ed.) (1975)

310   *Corporations, Classes and Capitalism*

Warren, B. (1972), 'Capitalist planning and the state', *New Left Review*, 72

Webb, S. and Webb, B. (1923), *The Decay of Capitalist Civilization*, London: Fabian Society and George Allen and Unwin

Weber, M. (1921), *Economy and Society*, 3 volumes, New York: Bedminster Press, 1968

Weber, M. (1923), *General Economic History*, Glencoe, Ill.: Free Press, 1950

Weinstein, F. B. (1976), 'Multinational corporations and the Third World: the case of Japan and South East Asia', *International Organisation*, 30/3

Westergaard, J. H. (1977), 'Class, inequality, and "corporatism"', in Hunt (ed.) (1977)

Westergaard, J. H. and Resler, H. (1975), *Class in a Capitalist Society*, London: Heinemann

Westney, D. E. (1979), 'Patterns of organisation development in Japan', in Dunkerley and Salaman (eds.) (1979)

Wheelwright, E. L. (1957), *Ownership and Control of Australian Companies*, Sydney: Law Book Company

Wheelwright, E. L. (1974), *Radical Political Economy*, Sydney: Australia and New Zealand Book Company

Wheelwright, E. L. and Miskelly, J. (1967), *Anatomy of Australian Manufacturing Industry*, Sydney: Law Book Company

Whitley, R. (1973), 'Commonalities and connections among directors of large financial institutions', *Sociological Review*, 21/4

Whitley, R. (1974), 'The City and industry', in Stanworth and Giddens (eds.) (1974b)

Whitley, R., Thomas, A. B. and Marceau, J. (1981), *Masters of Business?*, London: Tavistock

Whitt, J. A. (1981), 'Is oil different? A comparison of the social backgrounds and organisational affiliations of oil and non-oil directors', *Social Problems*, 29

Wibaut, F. W. (1913), 'De Nieuwste ontwikkeling van het Kapitalisme' (The latest development of capitalism), *De Niewe Tijd*, 18

Williams, K., Williams, J. and Thomas, D. (1983), *Why are the British Bad at Manufacturing?*, London: Routledge and Kegan Paul

Williams, R. et al. (1968), *May Day Manifesto*, Harmondsworth: Penguin

Williamson, O. E. (1964), *The Economics of Discretionary Behaviour*, Englewood Cliffs, NJ: Prentice-Hall

Williamson, O. E. (1970), *Corporate Control and Business Behaviour*, Englewood Cliffs, NJ: Prentice-Hall

Wilson, G. K. (1982), 'Why is there no corporatism in the United States', in Lehmbruch and Schmitter (1982)

Wilson Report (1977), *Progress Report on the Financing of Industry and Trade*, Committee to Review the Functioning of Financial Institutions, London: HMSO

Winkler, J. (1974), 'The ghost at the bargaining table', *British Journal of Industrial Relations*

Winkler, J. (1976), 'Corporatism', *European Journal of Sociology*, 17/1

Winkler, J. (1977), 'The corporatist economy: theory and administration', in Scase (ed.) (1977)

Winter, S. (1967), 'Economic "natural selection" and the theory of the firm', *Yale Economic Essays*

Wirth, M. (1973), 'Towards a critique of the theory of state monopoly capitalism', *Economy and Society*, 6/3, 1977

Wood, S. (1980), 'Corporate strategy and organisational studies', in Dunkerley and Salaman (eds.) (1980)

Wood, S. (ed.) (1982), *The Degradation of Work*, London: Hutchinson

Woodward, J. (1965), *Industrial Organization: Theory and Practice*, London: Oxford University Press

Wright, E. O. (1978), *Class, Crisis, and the State*, London: New Left Books

Wright, E. O. (1979), 'Class, occupation and organisation', in Dunkerley and Salaman (eds.) (1979)

Wright, E. O. (1980), 'Varieties of Marxist conceptions of class structure', *Politics and Society*, 9

Wright, E. O. (1983), 'A general framework for the analysis of class', Comparative Project on Class Structure and Class Consciousness, Working Paper, no. 16

Wright, E. O., Costello, C., Hachen, D. and Sprague, J. (1982), 'The American class structure', Comparative Project on Class Structure and Class Consciousness, Working Paper, no. 3

Yaffe, D. S. (1973), 'The Marxian theory of crisis, capital, and the state', *Economy and Society*, 2/2

Yamamura, K. (1978), 'Entrepreneurship, ownership, and management in Japan', in Mathias and Postan (eds.) (1978b)

Yanaga, C. (1968), *Big Business in Japanese Politics*, New Haven: Yale University Press

312   *Corporations, Classes and Capitalism*

Yasuoka, S. (1977), 'The tradition of family business in the strategic decision process and management structure of zaibatsu business', in Nakagawa (ed.) (n.d.)

Yazawa, M. (1963), 'The legal structure for corporate enterprise: shareholding–manager relations under Japanese law', in von Mehren (ed.) (1963)

Young, S. and Lowe, A. V. (1974), *Intervention in the Mixed Economy*, London: Croom Helm

Zald, M. N. (1969), 'The power and functions of boards of directors', *American Journal of Sociology*, 75

Zamagni, V. (1980), 'The rich in a late industrialiser: the case of Italy', in Rubinstein (ed.) (1980)

Zeitlin, M. (ed.) (1970), *American Society Inc.*, Chicago: Markham

Zeitlin, M. (1974), 'Corporate ownership and control: the large corporation and the capitalist class', *American Journal of Sociology*, 79/5

Zeitlin, M. (1976), 'On class theory of the large corporation', *American Journal of Sociology*, 81/4

Zeitlin, M. (ed.) (1980), *Classes, Class Conflict, and the State*, Cambridge, Mass.: Winthrop

Zeitlin, M. (1980), 'On classes, class conflict, and the state: an introductory note', in Zeitlin (ed.) (1980)

Zeitlin, M. and Norich, S. (1979), 'Management control, exploitation, and profit maximisation in the large corporation: an empirical confrontation of managerialism and class theory', *Research in Political Economy*, 2

Zeitlin, M., Ewen, L. and Ratcliff, R. (1975), '"New princes" for old? The large corporation and the capitalist class in Chile', *American Journal of Sociology*, 80/1

Ziegler, R. (1982), 'Market structure and cooptation', Working Paper for Analysis of Social Networks Project, Ludwigs-Marximilians-Universitdt, Munich

Ziegler, R., Bender, D. and Biehler, H. (1985), 'Industry and banking in the German corporate network', in Stokman *et al.* (eds.) (1985)

Ziegler, R., Reissner, G. and Bender, D. (1985), 'Austria incorporated', in Stokman *et al.* (eds.) (1985)

Index

There are no entries under such frequently recurring words as 'company', 'enterprise', 'capital', etc. Similarly, references are not indexed, only substantial discussions of a writer's work.

British Home Stores   81
Broken Hill Proprietary   123
Bukharin, N.   23
Burch, P.   64–7, 189, 253
bureaucratic control   174, 182
bureaucratization *see* divisional
   organization; functional
   organization; management
Burnham, J.   228–9
Burt, R.   192
business class *see* propertied class

Canada   116, 117–22, 125, 193,
   207, 210, 212–14, 217, 252, 260–1
capitalist society, theory of   16,
   21ff., 39, 196, 228, 259ff.
Carchedi, G.   230–1
career, concept of   174–5
Carrington, P.   192
Carroll, W. K.   118, 120–1, 157n
Chandler, A. D.   162, 163ff., 178
Channon, D.   172
Chevalier, J. M.   70, 73
Child, J.   75
City of London   85, 95ff., 102,
   178, 206, 222–5, 227n, 251, 260
class   17, 23, 26, 228ff., 266–8; *see*
   also inequality; propertied class;
   status
Clement, W.   121, 252
close surveillance   168, 169
closure   235–6, 246ff., 254
Cole, G. D. H.   233
Collett, D.   81
combines   141, 142ff., 149, 208
communication and interlocks
   55–6, 109–11, 252
competition   29, 197–8, 200, 218
concentration and centralization
   29, 197ff.
Confederation of British Industry
   224–5
control *see* operational
   management; ownership and

possession; strategic control
control through a constellation of
   interests   49–51, 54, 67, 68–71,
   74–5, 78–80, 81–3, 84n, 120, 123,
   124, 125, 138, 146, 156, 179, 188,
   206, 260, 265
corporate paternalism in Japan
   168, 194n
corporate strategy   44, 62, 150,
   160, 163ff., 179, 183, 243; *see*
   also divisional organization;
   functional organization; strategic
   control
corporatism   131, 218ff.
Courtaulds   80
credentialism   236–7, 254–5
Crosland, C. A. R.   37, 75
Cubbin, J.   81, 84n
Cutler, A. *et al.*   231
Cuyvers, L.   139, 193

Dahrendorf, R.   17–18, 183
Dai-Ichi Kangyo Bank (DKB)
   150, 159n, 203
Daumard, A.   241
Denmark   155
deskilling   162–3
De Vroey, M.   63, 138
directors   15, 43–4, 50, 53–4,
   54–5, 66, 75–6, 80, 108–9, 113n,
   116–17, 180–2, 243–4; *see also*
   interlocking directorships;
   management
disarticulation of national economy
   212–13
diversification   144, 172, 175,
   201–2, 204
divisional organization   162,
   171ff., 202, 260, 262; *see also*
   functional organization; holding
   company
Domhoff, G. W.   238
dominant coalition   43, 179–80,
   187, 192, 266